Classic Novels:
Meeting the Challenge
of Great Literature
Part III

Professor Arnold Weinstein

THE TEACHING COMPANY ®

PUBLISHED BY:

THE TEACHING COMPANY
4151 Lafayette Center Drive, Suite 100
Chantilly, Virginia 20151-1232
1-800-TEACH-12
Fax—703-378-3819
www.teach12.com

ISBN 1-59803-389-1

Arnold Weinstein, Ph.D.

Edna and Richard Salomon Distinguished
Professor of Comparative Literature
Brown University

Born in Memphis, Tennessee in 1940, Arnold Weinstein attended public schools before going to Princeton University for his college education (B.A. in Romance Languages, 1962, magna cum laude). He spent a year studying French literature at the Université de Paris (1960–1961) and a year after college at the Freie Universität Berlin, studying German literature. His graduate work was done at Harvard University (M.A. in Comparative Literature, 1964; Ph.D. in Comparative Literature, 1968), including a year as a Fulbright Scholar at the Université de Lyon in 1966–1967.

Professor Weinstein's professional career has taken place almost entirely at Brown University, where he has gone from Assistant Professor to his current position as Edna and Richard Salomon Distinguished Professor of Comparative Literature. He won the Workman Award for Excellence in Teaching in the Humanities in 1995. He has also won a number of prestigious fellowships, including a Fulbright Fellowship in American literature at Stockholm University in 1983 and research fellowships from the National Endowment for the Humanities in 1998 (in the area of literature and medicine) and in 2007 (in the area of Scandinavian literature). In 1996, he was named Professeur Invité in American literature at the École Normale Supérieure in Paris.

Professor Weinstein's publications include the following: *Vision and Response in Modern Literature* (Cornell University Press, 1974), *Fictions of the Self: 1550–1800* (Princeton University Press, 1981), *The Fiction of Relationship* (Princeton University Press, 1988), *Nobody's Home: Speech, Self and Place in American Fiction from Hawthorne to DeLillo* (Oxford University Press, 1993), *A Scream Goes Through the House: What Literature Teaches Us About Life* (Random House, 2003), and *Recovering Your Story: Proust, Joyce, Woolf, Faulkner, Morrison* (Random House, 2006). He has just completed *Northern Arts: The Breakthrough of Scandinavian Literature and Art from Ibsen to Bergman*, to be published by Princeton University Press in 2008. His latest project is *Literature and the Phases of Life: Growing Up and Growing Old*, under contract with Random House, with an expected completion date of 2009.

In addition to his career in teaching and writing, Professor Weinstein has produced a number of courses for The Teaching Company, including *The Soul and the City: Art, Literature and Urban Life*; *Drama, Poetry and Narrative: Understanding Literature and Life*; *20th-Century American Fiction*; and *American Literary Classics*.

Table of Contents
Classic Novels:
Meeting the Challenge of Great Literature
Part III

Classic Novels:
Meeting the Challenge of Great Literature

Scope:

The title of this course, *Classic Novels*, indicates the stature of the books we will cover. Beginning with Defoe and closing with García Márquez, our aim is to illuminate some of the most influential works of fiction in Western literature, yet works that challenge our sense of what a novel is, what it does, and why we have it. Those issues are represented in the subtitle of the course, *Meeting the Challenge of Great Literature*; our goal will be to grasp the intellectual ferment and power—social, emotional, and artistic—of these famous books. Hence, this course is more than a history of the novel; rather, it is a series of encounters with fictions that may be old but are far from dead. Our clichéd notion of a novel as simply "a slice of life" needs to be upended and rethought. Classic novels are restless creatures, trying out new forms of expression, challenging our views on how a culture might be understood and how a life might be packaged. What is the shape of experience? How would you represent your own? These books help us toward a deeper understanding of our own estate.

The virtue of beginning this course with three premier 18th-century writers—Defoe, Sterne, and Laclos—is to realize how wildly experimental the novel form is in its early phase. Defoe is our great journalist-author, and in *Moll Flanders* he tells the modern story of an underprivileged woman in a bustling metropolis, yielding a tale of streetsmarts and masquerade as the condition of survival in London. If Defoe's book is straightforward narrative, what are we to make of Sterne's *Tristram Shandy*? Nothing seems finishable or tellable in this confection of digressions, mishaps, and sexual innuendo. Sterne is a tonic figure: He exposes all the wiring, reminding us that *stories* are actually weird constructs, that *thinking* explodes most forms of expression. Then comes the dazzling epistolary *Les Liaisons Dangereuses*, rich in parallels with our modern culture of e-mail and text-messaging, wise about the lies we tell both others and ourselves. Seen together, these three narratives show us how unpredictable, how unhinging the *life story* might be; in these mirrors, we recover the depths and unruliness of our own condition.

The second phase of the course tackles a number of the greatest 19th-century novelists. These books constitute the heyday of the genre itself, functioning somewhat like the Internet of today, as sources of information about a rapidly changing world. They also explore something we are unequipped to see with our own eyes, the relations between self and society. Balzac's *Père Goriot* offers us the archetypal capitalist story: An innocent young man comes from the provinces to Paris to make his fortune, but at what price? Brontë's *Wuthering Heights* wins the prize as primitive fable: a story of crazed and ungratifiable longings, of the clash between appetite and culture. With Melville's *Moby-Dick*, American fiction enters both our course and literary history. This exuberant book, at once Shakespearean and mercantile, goes right off the charts of realism into metaphysics. Flaubert and Dickens appear as mid-century prophetic figures. *Bleak House* is an anatomy of the modern city: anonymous, inscrutable, corrupt, yet dreadfully interdependent. Flaubert seemingly returns us to a realist mode of writing but in a merciless, scalpel-like fashion; *Madame Bovary* rings the death knell on our dearest fictions, romantic love and bounded self. The Russians Tolstoy and Dostoevsky extend the canvas of fiction further than any other 19th-century practitioners. *War and Peace* offers a modern epic of the convulsive changes affecting Russian history and society, whereas *The Brothers Karamazov* uses the story of a parricide to explore the spiritual and psychological reaches of the human soul, yielding the most dimensional fiction of the century. At the century's close, the novel turns inside-out; Conrad's brief but bottomless *Heart of Darkness* is at once a moral anatomy of the "European project" and a crisis in storytelling. The 19th century ends on a deeply nihilistic note: An ethos and a way of writing are both in their death throes.

The last phase of the course begins with Thomas Mann, then zeroes in on five masters of the modern age—Kafka, Proust, Joyce, Woolf, and Faulkner—and closes with the magic realism of García Márquez. Mann's *Death in Venice* extends the Conradian anatomy of a sick Europe, and it points toward the libido-driven Freudian legacy that is our own. At this point, the novel form seems to explode with new vistas and new challenges. Kafka is the most sibylline of the group, as he packages spiritual fables and quests in relentlessly materialist frameworks. Proust's huge novel is the *ne plus ultra* of subjective vision, as if the inner world simply gobbled up the older regime of landscapes and surfaces. Might this be the great untold story that earlier fiction never accessed? With Joyce's *Ulysses*, we arrive finally at what may seem an unreadable fiction. In fact, this monumental text is, aside from its erudition and high jinks, the funniest and most carnal story in our literature, wise about both mind and body, offering us a shocking view of our actual song and dance. Woolf's *To the Lighthouse* takes the inside story further still, making us aware that our inner pulsions and responses have a fierce language of their own, that the enduring reality of others lies strangely within our own subjectivity. We then go to Faulkner's *As I Lay Dying*, a stream-of-consciousness masterpiece that chronicles, via the death of a mother, a still larger tragedy: the cashiering of self altogether. Our final text, García Márquez's *One Hundred Years of Solitude*, is the crazy quilt of the course, showing us a new world altogether, one in which family fate and human desire mock the old laws of time and flesh. Could this be a new freedom?

By course's end, a cartography of fictional projects and possibilities will have come into focus. The novel lives. Its practitioners have much to teach us, not only about the ways stories are told, but about the actual resources of our own lives. This storehouse of fictions is something of an "open sesame," because it enriches our sense of our own form and fate. A knowledge of their accomplishments widens and deepens—forever—one's sense of what classic novels do and what we gain by responding to the challenge of reading them.

Lecture Twenty-Five
Proust—*Remembrance of Things Past*, Part 2

Scope:

Love is one of the great themes in Proust's novel. The child's love for his mother and grandmother expresses a need that seems both infinite and gratifiable, as is clear in the famous scenes of the goodnight kiss and the visit to Balbec. But adult love is another matter; over the course of the novel, Proust stages the strange evolution of the protagonist's love for Albertine. Is love possible? If not, why?

Habit appears to most of us as an innocuous notion, but Proust makes us realize how it functions as a cocoon for us, keeping us ensconced in our own private head-world. But what happens when habit is disrupted, when the world breaks in? These matters can have great pathos, especially when it comes to our perception of our loved ones. Here is the logic that accompanies Proust's staging of the grandmother's death.

Outline

I. The familiar title that we use for this novel is probably a mistranslation. The title in French is *À la recherché du temps perdu*, "In search of lost time." Much of this lecture will focus on how the work of time takes place, along with a subject that doesn't seem to be connected, human love.

   A. We cannot see the work of time, although we can see its effects. In fact, it may not even be bearable for us to see the work of time in the faces and bodies of those we love.

   B. The love of the mother and grandmother for Marcel is the anchor of this novel. We see the child's voracious need, and the selfless women who answer it. Does this endless supply of love and support equip the child for adult life? How likely is it that this relationship will find its match in adult love?

   1. A famous early episode is the goodnight kiss between Marcel and his mother. We get a sense of jealousy here—that the boy cannot bear for his mother to have a life of her own. We also get a sense that the relationship

is almost erotic, not from the mother's point of view but from the boy's.

2. Later in the novel, on vacation in a seashore hotel room, the sickly Marcel is almost overcome by the alien environment. The strange room seems as if it is assaulting him, and he "longed to die."

   a. Then his grandmother comes into the room, and the boy says "to the expansion of my constricted heart, there opened at once an infinity of space."

   b. We almost feel as if the grandmother exists only as a source of endless love and nurturance for Marcel.

   c. The alterity—otherness—of the world threatens who we are, and we can find salvation only in love.

C. The Albertine saga constitutes the adult love relationship at the heart of the story.

1. Marcel first sees Albertine and her band of friends at Balbec. He is infatuated with their vitality and beauty, their potential to become almost anything.

2. Albertine invites Marcel to her bedroom for what he assumes will be a session of lovemaking, but he has misread her signals.

3. Later, when Albertine comes to visit Marcel in Paris, she is more experienced, but when he goes to kiss her, he finds that his lips are ill-suited to the job. As he closes in, he can't see what he's doing, his nose gets crushed, and his kiss lands on her cheek.

4. Still later, Albertine moves in with Marcel, but he finds that her consciousness is a barrier for him to sex. He can have sex with her only when she is asleep.

   a. For Marcel, sex depends on the exclusion of her subjectivity, which would distract him from what he needs to be able fully to love her.

   b. Of course, this idea is monstrous in normative terms, but there is a strange logic here: Subjectivity is the enemy of love, not the ally of it. Love can only be fully actualized when there is no distraction or competition.

5. Marcel suspects Albertine of lying about her sexual tastes and adventures and, thus, sequesters her in his

apartment. He suspects that she is a lesbian and believes that he cannot compete with female rivals.

6. Albertine has an accident on a horse and dies, but her relationship with Marcel is still not over. He asks his friends to investigate the rumors of her lesbian affairs. Even in death, she continues to romp freely in his imagination, and he finds that he can still be deceived and humiliated by her.

7. Ultimately, we learn that even loving someone does not give us access to their thoughts, their dreams, their fantasies. We think of love as the deepest expression of mutuality and human connection, but our love objects will always remain "others" to us, reaching inward themselves to infinity.

8. Jealousy emerges here as our worst creative fiction, as the unverifiable and endless novel that we invent on our own.

II. Proust is among the rare writers to explore the notion of *habit*.

A. Proust calls habit a "skillful arranger"; we might also think of it as "feathering one's nest." Birds feather their nests by taking random twigs and making a home; so do people.

B. Habit is the protective lens that shuts out the world's alterity so as to make it into a personal cocoon, to preserve our status quo. Are we equipped to see the world when the lens becomes broken?

C. In writing about Proust, Samuel Beckett said, "The boredom of living is replaced by the suffering of being." This quotation delineates the seesaw directionality of Proust's novel, those moments when habit fails in its mission, and the world jumps in.

1. Suspecting that his grandmother is ailing, Marcel plans a surprise visit, but he is shocked by the sight of her. As he enters her room, he suddenly stumbles into the recognition that she is old, sick, and dying. He has kept this knowledge from himself because of his love for her.

2. Proust says, "Every habitual glance is an act of necromancy. Each face that we love, a mirror of the past." This brings us back to the beginning of the lecture and our inability to see the work of time.

3. Our love for people preserves them in a certain way, enabling us to deny time and deny death.

III. Death, however, is the somatic endgame for all of us. We see, in the long and painful account of the grandmother's decline, a brutal physical lesson about mortality and the entropic treadmill all of us are on.

A. The grandmother experiences a stroke while walking in the Tuileries Garden with Marcel. She tries to convey to him that she is still the same woman of refinement, but the assault on her body has begun, and she is unable to make herself understood.

B. One by one, she loses her sight, her hearing, her ability to speak. We see her body as a fortress that is being stormed by the forces of entropy, and we realize that she is fated to lose this battle.

C. A "beast on a bed" is the final image we get of the grandmother. Awakened in the middle of the night, Marcel comes to her sickroom to say farewell, but she doesn't recognize him. Is this a replay of the "Little Red Riding Hood" story? We'll look at that question in the next lecture.

Essential Reading:

Marcel Proust, *Remembrance of Things Past*, Moncrieff, Kilmartin, and Mayor, trans.

Supplementary Reading:

Samuel Beckett, *Proust*.

Leo Bersani, *Marcel Proust: The Fictions of Life and Art*.

Alain de Botton, *How Proust Can Change Your Life*.

Roger Shattuck, *Proust's Way: A Field Guide to In Search of Lost Time*.

Arnold Weinstein, *Recovering Your Story: Proust, Joyce, Woolf, Faulkner, Morrison*.

Philip Weinstein, *Unknowing: The Work of Modernist Fiction*.

Questions to Consider:

1. Some would argue that there is no such thing as love in the Proustian scheme. Rather, they claim, it is all egomania, hunger, and pathology. Given what you know about this novel, does this tough criticism make some sense? Consider the examples of both the grandmother and Albertine as key instances for your argument.

2. Vision, Proust seems to be saying, is incapable of integrating *time* into its operation. Do you factor time into your perception of people, especially of loved ones? Is this possible? Is it desirable? What are its consequences?

Lecture Twenty-Five—Transcript
Proust—*Remembrance of Things Past*, Part 2

Proust scholars like to point out that the familiar title that we have of his great work, *Remembrance of Things Past*, is probably a mistranslation. The actual French is *À la recherché du temps perdu*, and the title that most people feel is the most accurate one is "In search of lost time." But even "search" doesn't tell us, because *recherché* in French also means "research." You get a sense of effort involved in it. So, a lot of this lecture is going to be about how the work of time takes place and how it is we might approach it. I want to link it to something that doesn't seem prima facie to be connected with it, which is human love. I'm going to start with an obvious remark but one that I think can be unpacked, which is we cannot see the work of time. We can see the effects of time, but we cannot see the actual dynamic of time. If you look at a photograph or if you look at anything—if I look at your face and you look at mine, we cannot see the actual workings of time. The retina gives us a snapshot picture of the world, but the corollary is—is it desirable? Is it even bearable to see the work of time in the faces and bodies of people that we love? So, there's nothing very esoteric about this. It's really quite basic, it seems to me, from an emotional and moral point of view.

Let me talk about the way the emotional and moral issues work in Proust along these lines. We get a sense that there is a very idyllic form of nurturing happening in this novel—that the two figures who embody that are the grandmother and the mother. Sometimes they almost merge with each other, and each one of them is presented as a kind of endless fount of nurturing and love, selfless love, for the narrator, this child, the boy, Marcel. You get a sense of parental love as being essentially infinite and perfect—that they are always able to shore him up and he is what the French call "neurasthenic." He needs shoring up. He is over-sensitive. He's fragile. He has his problems, and so he draws a lot on their support. They are the two beacon lights of the novel, the mother and the grandmother, and their love, as I said, seems like nourishment, like balm, like manna. Some critics have asked, well, what kind of an image might this be of one's grandmother or mother? In other words, they obviously had to have lives of their own, but from the novel's perspective, you'd never know that. All that really matters, and maybe this is the way we look at our mothers and grandmothers—how often do we say, what are their own lives like? What we look to them for is the nourishment and support that they give us. And so from that point of view, the novel is accurate.

What the consequences might be of that is a separate issue. If we have, in fact, received—maybe this is a fiction, maybe one never gets it—if you have, in fact, received an endless supply of nourishment and support from your parents and grandparents, does that equip you or does that, in fact, spell trouble for the life ahead? In this sense, how likely is it that you're going to match that with an adult love need and relationship of your own? In Proust, it's definitely going to spell trouble. There's one well-known sequence called the goodnight kiss where the boy is desperately trying to have his mother come up into the bedroom and kiss him goodnight. That's where we begin to see that there could be a little paranoia in all of this as well, a little bit of jealousy—that the boy can't seem to bear that mother could have a life of her own, that she is mixing with her own friends. There's something almost crazed about it, and at times it really looks a little bit erotic like this is almost a kind of lover/mistress relationship as well, not from her point of view but from his.

But I'd like to focus more on the relationship of the grandmother, because some of the most beautiful passages are in that category. In particular, I want to talk about a passage that happens when the boy and the grandmother make a trip to Balbec, which is the name that Proust gave to this lovely area on the seashore right between Normandy and Brittany. I have mentioned the word "neurasthenic." I have said that the boy has his own great nervous problems, and one of the most obvious ones is that—of course, he and his grandmother—he is too old to stay in the same room with her, she has her room right next to his. He has trouble going to sleep. Now, we don't have a count on how many people are insomniacs, but one of the reasons that people have trouble going to sleep, or at least in this case, has to do with whether you're sleeping in a strange room. There too, I don't know how much scientific or statistical data we have, but most people who have trouble sleeping in a strange room have it for this reason in my opinion, which is that sleeping in one's own bedroom is a case where the bedroom itself barely exists. The bedroom is like a cocoon. That's what we do to the rooms that we live in. We make them extensions of our own minds and bodies, but if you go to a strange hotel room, or you're spending the night or nights at somebody else's house, everything in that room is alien— that is to say it doesn't know you. You haven't domesticated it. You haven't turned it into a cocoon. You hear the clock ticking in a hotel bedroom that you would never hear in your own house. You look at a strange mirror, and it seems strange. The furniture jumps out at you. What you are seeing is the alterity, the otherness, of the room itself, which is exactly what we gradually grow able to stop seeing in our own domestic setting.

So, in Balbec at the hotel he's going crazy. This room is assaulting him. He can't bear it, and in Proust's case it sounds like it's really getting ready to kill him. At its worst, he says, "Having no world, no room, no body now that was not menaced by the enemies thronging around me, penetrated to the very bones by fever, I was alone and longed to die." It's a case really of the environment being so strong that it is penetrating him, invading him, and it's going to snuff him out. He can't offer resistance to it. It's as if his own ego, his own subjecthood, is getting ready to be annihilated just by the presence, in his view the aggressive presence, of a strange room. Now, you may say this is awfully coddled, awfully precious, and maybe it is. But that's the way the Proustian psychology works. Well, what solution might there be to that? By the way, let me just say this too as an extension. How many times do we know of cases where very old people who have certain infirmities refuse to leave their homes and go into nursing homes? And we know of people who are almost blind who can still negotiate their own houses, their own apartments, and their own corridors. But frequently you put these people into new settings, hospital settings, so-called "safe" settings, and they bump into walls, and they fall, and they die. I mean I'm exaggerating to make a case that what I'm arguing about, the way in which we domesticate our setting and can orient ourselves in it because we now have made it an extension of ourselves, I think that common experience will bear this out.

Well, let's return to the boy who is getting ready to die because the room is encroaching on him so much. The grandmother comes into the room, and this is what he writes. "Then my grandmother came in," and listen to this language, "and to the expansion of my constricted heart," it almost sounds cardiological, "there opened at once an infinity of space." That's what love might be, the kind of endless, nourishing, parental, grandmotherly love here. It's as if his heart is being squeezed into nothing, and she comes and it opens to an infinity of space. It's as if that were the answer, and he describes the embrace that she gives him. He describes himself as being in a kind of blissful state the way an infant that is suckling at its mother's breast might be. He feels it as a kind of transparent moment, not that he can read through into the grandmother but that she is only a source of love. She is not any kind of competing subjectivity. She is there only as a source of endless love and nurturance for him.

So, it's important, I think, to see what happens in the sequence that I read to you—that the alterity of the world, the otherness of the world, and you can see I'm only a short step away from the otherness of people, is such that it threatens who we are. In the passage I read to you in the hotel room, it threatens him to the point of capsizing. It threatens him in the sense of when one thinks of infarct or seizure, and then the grandmother comes in with her embrace, enfolds him, and this is a moment of total expansion and freedom.

Let me move from that love relationship to the adult love relationship in the novel, which takes place over many volumes with the girl called Albertine. It starts out when he first meets her at Balbec, and she's with a band of other girls and boys, mostly girls. He falls in love really with the whole bunch. They represent a kind of swirling mobility. It's the mobility of adolescence—when young people could become almost anything. There is something magic and magnetic about it, and he is filled with a sense of their beauty, their mobility, and their potential. He has a lot of trouble selecting out the girl that he wants to go for, which is Albertine, but he does. So, he flirts with her. They get to know each other a little bit. He thinks that she likes him. He is not sure, and then one fine day she invites him to her bedroom telling him that her aunt whom she is staying with is going to be gone. Well, in his lexicon this is a pretty clear kind of invitation. He thinks he knows exactly what he is in for, which sounds pretty good. So, he goes into that bedroom to approach her. She is lying in bed. Her cheeks are sort of inflamed a little bit. He figures this is perfect, and it's really a sweet moment in the book because he is filled with the kind of desire that is almost cosmic in scope. It relates to the sea that is outside the window, and he looks at the cliffs and the mountains in the background.

All of this sort of becomes a version of her own luscious, appetizing body, and as he's reaching over to her to get in bed with her, to leap onto her, she rings the bell. These are the old hotels at that time—rings the bell for help. He has obviously totally mistranslated the signs. So, this relationship gets off to kind of a rocky start. Well, the book is going to give us various stages of it. It turns out that later in Paris she comes to visit him, and she is a changed person. He doesn't really want to get the details, but she has obviously had a little more experience. So, she comes in, and she hops in bed with him. You would think, well, now things are going to get on a better basis here. They're going to get it on, and yet—this is Proust, a man and a woman or a boy and a girl on a bed together—that's just the beginning of the story. There can still be problems, and in particular how do two people make contact together? Most of us think we know the answers for that. Well, Proust being who he is says that the boy is thinking that finally he is going to be able to taste this girl that he has been desiring.

But it says that he hadn't yet stopped to reflect that he may not have all of the appropriate organs to do this. He says that a man "lacks a certain number of essential organs, and notably possesses none that will serve for kissing. For this absent organ, he substitutes his lips." Okay, lips won't do it. That's all we seem to be equipped with. Most of us never realize that there was supposed to be something better, but there is in Proust. The lips just get you onto the surface. You're sort of landlocked. You can't get in, which is where Proust always wants to go. So, then they get close up for a better kiss where it's going to be a fuller embrace, and as it's described with aeronautical detail, this is exactly like a plane coming in for a landing, except it's describing an erotic scene where one face is gradually, slowly, maniacally approaching another. He is coming in for an approach, and as he gets closer, her head starts to change. He sees her from different angles. He sees features of her face that he had never seen before. I mean he is like a cartographer coming in, and then the perfumes that are on her begin to assault him. Remember, this guy—remember the madeleine, things like that, the smell of the room he's in. But the last piece of it, of course, is when he is closing in for the kiss. But there too, nothing works as it should. It says in this matter of kissing:

Our nostrils and eyes are as ill-placed as our lips are ill-made—suddenly my eyes ceased to see, then my nose, crushed by the collision, no longer perceived any odour, and, without thereby gaining any clearer idea of the taste of the rose of my desire, I learned from these obnoxious signs, that at last I was in the act of kissing Albertine's cheek.

It's like a crash landing. He has just simply landed on the surface of her skin. Ever since I have read this passage, when I look at films because I don't want to look at myself this way and I see men and women kissing, I'm always looking—where does the nose go? What kind of a fit really is this? Proust is just delicious along these lines.

This is where we had thought things were going to come together. Well, they don't quite come together so well, but that's okay because there's more to come. Later, their relationship moves into a fuller gear, and in this fuller gear it turns out that they do have some kind of sexual relationship. But to use the pronoun "they" is probably a little bit misleading. I've lectured on this at universities, and I've had a lot of problems with women students who have told me—do you realize how completely diseased what you're talking about is? I keep answering feebly—this isn't me, I'm quoting Proust. I'm talking about Proust; I want to make that disclaimer clear. In this relationship, the only way sex can happen is if consciousness gets out of the way because consciousness is the great barrier. So, unsurprisingly, he waits until she falls asleep. They are in bed together. They are obviously embracing each other. She falls asleep, and at that point her body becomes something quite different. There is no longer any antagonism. There is no longer any independence on her part. She exhibits what he calls the "unconscious life of plants, of trees," and he awaits her descent into deep slumber so that he can examine her at great leisure. He caresses her, and then he mounts her, embarking on what the text calls the "tide of Albertine's sleep."

Believe it or not, it's described with great beauty. It's very serene, and I would even say at some level it's consensual, except that the consent she has made to it is to sleep. By the way, it casts a strange light on our old idiom—I slept with her, she slept with me, they slept together, because every time you say that you don't mean sleep at all. You mean something else going on in that bed. In this case, it does mean sleep on her part, and it means sex on his. What it really depends on, as you've seen, is the exclusion of her subjectivity, which would distract him from what he needs to be able to fully love her. Now, this is what people have said is monstrous, and it is monstrous along any kind of normative lines. Yet, there is a kind of weird logic in play here that subjectivity is the enemy of love, not the ally of it—that instinct will only work in a sense when the mind leaves, or that one's own love can only be fully actualized, brought to fruition, where there is no kind of static, distraction, competition, et cetera. What you make of it ethically, personally, is up to you. I just want to bring out how Proust writes this. Well, you would think, well now at least we see what that relationship is like, but we don't because it goes on even further.

After this, it turns out that she starts to lie to him more and more. He sequesters her. He locks her up in his own apartment. She comes to live with him. He closes the door. This is considered normal in this book. This book never says, my god, what kind of a monster is this? We would arrest this guy in two weeks today—not in this novel, and therefore she is more or less what the title is, the "captive" of that volume—not that she's trying to get clear. She comes back, but he watches her like a policeman. Every time they speak together, he is trying to decode what she's saying because he knows that she's lying. He suspects her of being a lesbian, and that's what is most painful to him because it's one thing if he had male rivals. But if he has female rivals, he feels like he can't even compete. Whatever kind of pleasure they are experiencing is one that he is not equipped to offer her. Then in a kind of remarkable follow-up, aftermath, she dies. She does offstage in the novel. She's riding a horse, and she collides with a tree. She's dead, and you say, well, now it's over. But it's not over even now because once dead—this is how diseased this book can become, he sends his friends out, his allies, to check up on her to find out if all of the rumors he had heard about her having lesbian relationships are true or not, which begins to tell us that at some crucial level in him she is not dead, even though she is dead, because she is continuing to romp freely in his imagination. We have a word for this. We call this "jealousy," and I want you to realize that jealousy doesn't require the person to be alive that you're worried about. You can still be tricked, deceived, humiliated, and hurt just by learning what they did to you when they were alive, and so he's trying to get the dirt on her. He gets more and more information about different kinds of rendezvous and assignations that she had with other women. This is a kind of horrendous afterlife, immortality, of love of the worst sort, that the loved one, if you want to call this love, is dead, and yet one is not clear. The cord is not cut, and in fact the betrayals continue to take place because one's self is imagining them. At one point in a very beautiful phrase he writes this—this is before she died:

> I could, if I chose, take Albertine on my knee, hold her head in my hands, I could caress her, run my hands slowly over her, but, just as if I had been handling a stone which encloses the salt of immemorial oceans or the light of a star, I felt I was touching to no more than the sealed envelope of a person who inwardly reached to infinity.

What a line. You can hold a body, you can love that person, but do you have access to what is inside of that person? Where are their thoughts, their dreams, and their fantasies even in that moment as you caress them, as you make love to them? That's what this book is getting at. We don't know. We cannot know. That's what subjectivity is about. We are marooned, locked, imprisoned in our mindset, our heart set, and even though love is an expression we think of mutuality, reciprocity, and human connection, even fusion, in this book no way. This book is about recognizing the alterity. I talked about the alterity of hotel rooms—now the alterity of people, particularly people that one might love. They are "other" to us. Even in moments of greatest intimacy, we cannot know what is inside of them. They reach inwardly to infinity, and the book is trying to track that, to chart that, to make a map of that—where they are. That's why the lies are so important. He asks her where she's been because he's trying to graph her entire itinerary.

It's a very interesting model of things. It's very close to what we think of as jealousy itself. What is jealousy but the imagination of the free acts of our loved ones when they are not with us? Jealousy has no floor. It has no bottom line. It's not even a false-bottomed suitcase because it is open to endless permutations and imagination by us. Jealousy is a novel. Jealousy is a creative fiction. Jealousy is when we cannot help spinning out scenarios of how other people have loved, and cheated, and hurt us. It's an inside job. We do it ourselves. There is no corrective evidence for it. This book is a great, great analysis—philosophical inquiry—about what jealousy might be as a kind of bottomless, creative fiction.

I want to shift from these hot topics to something that is going to seem to you more innocuous, which is a little five-letter word that none of us have thought much about—*habit*. I've already gotten close to it when I talked about the boy in the hotel room that seemed so different. It seems to be an innocuous term. Proust is one of the great explorers of what "habit" actually means. Habit is our way of domesticating our environment. Proust calls it a "skillful arranger." I'd like to invoke another notion we have, which is to "feather one's nest." We know that birds do that. They take little twigs from here and there, and then they make their own home out of it. I think Proust suggests that that's what human beings do. We go about first personalizing our world. We call it ours. I tell my students—you walk down the hall in your dormitory. You see two people talking, they glance at you, and you are certain they are speaking about you regardless of what they're talking about. There's no way of knowing. We relate the world to us because it's the only way we know how to go through life. Habit is the protective lenses that shut out the world's alterity and relates things instead to us. It makes the world back into our cocoon. Again, our bedroom is our cocoon. It preserves our status quo, but the corollary is are we equipped to see the world when the lenses, the blinders, of habit are broken and shattered? Again, going to sleep in strange rooms—obviously, every room is a strange room including your bedroom, but habit has turned it into something unstrange, an extension of you. Habit erases alterity. How often do you see the doorknob that you open up every morning to get out of your bedroom or to go into the bathroom? Well, let's extend it. How often do you see, really see, the faces of the people that you live with? We habituate everything. It is the law of perception.

What happens when the veil is lifted, I said. Samuel Beckett once beautifully said, "The boredom of living is replaced by the suffering of being." He was writing about Proust when he wrote that, and it's the seesaw directionality of Proust's novel. When the veil is lifted, our cocoon womb is broken because that's what it is. It's a return to the womb, and that alien world can no longer be domesticated. It happens in this book. It happens particularly with the grandmother. The boy speaks to her on the telephone long distance, and he hears in her voice, and it's because he can't see her, he hears in her voice that she's ailing, that she's lonely, and he elects to go to visit. He goes to Paris, and he walks into her room. He walks in before she knows he's there. He says it's as if he got there before her equipment was ready or his was ready to perceive her, and when he does see her, it is a shocking, horrible sight not because she is bleeding, or having a stroke, or anything but because he has not had time to prepare his own mental equipment. He all of a sudden stumbles into the recognition that she is frail, old, sick, and dying. This is what he has kept from himself forever, and not because he is repressive, because that is the law of love. Love is something that keeps people frozen in the way we have to see them, we want to see them.

Proust's extraordinary phrase is, "every habitual glance is an act of necromancy." That is the way we see our parents. We cannot bear to see them age. We continue to think that they still look the way they did earlier. He goes on to say, "each face that we love a mirror of the past." I started this lecture by saying can we see the work of time? That's what I've been talking about. Can we see the work of time? You may remember I said, would it be bearable to see the work of time? Often, photographs give it to us. We take a look at a photograph of someone who is old, and we see the lines in their face in a way that when we look at them in the room that we're sharing with them, we can't see. We won't see it. We refuse to see it. We edit it out of our image. Love is a kind of form of chloroform in some sense. That is to say that it preserves people in the way that we must see them because we must deny time because we must deny death. Time is the treadmill, the entropic treadmill that all of us are on. With young people, it can be very exciting. We are always shocked when we go home and a child that we knew is now a young boy or a young girl if we haven't seen them in a year or two, but with the older it is a much more grave and disturbing affair because that's when death is beginning to announce its presence. That's what occasionally by surprise we see in the mirror. Usually, mirrors hide this from us. Usually the mirror sends back an image that we want to see, but occasionally, usually by slip or something, we see the wrinkles, we see the things that we didn't want otherwise to take account of. Seeing people in time—we're not equipped to, we do not bear it easily.

Well, death is the somatic endgame, obviously, and so a chunk of this book depicts the dying of the grandmother. It is awful. It's moving. It's beautifully written, but it's unbearable. The boy goes with his grandmother for a walk in the Tuileries gardens in Paris, and he's only interested in meeting his friends. He's very impatient with her, and she says she has to go to the *cabinet*, the bathroom, in the gardens. She's in there for a long time, and she comes out. He's embarrassed, and he's waiting. He's impatient, and she can't speak properly. Her face is all disheveled. This is a woman of great culture as well as of great love, and she tries to even quote one of her great authors, Madame de Sevigne, to the boy. But what she says to the boy—she is trying to quote a piece of literature to tell him, my mind is intact. I'm still your grandmother. I'm still the person you knew. He can't understand a word she says because she has had a stroke, and it's where we see the encroachment that physiology and time has on human life. We watch this woman be assaulted in this novel because that's really what the book does. She is the figure of love, rectitude and culture, the most admirable figure in the novel. The book is going to absolutely smite her, and so we watch her resist disease. We see her take particular medical protocols. One removes her sight. One removes her hearing. One removes her smell, her talking. It's a fortress that's being stormed, and we see how unequal the fight is between the human body and entropy—how age is coherent and logical and therefore all the more awful, particularly age as it approaches death. Sherwin Nuland has written a wonderful book about how we die showing just how cogent dying is. We watch that, and we realize this is a kind of terrible contest that she is fated to lose.

In the last scene of the book, which I'll close this lecture with—not of the book but of this portion, where he is told to come down to the room to say farewell to his grandmother, she is called a "beast on a bed." She doesn't recognize him, a beast on a bed, and it's the fable of Little Red Riding Hood. Where has Grandmother gone? I want you to reflect on that before I do my next lecture on Proust. Thank you.

Lecture Twenty-Six
Proust—*Remembrance of Things Past*, Part 3

Scope:

Sickness and death are signature themes in Proust: The boy watched, helplessly, the grandmother's stroke and dying, yet he now discovers that she still lives inside him, via memory. Memory is a double-edged sword: The dead live, but we ourselves are graveyards. Time itself is on the docket: Do we dare factor time into our perception of loved ones? What would we then see?

Proust's legacy hinges on his view of art and artists as the source of that inside story that eludes us in life, an inside story that has no truck with the material surface world we all see. Can it be written? Do you know your own? Proust leaves us with a form of fourth-dimensional portraiture, suggesting that it dwarfs anything we might find in our retinal perception or in photography or film. Can you see the fuller figure of your life?

Outline

I. The crucial thing that precedes remembering is, of course, forgetting. What does it mean when we forget the past? How much of our lives have been forgotten? What happens when we forget our dead—both the people we have loved and our prior selves? Do the dead live on in some way—in photographs, in graveyards, or in us?

   A. We closed the last lecture with the grim scene of the death of Marcel's grandmother, in which she is described as a "beast on a bed." Two calendars are in play here: One marks the physiological death of the loved one, but the other marks the death of the loved one in us.

      1. Proust is interested in this second form of death because it is also a life—the life that people live inside of us even though they are physiologically dead. We experience this life as mourning.

      2. Successful mourning usually signifies that one's own ego becomes free and uninhibited again. Freud put forth this view in his essay "Mourning and Melancholia"; the

"work of mourning" is a systematic process in which the unconscious cuts the ties that connected us to the loved one; dead tissue cannot nourish living tissue.

3. When grief ebbs to the point that thoughts of the dead loved one no longer hurt to the same degree, successful mourning has taken place. We are then free to cast our love elsewhere. Living ultimately trumps grief, allowing us to get past the deaths of those we love. We will honor and remember them, but we will become, in some sense, free of them.

4. In this novel, Marcel continues to have adventures after the death of his grandmother. He completes the process of mourning and, to a degree, forgets his dead loved one.

B. Then, however, Marcel returns to Balbec, to the same hotel room where he and his grandmother had tapped messages on the wall to each other a year earlier. While in the room, he is struck by what he feels is an invading spirit; it's almost as if his grandmother has come back to life in the setting where the two of them had experienced so much intimacy and love.

1. Marcel sequesters himself in the room to process her death, to do the work of mourning, and he encounters the double-edged sword of memory. Memory is, on the one hand, a magic retrieval, a presence of loved ones who are dead. At the same time, it never blinds us to the fact that our loved ones are only present in a virtual sense.

2. Proust helps us to see the poignancy and inseparable nature of this presence/absence.

3. Only in Balbec for a second time does Marcel fully feel and understand what his grandmother was. He learns that she was already ill when the two visited the town earlier, and remembers moments when he was unkind to her.

4. Proust tells us that these memories are a form of self-punishment: "For as the dead exist only in us, it is ourselves that we strike without respite when we persist in recalling the blows that we have dealt them."

C. In the hotel room, Marcel fully realizes that his grandmother is no longer alive, and he realizes what he has lost with her. He knows what she was and that she is gone for good.

1. Marcel has had dreams in which he pursues his grandmother, who is dead but not fully gone. In his dream, he is told that the only way to find her is to enter his own bloodstream, the River Lethe. The dream reminds us of the myth of Orpheus and his journey to Hades to retrieve the dead Eurydice.

2. For Marcel, the dream is about saying farewell. Like all of us, he regrets not having fully shared his feelings with his grandmother while she was alive. He relives her death on his calendar time, not hers, now experiencing what she meant in life and the meaning of her death.

3. This type of farewell dwarfs what is said at the deathbed. There, we are helpless; we can do nothing for the dying bodies of our loved ones, and they are in no condition to hear our feelings. Marcel now experiences the act of saying farewell within himself.

D. The French word for oblivion is *oubli*, the place to which we consign those who have died or whom we have forgotten. Our past selves may be stored there, as well, but through memory, they are all accessible. *Oubli* is a form of death in life.

1. We are always locked out of the plenitude of our own lives. If we think of our résumés, we might ask: To what extent can we remember and relive this trajectory, which is, in fact, nothing other than our own lives? A résumé represents the markings of who we once were, yet how often is that invested with life; how many of these selves still live in us?

2. Even in the present, we play any number of separate roles, focusing only on the one we are currently involved in.

3. Proust's word *oubli* is the operative notion that makes life possible for us to become something now and rule out all the other things that we are or were. In this novel, we get a sense of the beauty and necessity of having to make this kind of vertical retrieval to recover something of the scale and scope of our lives and loves.

4. This novel is about recovering what is buried within us; it also deals with hallowing the temporality of life and the ability to see others in time. Can we look at someone

we love and see what the curve of time would tell us about that person? It's not clear that any of us is able to see the roundedness of the lives we look at.

5. Proust tells us that if we could see our loved ones existing in time, they would appear covered with the "velvety patina of the years." We would see the richness, the length, the fullness, and the dimensionality of their lives, which we cannot now do in our "snapshot world."

6. We are even unable to see our own stories fully, the motifs that make our lives cogent over time.

II. Proust would tell us that our truth is not in photographs or résumés; it's in our inner memories, which we must find a way to access.

A. Proust was critical of photography and realist literature, which he would have said doesn't capture anything. It doesn't tell us the private human story. Someone walking into your home and seeing your mementos couldn't possibly know what they meant to you, but such things are markers for you of your life, your emotions, your experiences, and your past. No faithful rendition of outside surfaces could render that inside story.

B. Proust argues that each of us has an inner history that we know nothing about which may be brought to the surface by association. We all have private markers—a smell, a sound—and Proust's project is to get in touch with those to enable us to recover our own lives.

C. For Proust, even a detailed biography is a fraud, because our lives are more than just a series of conventional events and ideas. The real story is what's inside of us.

D. In the last segment of the book, Marcel goes to a reception with people he has known all his life, but they look like they've been transformed. He sees two women whom he once loved when he was young; they have become dowagers, but he is able to look past what life has done to them and to himself and recapture his earlier love. As with F. Scott Fitzgerald, America's writer of desire, desire for Proust—that passion, that intensity—is more important than what one receives.

E. Proust finally says that his book is a mirror for his readers; they will see in themselves, perhaps, a door opening to their own unstoried, untold, unmapped inner lives.

　1. Marcel remembers his aunt having dinner plates with an Ali Baba motif, and he believes that if she had known the fuller lives of her guests, she would have thought she was having Ali Baba to visit, the man who finds magic treasure in a cave.

　2. The treasure, for Proust, is simply our own lives.

Essential Reading:

Marcel Proust, *Remembrance of Things Past*, Moncrieff, Kilmartin, and Mayor, trans.

Supplementary Reading:

Samuel Beckett, *Proust*.

Leo Bersani, *Marcel Proust: The Fictions of Life and Art*.

Alain de Botton, *How Proust Can Change Your Life*.

Roger Shattuck, *Proust's Way: A Field Guide to In Search of Lost Time*.

Arnold Weinstein, *Recovering Your Story: Proust, Joyce, Woolf, Faulkner, Morrison*.

Philip Weinstein, *Unknowing: The Work of Modernist Fiction*.

Questions to Consider:

1. Grandmother's death in this novel turns out to be a "double-death," inasmuch as she first dies for herself but only later dies within Marcel. Do you agree with this model of a double calendar for processing deaths? What seems to you most awful or most beautiful about such a vision?

2. Proust offers as his final image of the human being in time a man on stilts. It is a circus image. Why do you think Proust chose it? Does this trivialize his great theme, or does it bring it home to us in a special way? Can you see your own life as being on stilts? Does this perception soothe or hurt?

Lecture Twenty-Six—Transcript
Proust—*Remembrance of Things Past*, Part 3

In this last lecture on Proust, I want to talk about the crucial thing that precedes remembering, which is, of course, forgetting. What does "forgetting" really mean? What does it mean when you can't remember your past, or you forget your past? What does it mean when you forget about other people? What does it mean when you forget to do things? How much, do you think, of your life has been forgotten? I mean how much can we possibly retain in our memories? You could argue that our system is equipped only to allow us to keep a certain amount of material current, as it were—available on sort of the top of the heap. I've read somewhere that is the way memory is sort of structured—like layers. It depends on how many we can access. What happens when we forget our dead, "our dead" being the people that we have loved, but also our dead prior selves? And where do they live if they live—in photographs, in graveyards, or in us?

I want to return to where I closed the last lecture about the grandmother's death, the brutality of it. I tried to not exaggerate it but to do justice to Proust's own really grim picture. It's grisly that she is described as a beast lying upon a bed. Her eyes—one is not quite closed, but it won't really open. It reminds me even of the Legrandin scene that I mentioned earlier where the man is lying out of the chink of his eye. I said lying is a form of creative activity. The grandmother in her last sort of gasp before she dies fully, her one eye is partly open, but she can't even recognize the people that she's looking at. And they can't recognize her. The boy says, but this was not my grandmother, and if it was not my grandmother, where was she? That's what led me to say this is a bit like Little Red Riding Hood's story.

So, let's think about the kinds of calendars that are in play. The scene of grandmother's death is her death, her physiological death. The beast on the bed is unfortunately the way we will frequently if we attend the deaths of those who are older than us perceive them, as bodies that are being played out and finally expiring in front of our own horrified eyes, whether we see this in a hospital room or in a bedroom.

That's one form of dying, and there's no question about it. That's the one that will be followed by a funeral and a gravestone probably. But the other calendar is different. The other calendar is inside of our heads, and it is when the loved ones die in us. It may or may not be the same thing as the date on your calendar as to when someone died, or the date written on the gravestone. That other death is the one that Proust is most interested in because it is also a life—the life that people live inside of us even though physiologically they are dead. We are now talking about mourning, aren't we? Successful mourning usually signifies that our own ego, our own system, finally succeeds in becoming free and uninhibited again. That's what mourning is about. Freud has written the most famous essay on that called "Mourning and Melancholia." He talks about the "work of mourning." That's his phrase, *die Trauerarbeit*, the "work of mourning." But it's not work that we consciously do. It's work that Freud says our organism does. It systematically goes about cutting the ties that connected us to the loved one, because the organism knows that the loved one is dead and that dead tissue, as it were, cannot nourish living tissue. It's a brutal, brutal biological picture of things, of the psyche. It's brutal partly because in our hearts and minds we want to think that love is eternal, imperishable, but flesh, of course, is perishable and that, of course, is the kind of paradox that we're talking about here.

When I said that successful mourning means that we become free and uninhibited, those are Freud's terms, free and uninhibited. The ego finally is emancipated from the weight of the dead one. It doesn't mean you forget the dead person, but when you can say it no longer hurts the same way, then you can say that the ties have finally been cut. Then you are free, as it were, to cast your love, and your affection, and your needs elsewhere. It's a kind of deference to the reality principle. It's a way of saying that living trumps everything and that ultimately we will toe the line and finally get past the deaths of the ones that we love. They will not bring us also to die. We will honor them. We will remember them, but we will become in some sense free of them.

Well, let's think about the way Proust handles all of this—you remember the beast on the bed. That's the way she died. Then the book continues. It's a long book. There are lots of advantages to having a 3,000-page book. You can do a lot of things with it, and among the things you can do is you can go past the death of one character and continue building on the life of the younger person, Marcel, the protagonist. So, he continues to have adventures. He has lived at least a full year past her death. There is a sense in which the successful mourning has been completed, and in some sense, I don't want to overstate this, he forgets the grandmother. That's what successful mourning means. In another sense that Proust couldn't have intended, we forget the grandmother. We have read pages and pages of this young boy continuing to go through this adventure in his life, and so she seems to be gone.

Then, we have a second trip to Balbec. He goes back. This is the place, you remember, where he had this sense of almost being annihilated, asphyxiated by the strange room, and his grandmother had come in to see him, had embraced him and had given him a kind of infinity of space to his constricted heart. The way they had done this was quite interesting as well. The grandmother and the boy couldn't stay in the same room. I said that, but they stayed in adjacent rooms and the wall between them was used as their little Morse code wall. The boy would have his attacks of anxiety and panic, and he would tap on the wall usually early in the morning, sometimes late at night. He wouldn't tap very loudly because if he thought maybe she was really deeply asleep it was a cruel thing to do, but he would tap loud enough for her to hear. Invariably, she would tap back, and her little message to him always meant "Don't fuss little mouse," This is the way Proust writes it. "I know you're impatient, [but] I'm just coming."

I love the image of the wall between the two rooms because it is the wall of human skin that separates human beings in life. It's the wall that he collided with when he tried to kiss Albertine. That wall in the hotel room says, no, this is penetrable. This is a membrane that unites two people. It doesn't divide them, and that's what had happened to them when they were in Balbec. But now she is dead, and he's back there. He is in the room, and we have almost a replay of how the novel begins—a middle-aged man who is tired and depressed bends down. In this case, he doesn't take a cup of tea with the madeleine. He bends down to take off his shoes, and he is struck. Just as the middle-aged man was struck by a feeling of eternity with the madeleine, in the room at Balbec again, he is struck by some kind of invading angel, an invading spirit. He knows who it is. It's her.

It's as if she comes back into his life because they have recreated the setting where the two of them had experienced such intimacy and love, and he bends over and is almost struck dead by it. It's almost too much for him. He stays in the room. He sequesters himself in the room. He doesn't go out at all. He stays there because this is the work of mourning. He is now going to actually process her dying. It's called an unknown, a divine, presence, which floors him. How will he do that?

He is encountering the double-edged sword of memory. What is memory? Memory is on the one hand a magic retrieval, a magic presence of those who are dead or gone elsewhere. We can't remember what's in front of us. We don't need to remember it. Whether you're remembering the book that you left in your room or whether you're remembering your grandparent who is dead, they're not there. Yet, the double-edgedness is that memory never ever blinds us to the fact that they are only there in some virtual sense. They are only there in our minds—that the book is still in the room and that grandfather or grandmother is still dead. That's the kind of remarkable poignance it seems to me that memory possesses and that Proust helps us to see, a kind of presence/absence. They are inseparable from each other.

Only now in Balbec a second time does he fully grasp, and measure, and feel, and understand what this woman was. The beast on the bed where he is standing with his parents and seeing this woman move from the living to the dead with the parade of doctors who had been coming and going is not a place for understanding or measuring love. But later, after she is long dead, he finally begins to fully process what has happened. He remembers the two of them being in Balbec together. He even learns from other people that she had been sick already then and in fact was already beginning to die. He had no idea. He wasn't interested. He didn't care. Now later, too late—she's dead. He realizes what a tragic situation it was. There's one episode in particular where she wanted to have a photograph taken of the two of them. He was inpatient. Why waste this time taking a photograph? It's because she knew that she wasn't going to live much longer. These are the things that you learn belatedly. They do you no good for the person who is now gone. All they can do is inflict pain on you. He remembers other ways in which he had been mean to her, nasty to her, as we are to the people we love. And yet, remembering it later is only a form of self-punishment. I quote Proust, "for as the dead exist only in us, it is ourselves that we strike without respite when we persist in recalling the blows that we have dealt them." When you remember how you have been cruel to your parents or grandparents who are no longer here and who probably forgave you even, the harm is being done to you. It's yourself that you're punishing. It's your own misdeeds, your own cruelty that you're now measuring, and you are the sounding board for it. You are the place where it's happening—laceration, self-laceration.

It's now that he realizes two things, and this is going to sound simple but it's not. He now knows that she's not there because that's what the memory shows him. He's known it in some conceptual way as voluntary memory, but when this spirit comes to him as he bends down to take off his shoes and realizes the presence of this woman, the love of this woman, the magnanimity of this woman, that's when he realizes what he's lost. At the same time, he knows that he has lost her for good. He knows what she is and that she's gone for good.

Maybe that's what ultimately farewell is supposed to be about if it is to be commensurate with the actual life of our heart and the death of those that we love because what happens, and this is a famous chapter in Proust called "*Les intermittences du coeur*," which means the "Intermittencies of the Heart," or the "Intermissions of the Heart." It's been called both. He has these dreams, and one often has dreams at the death of loved ones. He has these dreams in which he is pursuing her. He's pursuing her because he's been told that she's dead, but because this is the logic of dreams, she is not fully gone. She is in some strange little room where she is being kept, and he is trying to find her. How do we find her? He is told that the only way to find her in the dream is to enter into his own blood stream. His own blood stream is called the "River Lethe," and he has to move into it, travel it, and voyage it in order to find where she is hiding, the room that they've taken her to, the room where she is outfitted with a nurse, a tiny, little room because she's paralyzed. He thinks she must think that he's forgotten her. There is something exquisite about this. She is, in fact, dead, but in the dream he is thinking there she is trapped in this little room. And she's thinking that I, her grandson, have forgotten her now that she's dead because the logic of the dream allows all of that. He goes trying to find her, and he has his father come in the dream as well because the father knows her address. But the father keeps saying, no, I don't think you should see her. I don't know that you would really recognize her. I don't think it's quite right. It's an awful dream, but it's a dream of pursuit of the dead. It's almost like Orpheus and Eurydice going into Hades, going into the dead, in order to retrieve the ones that you have lost. At the end of this dream he wakes up, and this dream I want to say is about farewell. It's a dream about trying to tell somebody that you love them enough, something that we never do in life. It's when they're dead that we realize that we didn't say it enough. We simply are incapable of being commensurate with our own feelings or sharing them fully. Afterwards, it's when we regret, when we think through, when we are pained and hurt, we suffer from it. This sequence here of reliving her death on his calendar time, not hers—she is again in the earth, but now he is experiencing what that dying really meant and what she really meant. It's at that moment that we see the kind of plenitude, the fullness, of Proust's view of things.

This is a farewell that in my opinion dwarfs the scene of a "beast on a bed." That's where we're helpless. The dying body of our loved ones we can do nothing for. We can't even tell them anything. They're in no condition to hear it, to respond to it, but later, and it's true it's only in him, it's not in her—we don't know what possibly she could, dead, be experiencing, but in him he is trying to say farewell. That is about the most orderly thing in human affairs is to be able to say farewell to the ones that we love who die. Then, he wakes up more or less from this dream of pursuing her to tell her how much he loved her, and he looks at the sea and then he looks at the wall. It's exactly the wall that the two of them used to tap their little messages of love on. It's an exquisite scene.

That's part of the richness, pathos if you want, and beauty of Proust's world and Proust's novel. He is often thought of a kind of maniacal egoist, and he is. Even in this scene that I've just described it's still all taking place within him, and yet it's a scene of great beauty. So, one understands the role of Forget—the French have a word for it, we don't. *Oubli* is their word, and our only translation is "oblivion." It's where the people go whom we have lost if they're dead, or whom we've forgotten if they're alive. It's like a huge storeroom where all of the experiences, and others, and perhaps past "selves" are stored, but through memory they're all accessible. *Oubli* is a form of death in life. Oblivion is a form of death in life, and I want to expand on that a little bit and to say that Proust is touching on things that have much more to do with our everyday lives than we may suspect. It's not simply a question of the lovely story of a boy and his dying grandmother and the kind of exquisite retrieval that takes place in the dream.

It's also a question of how we are locked in and locked out of the plenitude of our own life all the time. If you look at your CV or your résumé, look at the various selves that you have been, look at those jobs that you've had, the degrees that you've had, the stages you've gone through, all of us are skilled at writing these things, and ask yourself to what extent are those living creatures who are listed there and named there? To what extent can we remember and relive this trajectory, which is in fact nothing other than our own life? Often this, too, is dead words, dead letters. These are the signs, the markings, of who we were, what we were, and yet how often is that invested with life? How many of these "selves" still live in us? I'd even be willing to leave time out of it and bring it right into the present moment. Think about the lateral dimensions of it, about any single life, how many separate roles each of us plays out every day, as husband, as father, as son, as teacher, as someone eating a meal, as someone going to church, as someone earning a living, as someone going to bed, as someone going to the bathroom, et cetera. All of us play out extraordinarily diverse roles, and we always forget about all of the other ones. I mean, again, it's the law being able to focus and do any one thing.

Proust's word *oubli*, or oblivion, is the operative notion that makes life possible for us to become this and therefore to have to rule out all of those other things that we also are or were. We have to forget our other selves to succeed in each narrow role. So, in this novel we get a sense of the beauty and necessity of having to make this kind of vertical retrieval, to recover something of the scale and scope of our life and our loves, and it's a sense in which, as I said, the only way the dream worked was for him to move into his own bloodstream. Proust actually calls it the "depths of those mysteriously lighted viscera." That has always struck me as a brilliant line because today we can go to doctors. We sometimes have to go to doctors, and they can go inside of our bodies. They can go into our channels and passages to see what kinds of blockages or growths might be there to get our equipment running right. You have to ask yourself—is that what's inside of us, blockage, passages, blood? Where does love live inside of us? Where's our life inside of us? Do we have an imaging tool that would give us that? Is there any surgeon who is able to give us that?

This is a book about recovering what is buried in us. Remember, I evoked the Titanic when I talked about the madeleine. It's our own life that is being retrieved here, and there's also a kind of hallowing of the temporality of life that has to do with being able to look at people and to see them in time. I don't mean to get there in time but to see them as existing in time, and as I said, the mind is not equipped for that or at least the eyes aren't. The retina takes in what you look like right at this moment. But could you look at the person that you see and love and try to remember what the large curve of time would tell you about that person—the plenitude of the lives that you're looking at? Most of the people, I'm afraid, that we look at are not even a fully developed photographic image. They're like silhouettes. It's not clear that any of us is able to see the roundedness of the lives that we look at. I think of the photographs of my children. I look at them, and now I look at these children and they are grown-up adults now. I see in those photographs something that is sort of magnificent—the mobility of who they might be and all the people they might be, and now I look at the wonderful people that they are. It's as if I'm getting a double vision when I look at pictures.

One thinks of the people that are old and dying, and it's important to try to remember what we know they were like when they were young, photographs of them earlier. Proust gives us an image of that. He said that if we looked at people and could see them as existing in time, then they would appear, he writes, covered "with the beautiful and inimitable velvety patina of the years." Isn't that wonderful that people would be covered with the patina like a painting has a patina of the years? It would give a kind of lovely, rich, luxuriant gloss to their faces as opposed to what dullness, and torpor and routine do, which is they thin out life for us. He gives us an analogy for it: "Just as in an old park a simple runnel of water comes with the passage of time to be enveloped in a sheath of emerald," a beautiful line—in a park, water that just passes into the greenery over time becomes enveloped in a sheath of emerald. Shakespeare wrote in the tempest, "Full fathom five thy father lies; of his bones are coral made." It's a lovely image that suggests that when we die, a sea change takes place, a transformation. We become precious stones. Proust is giving us something comparable.

Could we imagine the plenitude, the temporal plenitude of the lives of those that we love as turning them into a sheath of emerald, of helping us see the roundedness, the richness, the length, and fullness of their lives, the dimensionality of their lives? That's finally what this book is about. We live in a snapshot world, our selves, our own conceptions, and models and notions are that. We cannot take into account the plenitude, fullness, reach and dimensionality of lives. One of the notions I want to bring up is can any of us see our own story? In other words, anybody can write résumé, but can you see your story? Is there a story? Let me put it musically. Would there be a melody to your life? If there were, it couldn't possibly be what shows up in a résumé. It would be something that would require you to see what the leading strands are of it, what the motifs are that make your life something cogent over time. Can we access it? Could we share it? We live a long time. That's one of the things that Proust says, and I tell that to my students. They're usually 18 to 22, and I say you have lived so long. There is so much you have already forgotten that is no longer accessible to you.

So, this book is about recovering something of that plenitude, and it's also about the cheat or the fraud that we are often subjected to about where our own truths are. He would suggest that our truth is not in the photograph we have. It's not in that at all. It's rather in these inner memories that we need to somehow be able to reach where we can relive our past. Proust was a great critic of film, which was a new art form when he was writing. He was a critic of photography. He would have been a critic, and he was, of so-called realist literature, which describes the outside world, because he would have said that doesn't capture anything. It doesn't tell us the human feeling of these things. It's what things mean to us, it's that private story that if we don't ever find it and express it will never be known. It's the inside picture. Imagine someone walking into your bedroom, and let's say they see a doll there, or a photograph there, or a poster there. For that person it can't possibly mean what it has to mean for you because that's why you put it there. It's a marker for you of your life, of your emotions, of your experiences, and of your past. That's the inside story that no sort of faithful rendition of outside surfaces could possibly render.

What the world meant to us is what we know nothing about because we don't ever seem to share it and because it's inaccessible to the camera. Often enough, it's inaccessible to historians. Proust argues that there is a whole inner history we know nothing about, and it's often a kind of associative logic. He says that we can open up a newspaper, and we'll encounter something that will send us back to ourselves. We can walk down the street, and we will see in a poster, or a sign, or somebody else's face, or we will smell something that will send us back to us. You saw how the madeleine sequence worked. Everybody has private coordinates. The smell of a Gauloise cigarette for me reminds me of when I was 20 years old and a student in France. The smell of wildflowers will do something different for each of you. The sound of chalk going across a board will convey something to each of you. A sound, a look—everybody has their own private coordinates, their own private markers, markings, about their life, which are not public, which are not sharable, and Proust's project is for us to somehow finally get in touch with that and recover it because it's the recovery of our own life.

To put it most simply, who on earth could write your biography? They could do all of the obvious public data. They could say when you were born, what school you went to, who you married, if you married and what your income was maybe. Could they possibly tell your story? Who could ever know the extraordinarily complex, long, rich, coursing thing that is inside of every living person? That's the fraud he is talking about—that we are cheated out of that because we think life is just a series of received notions and conventional ideas. The quarry we should be going for is what's on the inside of us.

This leads him as well to value, as the last segments of this book are about a man who is quite old. He goes to a reception, and he sees all of these people around him. He thinks they're all in masquerade. They're all wearing white wigs. It doesn't seem possible that these are people he has known all his life. He hasn't seen them in years. They look like they're transformed. They're moving toward the grave. I see that at my university. I've been teaching at one place for 40 years, and I see people now that are old and bent making their way painfully to their labs or their classrooms. I remember, and in my mind's eye I see these people as stalwart and strong—and the people that I admired when I first came. They were the leaders of the campus. That's to be able to have a vision that is temporal, a vision that is cued to time. It is also a vision that valorizes our feelings, wants, and desires.

The American writer who resembles Proust is Fitzgerald. He's the writer about desire. At one point at this reception he looks at these two doughty dowagers. They were both women that he was in love with when he was young, and in a realist, critical novel you would say, well, that proves the folly of desire, doesn't it. Proust says the opposite. What I saw in those women was not what they had become, what life had done to them or to me, but what I recaptured in them was how much I loved them when I was young in an earlier point in my life. What I want to remember and valorize is what they then meant for me. It's a question of finally saying our desire is more important than what we got, our hunger is more important than the bottom line. Let's be faithful and commensurate to that. Let's not forget what we wanted in life, because that was our intensity and that was our passion. So, this book is about writing in such a way as to deliver the inside story of a life, all of the inner wants, passions, needs, and emotions that one has in a life and that rarely make it into the public domain. That's the story he wants to tell. That's the whole planet I said that the astronomers want to discover and that this man has tried to chart in his book.

He finally says his book is a mirror for his readers—that they will see in themselves perhaps a door opening to their own unstoried, untold, unmapped, inner life, past and history. He finally compares himself to Ali Baba. It's a lovely thing. He doesn't do it, but I'm going to. He remembers Ali Baba being a sort of motif on these dinner plates that his aunt used to use. He says that his aunt, if she had really known what strange lives the people whom she thought she knew actually had, she would have thought she was having Ali Baba to visit. I like that because Ali Baba is the man who has the "Open Sesame" expression and goes to his magic treasure in the cave. That's the vision of Proust. The cave is simply your own life. The treasure is simply your own life. It's a question of accessing those depths, that enormous space, and making it yours. I can't think of a more noble goal for any literary text than that.

Thank you.

Lecture Twenty-Seven
Joyce—*Ulysses*

Scope:

Ulysses is the most influential novel in the English literary canon, 800-pound gorilla or not. Joyce began his career with scrupulous realism, then wrote the swollen *Portrait of the Artist as a Young Man*, his most popular book, about self-making and freedom. *Ulysses*, with echoes of Homer, reprises Stephen Dedalus in drastically new fashion and questions the entire theme of self-emancipation by showing the past's hold.

Stephen is obsessed with the fate of flesh and/or soul, with "dogsbody" (our bodies rot at death) or "godsbody" (the immortal soul remains). Yet this heavy material is larded with hilarious humor, and Joycean prose succeeds in mocking its young protagonist, offering us a radically new kind of literature, illuminating a song and dance we rarely see. Stephen, brilliant, *Hamlet*-obsessed, is the son looking for a father.

Outline

I. James Joyce's (1882–1941) *Ulysses* (1922) is arguably the most distinguished modern classic in the English literary tradition and, perhaps, the most unread and unreadable.

   A. We know the book recasts the adventures of Homer's hero Odysseus as a day in the life of the characters in modern-day Dublin, but beyond that, the novel seems confusing. We don't seem to find any kind of plot or story; we flit in and out of bits of dialogue, description, and Joycean erudition. In these three lectures on *Ulysses*, however, we'll also see that it's a hilariously funny novel.

   B. *Ulysses* is a wake-up call for readers, and in it, Joyce awakens us to *our* genius, not his. He makes us realize that we, too, operate in the same way that his characters, Stephen and particularly Bloom, operate—we engage in a strange song and dance and talk back to life in ourselves in ways that we rarely attend to.

©2007 The Teaching Company.

II. Before we begin *Ulysses*, let's take a brief look at the curve of Joyce's work.

    A. Joyce's first narrative, *Dubliners*, is a lean portrait of straitened lives at the end of the 19th century, a somewhat unrewarding book.

    B. Then comes *Portrait of the Artist as a Young Man*, his most popular and manageable text. This essentially autobiographical text tells the story of Stephen Dedalus, a young Irishman torn between his desire to be a priest or to be a writer.

        1. In *Portrait*, Joyce moves into a subjective mode, writing the evolution of Stephen Dedalus.

        2. At the end of the novel, Stephen leaves Ireland for the Continent to make his career. The book tells a bracing, seductive story of liberation and self-emancipation.

        3. Of course, the name "Dedalus" recalls for us the myth of Daedalus, who constructed wings and taught himself to fly, and his son, Icarus. As we know, Icarus flew too close to the sun, melted the wax of his wings, and fell into the sea. Both flying high and falling low will be important in Joyce's work.

        4. Young people (perhaps particularly American young people) are drawn to *Portrait* because it confirms a view of life that they believe in: We can fly over the constraints of birth, class, and gender to achieve individual freedom.

        5. A great deal of modern thinking suggests, however, that culture is, in fact, contained within us. It is not something we can fly above. Joyce seems to subscribe to this model in writing his later books, such as *Ulysses*.

        6. We should also note that *Portrait* is not the clear emancipatory fable that it at first seems. It contains many passages in which Stephen has visions of a great future, leaving behind the sordid conditions of his life up to that point, but those passages are invariably followed by evocations of falling and of being trapped in a dense, material world. The directionality of *Portrait* is contrapuntal.

C. Joyce's next book, *Ulysses*, is our target in these lectures. Weighing in as the 800-pound gorilla in the English canon, *Ulysses* is the most significant, most celebrated, and most unread of the great novels in English.

1. The central features of *Ulysses* include the use of stream-of-consciousness writing, or the interior monologue, and a delight in mixing the inside world of thought and feeling with the physical and conceptual stimuli of the outside world, the noise of life.

2. As we've said, *Ulysses* is harder to negotiate than most novels we're familiar with. We usually think of novels as moving in a linear fashion, but Joyce tells us that life isn't like that.

3. In *Ulysses*, the autobiographical figure of Stephen shares the stage with two other major figures, Leopold and Molly Bloom. In fact, Bloom will dwarf Stephen in significance.

4. Joyce chose the story of Odysseus for his modern-day pilgrimage because he thought of that figure as well-rounded—a father, son, husband, farmer, warrior, and traveler. Perhaps most importantly, he is also wily, resourceful, and cunning.

5. This novel forces us to ask: Do we have Odyssean adventures ourselves? Could going to work or trying to get a raise be an Odyssean adventure? What about other kinds of behaviors, such as passing gas? Joyce prompts us to rethink what the Homeric hero model might mean when translated into modern life.

D. Joyce's last book, *Finnegans Wake*, is his nighttime epic. It is a book of *portmanteaux* (constructed or blended words) and is read almost exclusively by Joyce specialists and worshippers.

III. A new Stephen Dedalus appears in *Ulysses*, and he is a far cry from the swooning young protagonist of *Portrait of the Artist as a Young Man*.

A. Back from Paris, Stephen is living in a Martello tower with Buck Mulligan. He feels alienated, outcast, and unrecognized. His mother is dying, and Stephen has refused to kneel and pray at her deathbed, as she begs him to do.

Joyce undertakes to write Stephen's guilt about his mother's dying.

1. In an opening scene, Buck Mulligan, the Mephistophelean figure of the book, makes snide jabs about Catholicism and diminishes Homeric language. Instead of the "wine-dark sea," he speaks of the "snot-green sea." Stephen's guilt will be written in a way that merges the outside setting, the Martello tower and the sea, with his own anguished mental landscape.

2. Stephen has a vision of his dead mother coming to haunt him in her grave clothes. He looks toward the sea, now described as a dull green mass of liquid. This triggers another memory of his mother's green bile vomited into a china bowl. These dull green masses bring to mind the mass of the Church that Stephen refuses to attend.

3. In a Catholic mass, the body and blood of Jesus become the wafer and the wine. This is the miraculous transformation that Stephen refuses, and he does so because the dying body may become green bile instead of a wafer and wine. This returns us to the Homeric reference to the sea—our "great, sweet mother"—and reminds us of Stephen's own dead mother. We see here Joyce's approach to writing a character's inner emotion.

4. We tend to think that our deepest emotions are lodged in an inner sanctum inside of us that we visit only periodically. But Joyce tells us that this inner sanctum doesn't exist; instead, our emotions are awash in the way we see the world. They bleed into the outside scene, and anything we see can send us into our own hidden emotional story.

B. In *Portrait*, Stephen said that he would fly over the nets that threatened to constrain him, but in *Ulysses*, Joyce writes about collusion, about merging, and about the fact that we are porous; the outside world constantly enters us, and we constantly bleed into the outside world. The contours that we think of as binding the self are, in fact, mixed with external things.

C. Stephen has refused to pray and will be reminded of that fact constantly. He overhears a conversation on the beach about someone who has drowned and visualizes a corpse that has been in the water for nine days. His thoughts seem to be a meditation about the final outcome of the human body. Do we possess an imperishable soul that will be reunited with God, or are we merely physiological creatures that will decay after death?

　1. In *Ulysses*, the corpse appears on the beach, swollen with gas. This world seems to have no place for Jesus.

　2. In fact, the world of *Ulysses* is more like that of Proteus (the title of this chapter), the god of incessant change. Change is Joyce's picture of the human body and the human mind.

D. At one point, Stephen says, "Dead breaths I living breathe, tread dead dust, devour a urinous offal from all the dead." The air we take in is saturated with the decomposition of life, yet this is a remarkably vital phrase, filled with hunger, energy, and vibrancy. This is Joyce's dialectic: Life and death are locked together in a dance.

　1. Stephen develops two terms for this dialectic, the first of which is "godsbody," which is code for the mass. When someone dies, he or she becomes part of the larger body of God.

　2. The other term is "dogsbody," the idea of the physical body destined to rot.

E. We shouldn't think for a minute that Stephen's thoughts are esoteric. He is grappling with issues that are basic to us all.

IV. Let's turn now to some of the humor in *Ulysses*.

A. *Ulysses* is, foremost, a text that talks back. For example, Stephen doesn't answer Mr. Deasy when he asks whether Stephen has always paid his own way, but the text does, with a grocery list of Stephen's debts.

B. In *Portrait*, Stephen had seriously considered becoming a priest, but we now learn that he had prayed to the Virgin not to have a red nose and had asked the devil to have a woman in the street lift her skirt a little higher. We even get a replay of a courtroom scene, in which Stephen puts himself on trial for having yelled "Naked women" on a tram.

C. Joyce's wordplay in Stephen's reflections on the books he planned to write is another way in which *Ulysses* seems to stick its tongue out at the young man's most serious ambitions.

D. The Stephen Dedalus here is much better company than the figure in *Portrait*. In *Ulysses*, Stephen has a sense of humor about himself. We will see more of Joyce's humor in the next two lectures.

Essential Reading:

James Joyce, *Ulysses*.

Supplementary Reading:

Harry Blamires, *The New Bloomsday Book: A Guide Through Ulysses*.

Frank Budgen, *James Joyce and the Making of Ulysses*.

Clive Hart and David Hayman, eds. *James Joyce's Ulysses: Critical Essays*.

Hugh Kenner, *Ulysses*.

Arnold Weinstein, *Recovering Your Story: Proust, Joyce, Woolf, Faulkner, Morrison*.

Questions to Consider:

1. Stephen Dedalus is, essentially, a successful figure who comes of age and leaves Dublin for Paris in *Portrait of the Artist as a Young Man*. Why do you think Joyce would want to retrieve Stephen from Paris and bring him back in *Ulysses*? What does this tell us about the project of "flying over nets" that constituted Stephen's bid for freedom?

2. How many books do you know where the text "talks back"? Given how straightforward so much literary notation is, do you feel that the actual noise in our heads differs greatly from the accounts we read in books? Would you know how to tell your own story?

Lecture Twenty-Seven—Transcript
Joyce—*Ulysses*

James Joyce's *Ulysses* is arguably the most distinguished modern classic in the English literary tradition, but it's also, and this is unarguable it seems to me, the most unread, the most unreadable, or the most unfinished. Why? Why is that the case? I don't think it's at all because *Ulysses*, the modern book, recasts the adventures of Homer's hero, Odysseus, as a single day in the life of the characters in modern-day Dublin. That's not why. All you have to do is open the book and look at any page, and you realize this is trouble. How do you possibly make sense of this kind of layout? There doesn't seem to be any kind of plot. There doesn't seem to be a story. You're not sure where the characters are because you flit in and out of bits of dialogue, bits of description, and bits of Joyce's extraordinary erudition. So, it's a forbidding, foreboding kind of book, and the thing that I want to do in these three lectures that I'm going to devote to this book is to show you that it is also a hilarious book. It is a book that is perhaps more fun than any other book that I know. To put it really in a kind of consumerist way, there can be more pleasure per page in *Ulysses* than in any other literary text that you've read.

Let me extend that a little bit. It seems to me that what's fresh, weird, strange, and inebriating about Joyce's book is that it's a kind of wake-up call for us, for readers, and I'm going to say something that's going to seem bizarre to you. Joyce awakens us to *our* genius, not to his. He makes us realize that we, too, operate the same way that his characters, Stephen and particularly Bloom, operate—that we, too, in some strange way, have a song and dance that we have rarely attended to; that we, too, talk back to life all the time in ourselves. We rarely do it out loud. This book eavesdrops on exactly that kind of music, that kind of noise, and it's that, it seems to me, that is so astonishing and so gratifying to catch in a novel.

Before getting into *Ulysses*, let me say a few words about the curve of Joyce's work because it's a really marked curve that he starts with a book called the *Dubliners*, which in fact is an extremely, I think, unrewarding book. It's a very sort of mean portrait of straightened lives in Dublin at the end of the 19th century, early years of the 20th, and then he writes what is his most popular, manageable book, which is *Portrait of the Artist as a Young Man. Portrait of the Artist as a*

Young Man is the story of Stephen Dedalus, and we can't miss the fact with the title as well that this is essentially a kind of autobiographical text about a young person, a young Irish boy who is very much torn between wanting to be a priest on the one hand and finally deciding to be a writer on the other hand. In *Portrait*, in contrast to *Dubliners*, Joyce moves into a kind of subjective mode, and he wants to write Stephen Dedalus's evolution. Really, it's like the formation of a soul. Each of the chapters sort of describes a stage in Stephen's development, and it's written from the inside. Stephen's fate, as I said, looks like Joyce's.

At the novel's close, he leaves Ireland off to the continent to make his career. It is a bracing story of liberation, of getting clear, of self-emancipation, and for that reason it's an extraordinarily seductive story. I'll quote you one of the most famous passages in it because I think you'll see immediately why this is seductive. This is Stephen speaking:

> The soul is born, he said vaguely, first in those moments I told you of. It has a slow and dark birth, more mysterious than the birth of the body. When the soul of a man is born in this country there are nets flung at it to hold it back from flight. You talk to me of nationality, language, religion. I shall try to fly by those nets.

Well, I hope you can see just in the imagery itself of nets and flight and the fact that this character's name is Stephen Dedalus that Joyce is really working the old myth of Daedalus and Icarus, Daedalus who constructed the wings and could fly—taught himself to fly, and then his son Icarus, and he's an equally important figure here, who tried to emulate his father. The wings were attached with wax, and Icarus flew too close to the sun and fell into the sea. You're going to see why those two types of directions, flying high, falling low, matter a great deal in Joyce's work.

Let's leave for a moment the tropes, the figures, in this passage I read to you and think about what it says, because it's an astonishing passage, it seems to me, deeply American, even though Joyce was obviously Irish. "When the soul of a man is born in this country, there are nets flung at it to hold it back from flight. You talk to me of nationality, language, religion. I shall try to fly by those nets." This is the clarion call of independence, of emancipation, of getting clear, of flying over the things that would stop you from your own path toward self-determination. I'm using terms that sound extremely American to me. It is about individual freedom, maneuvering room, liberty, and self-enactment. Hence, young people when they read *Portrait* find it irresistible. It confirms exactly the view of life that they either have been told about or that they want to believe in—that we are able, in fact, to fly over the things that would constrain us and trap us. You can turn it into an American story by saying upward mobility—we're free of the constraints of our birth, of our class, of our gender, of any of the things that would in a more traditional society define you. Instead, it's a paean, as it were, to freedom. One wants to believe this. This is extraordinarily seductive.

However, much of what has been written about modern culture and modern psychology in the 20th century calls sharply into question exactly those notions. In other words, yes, this seems to say life, liberty, and the pursuit of happiness. We are free agents, and we are able to attain these things. At the same time, what we learn more and more about in modern thinking is that culture is not something that you can fly over because it's not out there. It's not on the ground and wings would take you over it. The startling modern thinking is culture is on the inside. If I had to use another model, it would be pollution. It's the air we breathe. It's what constructs our way of thinking. One of the great darling phrases of modern sort of ideology is "Subjectivity is constructed." Now, if culture is on the inside, how on earth do you fly over it? Because you take it with you, and that, I think, is the model that Joyce is going to subscribe to increasingly when he writes later books such as *Ulysses*.

I want to say one more word about *Portrait* before moving on to *Ulysses*, which is that *Portrait*, when looked at more carefully, is not the kind of clear, emancipatory fable that it looks like about someone named Dedalus who learns increasingly how to fly over these nets. Instead what we realize when we read *Portrait* is that it has a weird kind of seesaw of tonalities. It has many passages of Stephen swooning and having these visions of a great future, ecstatic visions in which he seems to leave the sort of sorted conditions of his own life, his family, his socioeconomic status, and fly into some other higher zone, but those passages are invariably followed by passages that have to do with falling, that have to do with being trapped in a kind of material world, a greedy, social world, but also a fleshly world that you cannot get easily clear of. So, the directionality of even *Portrait* is up and down, Dedalus, Icarus—contrapuntal. "Contrapuntal" is a word that I'm going to be using a lot as I'm talking about Joyce.

Ulysses is the book that we're going to speak most about. It is the 800-pound gorilla in the English canon. It is celebrated, and it is, as I said, unread. Its central features, if one had to sort of name them, would be things such as stream of consciousness, what is also known as interior monologue, which I think has been over-touted as the central sort of characteristic of *Ulysses*. We'll see that will only take us so far. It also delights in mixing the inside world of thought, and feeling, and sort of bubbling sensation—Joyce knows how to write those things like nobody else, and the outside world that all of us are always at every moment placed in, even if we're sitting in out own room or lying in bed. We're in an outside world, but we're in an outside world more than just physically. We're in an outside world also conceptually. We're always taking in stimuli from the world whether they're things that other people say to us, whether they're ditties and refrains of our culture, whether it's the advertisements that we see, whether it's the newspapers that we read. Joyce is extraordinarily alert to this traffic, to this give-and-take of a kind of inner song and dance on the one hand and then all of the noise that is life, the noise of the street, the noise of ideology, the noise of culture, the noise of the things that we have learned from parents and from school, from church, from everywhere. You put this together, and you get an extraordinary mix.

It's also hard to negotiate. We're used to novels being much more selective, much trimmer, more proper, more "edited," I'd like to say. They tell a story. It moves in a linear fashion. Character A goes through these particular obstacles and finally arrives at some kind of destination or goal, and we say we understand that story. That is a trajectory we can follow. It's usually the same trajectory that we tend to put in our own résumés. Yes, we got these degrees, and we did this kind of work. Now, look where we are. It is a fiction, according to Joyce. It's a fantasy. Life doesn't go quite that way.

So, we get in *Ulysses* a book that is going to take Stephen and put him in a larger framework that will be other characters, in particular Leopold and Molly Bloom. In particular, Leopold Bloom will dwarf, I think, Stephen in significance. Now, *Ulysses* is the book where the story of Odysseus is being recast as a modern story of several people living in Dublin. So, Odysseus' adventures are now going to be reconceived as the peregrination, the pilgrimage, of a character living in Dublin.

Why did Joyce choose Odysseus? He told us why. He thought of a lot of figures that he wanted to use as his central, heroic figure in *Ulysses*, and he thought that Odysseus, or Ulysses, depending on which name you want to use for him, was the most well-rounded of all. He is a father. He is a son. He is a farmer. He is a warrior. He is a traveler. He is a husband, and that's what Joyce was drawn to—this sort of multi-faceted nature of this particular hero. He is also, and for my money this is the most important of all, wily, resourceful and cunning. So, to re-imagine the *Odyssey* in terms of the lives of several modern figures living in Dublin, that's what Joyce is up to.

You may ask, well, why would one do this? You may ask as well, do we have Odyssean adventures ourselves? Could going to work be an Odyssean adventure? It certainly was in Kafka's story, "The Metamorphosis." He couldn't manage it. What about trying to get a raise? Could that be an Odyssean adventure? Let me really go low to the ground the way Joyce does—what about picking your nose when nobody is looking? Could that be an Odyssean adventure? What about farting when nobody is listening? Could that be an Odyssean adventure? Joyce is going to ask us to totally rethink what the Homeric heroic model might mean when translated into modern life, and of course it becomes very raunchy at times.

Well, those of you who know something about Joyce know that *Ulysses* is really his third novel, and then he wrote something even more extraordinary, and even more unreadable, and even more unread, which is called *Finnegans Wake*. That's the nighttime epic, and it is a kind of book of *portmanteau* words, "portmanteau" being a French term about words that you just construct. It's a book that is entirely, in my opinion, unreadable. It is much beloved of the Joycean specialists and essentially unapproachable by anybody else, and so I'm not going to approach it either because we're going to stay with *Ulysses*.

In *Ulysses*, Stephen Dedalus, who is the hero of *Portrait*, reappears, as I said, but he doesn't look like the same figure. He's not the swooning figure of *Portrait*. In fact, you may remember I said

Portrait ends with Stephen being emancipated and headed off for the continent to make his great career as an artist. At least that's what the young people who first read *Portrait* believe. Once you open *Ulysses*, you realize, well, things haven't gone so well. Instead, Stephen is back in Dublin, and he's pretty much a down and outer.

He is now living in a Martello tower with this fellow, Buck Mulligan. He feels alienated. He feels outcast. He feels unrecognized. Joyce then decides to try to write this Stephen in a way that is radically different from anything in *Portrait*. It turns out that Stephen has returned to Dublin because of his mother's dying. His mother is dying, and Stephen refuses—this is critical, refuses— to kneel down and pray at her deathbed as she begs him to do. This is the moment when Stephen rejects the teachings of the church. He refuses to pray, and this is known by some of his friends.

Now, Joyce wants to write what that can feel like, the kind of hauntedness, the kind of guilt feelings that you might have if you don't pray at your mother's bed when she's dying. So, the book opens with Stephen and Buck Mulligan standing together at the Martello tower, and Buck Mulligan, who is the Mephistophelean figure of the book, the mocker of the book, is shaving, and he's making his own little snide jabs about Catholicism. He calls the white shaving cream "corpuscles." He refers to himself as the "genuine Christine," a version of Christ, and he's looking out into the sea. Joyce writes the terms that they use for the sea, and these are Homeric. Homer is filled with these specific kinds of epitaphs, but Joyce is going to reconceive them. Instead of the "wine-dark sea," it's going to be "The snotgreen sea." Well, you can see that's not quite the same tonality, and even "The scrotumtightening sea." So, Joyce is clearly having a bit of fun with Homeric language. Mulligan continues to shave. Stephen gazes at his coat sleeve, and then Joyce begins to open up the scene. We begin to realize that Joyce is going to write Stephen's remorse and guilt in a way that totally merges the outside setting, Martello Tower, the sea, which they can look at, and on the inside Stephen's own anguished mental scene.

So, we read about a vision that Stephen has, a dream of the dead mother coming to haunt him in her grave-clothes reeking of wax, rosewood, and wet ashes. Then, Stephen looks out toward the sea, but now the sea is described as "a dull green mass of liquid." Then another memory is triggered of her death where we have a china bowl and a container that has "green sluggish bile," which she had vomited up as her liver gave out. In these notations, I think we begin to see what Joyce is achieving, because that dull green mass of liquid, we're supposed to realize that mass also refers to what Stephen refused to pray to. He refused to make his prayer. He refused to go to the mass. It's also the mass that Buck Mulligan is mocking with him.

Not only that, what does the mass stand for? The mass stands for the transubstantiation, so that the body and blood of Jesus becomes the wafer and the wine. This is the miraculous transformation that Stephen Dedalus is choking on that Stephen Dedalus has said no to. Why do you say no to that transubstantiation, to that transformation of the body and the blood into the wafer and the wine? Why? Because someone's dying body may not become a wafer and wine. It may become something quite different. It may become green, sluggish bile, and so even the earlier snot green sea gets worked up as green, sluggish bile. The reference to the sea, which is Homeric, our "great, sweet mother" we realize—wait a minute, that's not just Homeric. It's not just the Mediterranean, or the sea around Athens, or anything like that. Instead, it's also Stephen's own mother who is dead, so that what Joyce has done is to find another way of writing one's own inner emotions.

Now, let's think about that for a moment. We tend to think, we have been taught to think, that our deepest inner emotions are lodged in some sort of inner sanctum inside of us, and periodically, not all that often I think—Joyce knows not all that often, periodically we take out our little key, we open the door on the inside, and we visit this inner sanctum. This is when we deal with the deepest emotions that we have, perhaps emotions involving the loss of our loved ones or how much we love the ones that are still alive—things that are the most private and the most important in our lives. What Joyce says is, no, it doesn't work that way. That's not how we do it. There is no private, inner sanctum. Instead, our emotions are awash in the way we see the world. Our emotions bleed into the outside scene. They're a part of everything around us so that anything we look at, whether it's the sea, whether it's shaving cream, all of that can in fact send us to our own hidden emotional story. I said there's traffic in Joyce, and this is the kind of traffic I'm interested in—that one's own inner story is being written as a mix of public and private signs, markings.

It's a new way of cargoing human feeling onto the page. It makes, of course, reading rather difficult. *Ulysses* is written almost musically, so that things are out there and in here all at the same time.

As I said, it is a very shocking way of understanding that there is no private space. Now, remember again what I said about Stephen Dedalus from *Portrait*. "I will fly over those nets." That suggests a kind of self-enclosed, atomistic individual, the kind that is precious in American thinking, a free agent who can fly where he wants. Instead, Joyce's writing is about collusion, about merging, about the fact that we are porous and invadable because we live in a culture and because the outside world constantly enters us and because we always bleed into the outside world. It's really much more of an ecological picture where we are part of a larger stage, a larger setting, and we mix with it. We blend with it so that the contours that we are used to that bound to self, that make me me and you you, and we can easily see it and don't have any trouble with it—all of that is in fact in trouble in Joyce because things—it's not that they get blurred. It's that they mix. It's that they are promiscuous. It's that we find that we are in fact led out elsewhere and that elsewhere is inside of us. This is an extremely provocative picture of human feelings and also of how we might write the human story.

Well, Stephen has refused to pray, and it seems that everywhere he goes he is going to be reminded of that, which of course is the way that remorse and guilt work. Everything sends it back to us. So, he's walking on the beach, and he hears people talking about someone who drowned—that the tide will bring something in. He even hears a reference to five fathoms of water, and then for a moment in his mind he visualizes a swirling bundle that is his image of what a corpse that has been out there in five fathoms of water for some nine days is likely to look like when it washes onto the shore. He imagines it even speaking. It has a puffy face, and it seems to speak to him and say, Here I am. Isn't this also a kind of meditation about what is the final outcome of the human body? Are we some imperishable soul that moves into the heavens and is reunited with God, or are we a physiological creature that will essentially decay, rot, and turn into a swollen bundle and be washed up on the shore? "Full fathom five thy father lies." I quoted that in an earlier lecture from Shakespeare. Joyce is remembering that when he says that there is something out there in five fathoms of water. "Full fathom five thy father lies," Shakespeare wrote, and he continued, "Of his bones are coral made." That's the precious transformation that we turn into precious stone—that there is something beautiful and miraculous. A wondrous sea change is what Shakespeare calls it. That's beautiful isn't it? That's lovely.

That's lyrical, but what if we turn into a swollen bundle instead? That's what's going to happen in this text is that this corpse will, in fact, appear on the shore, and this corpse will look rather strange because we will see that it is puffed up, it is gaseous, and there are minnows that we can see that are going through the trouser fly. We get the sense that its genitals have been nibbled at, devoured.

This is a world that has no room for Jesus. In fact, this is a world that looks like Proteus, which is the title of this chapter—Proteus who was the god of incessant change, the god that you could not possibly grapple with or grasp because he is always altering. That's closer to Joyce's picture of the world. That's closer to what Joyce thinks the human body undergoes as well as the human mind, and so in this view of things it's bad news for any kind of transcendental model that would be inscribed in the mass that the body and the blood becomes the wafer and the wine. Instead, it is a form of rot, putrefaction, and you could say that even that is a form of life because that's the way Joyce is going to see it.

At one point Stephen says, "Dead breaths I living breathe, tread dead dust, devour a urinous offal from all dead." It's as if the air we take in is also saturated with the decomposition of life, and that is the cycle itself. It is what makes part of our breathing, and we exhale it and we continue to move and live. It's a remarkably vital phrase it seems to me. Just listen to it. It sounds like poetry. "Dead breaths I living breathe, tread dead dust, devour a urinous offal from all dead." Yes, there's lots of reference to death, but think about how much reference there is to life. I living breathe. I tread. I devour. This is hunger, appetite, energy, vitality, and vibrancy. It's all there. This is the dialectic that's in Joyce—that life and death are locked into this dance. That is the very sort of coursing of energy that we inhabit, that inhabits us. The two terms that Stephen develops for this are "godsbody" which is the very code for the mass. Godsbody is that when I die, when my physical body dies, it becomes part of the larger body of God. His other term is "dogsbody," and of course "dog" is just the word "god" turned inside out. Instead of g-o-d it's d-o-g. Dogsbody doesn't have much of a transcendent future. Dogsbody is destined for rot, and that's, of course, the kind of dialectic again that Joyce is showing us with Stephen.

Well, this is a text that therefore has a kind of intellectual mischievousness, prancing, moving, and skipping. It is willing to play with ideas that are central ideas, crucial ideas. Don't for a minute think that these are esoteric ideas. Don't think that you have to know anything about theology. Is there any human being who has lived even a little bit who doesn't wonder what's going to happen to him or her when they die? I mean these are meat and potatoes issues. These are those basic things on earth. It's not an accident, of course, that the church has always grappled with them as well. So, what Stephen Dedalus is going through about not kneeling to pray at his dying mother's deathbed or the other kinds of play of words such as godsbody and dogsbody may for a moment seem off-putting, but in fact it gestures toward absolutely basic elemental, literally about the elements, crises, traumas, and events in our own lives.

Now, I said earlier that this book is funny, and I want to spend the rest of this lecture trying to get across that it is funny. In particular, this is a book that talks back. Now, I don't know of any book that talks back. Most books are there for us to read and to see what is written on the page, but I'm going to give you some examples of how the book talks back. For example, in one chapter Stephen, who is a schoolteacher, is talking to the head of the school, who is a sort of puffed-up Englishman, and there is Stephen, the kind of rebellious Irish teacher. Mr. Deasy explains to Stephen that the Englishman's pride consists of having always paid his way. Heaven knows if this is true or not, but that's what Deasy says—always pays his way. Then he looks at Stephen right in the eye and says can you feel that? Stephen, who is the teacher, is not going to answer. He doesn't say anything, but the text answers. Can you feel that—always paid your way? And what the text answers is a kind of grocery list of all of the debts that Stephen has. It just lists all of the people that Stephen owes money to. The Englishman has always paid his way, and then you get a list of all of the people that Stephen owes money to. That's the way this text likes to stick out its tongue. That's the way this text is sort of free to move wherever it wants. If anyone has read the *Portrait*, one would remember Stephen wanted so seriously, so, so seriously, to become a priest in *Portrait*. We learn now in this later book, which is a book that is willing to stick out its tongue and even give the bird to the kinds of issues that it treated so seriously earlier, that Stephen also prayed to the Holy Virgin not to have a red nose or that he prayed to the devil that maybe the woman that he sees in the street might lift her skirt just a little bit higher. So, prayer has a slightly different function here. Stephen even remembers in this book having been on a tram yelling, "Naked women," and then because this book is so prancing, all of the sudden Stephen begins to sort of do his own courtroom attack. He has yelled naked women, and the other Stephen says, you know, wait a minute—that's not very nice. Why did you say something like that? Then he answers himself. Well, what else actually were they invented for—women, naked women? What else were they invented for? So, you get a sense that there is a kind of put-down in this book or let's say a kind of exposé of what it's really like. It can be pretty riotous and funny inside of the awfully serious Stephen Dedalus.

The most serious thing in *Portrait* is Stephen's ambition to be a great writer. He talks about epiphanies, and he talks about grand, grand fame that he will finally achieve. I'll read you this passage here. This is Stephen reflecting on himself.

> Books you were going to write with letters for titles. Have you read his F? O yes, but I prefer Q. Yes, but W is wonderful. O yes, W. Remember your epiphanies written on green oval leaves, deeply deep, copies to be sent if you died to all the great libraries of the world, including Alexandria? … When one reads these strange pages of one long gone one feels that one is at one with one who once.

And you begin to realize Joyce is sticking his tongue out at all of Stephen's most pious wishes from *Portrait*. This is the kind of number that Stephen is doing on himself in this text. This is the way Joyce goes inside and says, you know, it's not all high seriousness, and when it is high serious, you can be sure that it will be followed by a joke, by something raucous, by making fun, by pricking the bubble that has been inflated. That is the way Joyce is going to write this book. That's also part of the talking back that I had in mind.

This Stephen Dedalus who pricks his own bubbles, who deflates the things that he has inflated, this Stephen Dedalus is much better company than the figure in *Portrait*. He also tells us that he inhabits a book that behaves along very different kinds of lines that is willing to go inside of its people and give us may different stories about them. It says to me something wonderful about the way we don't let ourselves off the hook. Yes, we can be puffed up and preening, and at the same time, there's something in us that says, hold on—who are you kidding? So, this is the Joyce that I like, and it's the one I'm going to be talking about more and more.

Thank you.

Lecture Twenty-Eight
Joyce—*Ulysses*, Part 2

Scope:

The central figure of *Ulysses* is Leopold Bloom, ad man and modern-day Odysseus, with the liveliest imagination in literature. Bloom, like all of us, has much wrong with his life (a dead son and a cheating wife), and Joyce's gambit is to display this man's skill at dodging bullets, evading ghosts; such moves are termed "lotus solutions," and Joyce suggests that the Church has always been wise about strategies of evasion.

The novel treats us initially to Bloom's sorties, his down-to-earth wisdom that is at odds with transcendental formulas, but we increasingly measure—via driblets of text and rising memories—what Bloom has lost. Yet the novel moves from depictions of consciousness through a staggering set of pyrotechnical narrative ventures, yielding some of the richest and funniest displays in Western literature, shocking us with its views of how a story can be told. Our view of our own lives is energized.

Outline

I. If Stephen Dedalus is, in some sense, a younger version of Joyce, the main character of the novel, Leopold Bloom defies categorization. He has, perhaps, the liveliest, shrewdest, funniest imagination in literature.

   A. How can Bloom be Odysseus? To answer that question, we must revise our notions of heroism and, perhaps, survival in a modern world.

   B. Much of the pleasure in this novel consists of watching Bloom in action. He has been termed "polytropic," a man of many turns. Arguably, the chief delight of *Ulysses* lies in the sparkling rendition of Bloom's wily maneuvering through his day, his city, and his life.

   C. We meet Bloom as he wakes up and goes to the market to shop for his breakfast. While waiting in line, he admires a woman in front of him with ample hips—a "freebie" that life has offered him as he starts his day. On his way home, he fantasizes about her. This text is full of such small pleasures that are, in fact, significant pieces of our lives.

D. Bloom's perceptions are among the sweetest in literature. He wonders, for example, whether fish get seasick and whether birds choose particular targets for their excrement as they fly overhead.

II. Many people have trouble reading *Ulysses* because of the difficulty of finding its plot.

A. Rather than a direct storyline, this book is filled with scattershot, random notations. But Joyce seems to be asking us: Does life have a plot? If so, is it a grand plot that follows us from birth to death, or is the story of a life told in "plotlets"? Will the kids win the game today? Will I have sex tonight?

B. *Ulysses* also plays with the Homeric idea of the lotus. In Homer, the lotus blossoms cause Odysseus to fall asleep. Here, "lotus" is a code word that stands for a narcotic approach to avoiding difficulties in life or simply opting out of troubling situations. We might think of this as a negative reaction to experience, but it may be a superior form of wisdom. Joyce suggests that the most basic imperative in the human psyche is to find pleasure and avoid pain.

1. Bloom sees a sort of happy bargain for coach horses that have been castrated but are well fed via their feedbag.

2. In another scene, he observes the Catholic mass from the point of view of a former Jew and an advertising man. He admires the Church's use of effective strategies of persuasion to retain the faithful. Bloom's interpretation of the intricacies of Catholic ritual is hilarious.

3. Another form of the lotus idea is avoiding one's ghosts. For Bloom, these ghosts are his father, who committed suicide, and his son, Rudy, who died when he was 11 days old. Joyce tells us that, contrary to popular wisdom, facing up to such realities may be stupid and inadvisable.

4. Bloom tries to avoid thoughts of his father, Rudy, and Blazes Boylan, who is slated to make love to Bloom's wife, Molly, at 4:00 in the afternoon.

5. This strategy of avoiding trouble is a basic, elemental kind of wisdom. Dickens uses the phrase "artful dodger" in *Oliver Twist*, which describes, in some sense, what we all seek: to dodge the bullets of life and not think too much about what is happening in the world around us.

6. Homer's *Odyssey* was thought of as his comic text, a story about cunning, wiliness, and avoidance of direct confrontation. This seems to be the side of the epic that interested Joyce.

III. As we saw earlier, Stephen is haunted by issues of life versus death. Do the same questions haunt Bloom?

A. In addition to the two deaths associated with Bloom that we've seen already, those of his father and his son, he is also attending a funeral on this day, that of his friend Paddy Dignam.

B. Thoughts of the funeral trigger, in Bloom, the image of a cemetery as a picnic grounds or a processing plant that receives a daily ration of dead bodies. We might contrast Bloom's musings with Stephen's obsession with "godsbody" and "dogsbody."

C. As Bloom is leaving the ceremony, Mr. Kernan quotes to him the Protestant phrase "I am the resurrection and the life," saying, "That touches a man's inmost heart." Bloom's response: "Your heart perhaps, but what price the fellow in the six feet by two with his toes to the daisies?"

1. We see Bloom's materialist view of the exalted afterlife of the body: The cemetery is merely a storehouse for broken organs.

2. Finally, Joyce ends the scene with a pun: "Come forth, Lazarus! And he came fifth and lost the job."

IV. *Ulysses* is also a book of great appetite. The "Lestrygonian" chapter follows Bloom into a restaurant, where he watches people eating.

A. As Bloom sits at a table drinking wine, he experiences a remarkable memory of the first time he made love with Molly. Their life since Rudy's death has been without sex, but his recollection of their first time together is lyrical and richly evocative. The passage ends with the words "Me. And me now," a comment on Bloom's passionate past and the life he leads in the present.

B. Such moments of grandeur and lyricism are often squeezed in between the other flotsam and jetsam of this book. Again, Joyce is telling us that this is the way life works: It bleeds through our everyday experiences.

C. Three pages later, Bloom sees a dog vomit on the street and lap up the mess. He thinks to himself, "First sweet, then savoury." This gastronomical injunction brings us back to Bloom and Molly exchanging the seedcake in their mouths. That was the sweet, and the episode with the dog is the savory.

D. This is an example of Joyce's contrapuntalism, and it's also a formula for life. How often do we experience or remember moments of lyricism that are followed by episodes that are much more pungent and cynical?

V. Joyce has a huge bag of literary tricks that goes beyond the use of stream of consciousness that is usually associated with *Ulysses*.

A. The "Aeolus" chapter takes its name from a Greek god of winds. The chapter takes place in a newsroom and is divided into headlined sections. For Joyce, words can be windy, in some cases even flatulent.

B. The "Wandering Rocks" chapter gives us a bird's eye view of the characters as they make their way across Dublin, but the characters lose their depth and humanity from this perspective.

C. Why does Joyce write this way? The best answer seems to be: because he can. He sees life from countless vantage points and angles.

D. Probably the most infamous chapter in the book is "Oxen of the Sun," which focuses on the labor of Mina Purefoy in a maternity hospital. Joyce writes the chapter in terms of the birth of the English language, from Anglo-Saxon to the English of his own day. By writing the chapter in this way, Joyce makes us realize how storied, historical, and layered language is.

E. In the "Sirens" chapter, the world consists solely of sound. Bloom sits in a bar, thinking about Blazes Boylan and his wife, and the words running through his mind become music: "Tipping her tepping her tapping her topping her," "Flood, gush, flow, joygush, tupthrob." Joyce is not constrained to use an ordinary dictionary here.

1. In this same chapter, Bloom also thinks about the ravages of his life as if it were just words: "Hate. Love. Those are names. Rudy. Soon I am old." These are the words that perhaps signal Bloom's life, but they are, at the same time, just words.

2. What if we could imagine that "hate" and "love" were just words? What if we could reduce the pain of a dead loved one to nothing more than words? "Sirens" and Joyce's other chapters seem to give us a kind of esoteric showmanship, but they also bring us a profound, basic wisdom.

Essential Reading:

James Joyce, *Ulysses*.

Supplementary Reading:

Harry Blamires, *The New Bloomsday Book: A Guide Through Ulysses*.

Frank Budgen, *James Joyce and the Making of Ulysses*.

Clive Hart and David Hayman, eds. *James Joyce's Ulysses: Critical Essays*.

Hugh Kenner, *Ulysses*.

Arnold Weinstein, *Recovering Your Story: Proust, Joyce, Woolf, Faulkner, Morrison*.

Questions to Consider:

1. Leopold Bloom is Joyce's candidate for Odysseus/Ulysses, Homer's wandering hero. Bloom is an ad man, and his voyage takes place in one day in Dublin. Does a procedure like this seem to you to belittle Homer's heroic text? Further, would you call Bloom "heroic"? Does this make a difference?

2. *Ulysses* is often thought of as a stream-of-consciousness masterpiece. Yet after the first six chapters, Joyce appears to sign on for an entire bag of narrative tricks and high jinks that have little to do with the representation of consciousness. Why would he do this?

Lecture Twenty-Eight—Transcript
Joyce—*Ulysses*, Part 2

If Stephen Dedalus is in some sense a version of the younger Joyce, and he clearly is an intellectual figure, the main character of the novel, Leopold Bloom, defies categorization. In my opinion, he has the liveliest, shrewdest, and funniest imagination in literature, and that's a large claim. I've read a lot of literature and, of course, you may not agree, but I'm going to try to make you see it that way. You have to wonder—how can he be Ulysses? In order to make sense of this, you may have to revise quite sharply your notion of what heroism is, perhaps even what survival means in a modern story, perhaps even forgetting about Ulysses or Odysseus altogether. In fact, one critic once said, if Joyce hadn't called this novel *Ulysses*, most readers reading it would never have even thought to relate it to that story of Homer's. That's a separate issue, but I want to get back to Bloom.

Much of the pleasure of this book consists of watching this man in action, and I once quoted Kafka and I will quote him again before I'm through with this course, about art being the ax that chops into our frozen sea. Reading Bloom on the page makes you realize how much frozen sea, how much torpor and complacency, is inside of you because this man is so alert, and lively, and bubbling. He has been turned "polytropic." It's an odd word, but it means man of many turns. It seems to me it's a good phrase for him, and the greatest delight of this book is following this man's sort of wily maneuvering in the day that he spends in Dublin and also maneuvering through his life.

So, it starts with Bloom waking up and getting ready for breakfast, which means going out to buy the kidney that he wants to have for his breakfast. Now, most people would think this is not really material for serious literary treatment, but in Joyce's view, early morning breakfast shopping can be a quite exciting kind of proposition, showing us how much we may have missed. So, Bloom goes out to buy a kidney, and he's standing in line behind a woman with ample hips—already off to a good start. This is one of the little "freebies" that life has offered him, and then when he's waiting for his kidney there is this woman with the hips that he is quite drawn to and would enjoy watching a little bit longer with no plans of saying anything to her—just get the visual freebie there, and he gets a little irked because after all it's taking too long for the man to wrap up his kidney. The guy is talking to him. He wants to get out of that shop and follow this woman back—too late, won't work. So instead, being Bloom, he fantasizes about this woman—that she will, in fact, be approached by some kind of off-duty constable. He thinks that those guys, those constables, like them big, these woman—"prime sausage," he even says, which picks up the idea of the kidney again. This is the way this text works—that life is full of little, bitty, low-to-the-ground pleasures all the time, and that's what people are into. That's how we live our lives. That's the way we sort of manage to orchestrate things for ourselves.

Well, Bloom's perceptions are among the sweetest, I think, in literature. How many characters do you know in novels, how many characters do you know in life, who might come to the query—do fish get seasick? It's the sort of thing that Bloom thinks about. I admit I have never thought about that before. Or, when Bloom sees a bunch of pigeons in the air he begins to wonder what they're actually saying to themselves. He watches them flying over Parliament, and he figures they're probably discussing among themselves who they're going to drop their load on. He thinks of it as a group conversation, each pigeon selecting his target, taking aim, and letting go. Finally, we get this lovely little phrase, "Must be thrilling from the air." This is a really elastic kind of imagination to project yourself up into the pigeons who are presumably having this conversation about where to let their charge go and then to have them saying, "It must be thrilling from the air." What's thrilling, to select your target, to let go? This is going to have a scene, this book, where Bloom goes to the outhouse and let's go of what's inside of him. So, that also has its own interest. That could be thrilling as well or scoring—the pigeon who may actually watch it go all the way down and see that it hits on target. Very few novels would treat us to material of this rather low sort, and yet to me this is where we go for the fun and games, and perhaps even for the riches, of this book.

It's difficult to find a grand plot in this book, and that's the staggering challenge of the novel. That's why many people have trouble reading it. It seems to be filled with scatter-shot random notations. Books have plots. We know that. But does life have a plot? That's the question that Joyce is actually throwing at us. Does our life have a plot? Does your life have a plot? Where would you locate that plot? Is it some grand plot that from birth to death you've been programmed for this grand trajectory, or are there instead only little "plotlets," tiny little plots such as am I going to avoid traffic today? That could be a plot. Did the kids win the game today? Might there be sex in store for me today, or this week, or this month? Those are the little plots, in fact, that make up most of our lives, and Joyce is saying you just have to have a much finer-meshed picture of what a plot is and how you get them.

The book also enjoys a notion that is called "lotus." Now, in Homer the lotus blossoms are what make Odysseus fall asleep, but in this book "lotus" is going to actually be a code word that stands for narcotics in the sense of sort of being buffered from experience, avoiding difficulties, a way of simply opting out when trouble comes your way. Now, I just put it in negative terms, which is the way we usually see it, avoiding experience, opting out when trouble comes your way. Has anybody considered the fact that this may be a superior form of wisdom? Well, let's go further. This may be, in fact, what Odysseus or Ulysses would today in fact be doing. I think Joyce suggests that the most basic imperative in the human psyche, and there's nothing volitional, nobody decides this, is really simple—find pleasure and avoid pain. That's the way our craft goes through life. That's the way our little machine operates. Now, we know that these things, and they will in fact turn out this way in *Ulysses*, can be complicated. Sometimes we look for pain. Sometimes pain gives us pleasure. We call that sadomasochism, and we're going to see some of it. But nonetheless the principle of lotus, of avoiding trouble, is going to be a major principle in this book, and it's going to have a lot to do with the maneuvering of Leopold Bloom and also with the way he interprets what he sees.

He walks, for example, past a hackney. He sees the horses there with their heads deep in the feedbag, and he also sees wagging between their legs what the text calls, "little black gutta-percha." In other words, they've been castrated, and he makes the connection between them. They've been castrated. They've sort of been robbed of their own sexual lives, but they've got their noses deep in the feedbag and they're getting food. This is life's little bargain that's been worked out for them. This is also a version of "lotus." A more serious and equally funny version of lotus is when Bloom strays into the church.

He thinks maybe church is a place where you might meet some nice girl, or maybe a girl who is not so nice. He strays in there, and he is a former Jew. He is a converted Jew, but he still doesn't understand much about Catholicism. He's looking at the ceremony of the mass, and he sort of gets it all wrong. He thinks that the priest is dispensing communion as he hands out the wafers, and he's an ad-man, don't forget. He's interested in strategies of persuasion, and so he understands in his view that the mass itself may be some remarkable strategy of persuasion the church long ago worked out. Rule number one—speak a language that nobody understands. So, give the whole service in Latin. Smart, thinks Bloom. Secondly, he looks at these people with their eyes closed and their mouths open, and he says this is working. They're sort of stupefied. He also thinks of it as a form of consumerism in the literal sense—consuming something, ingesting something. He figures these guys think that they're ingesting the kingdom of God. All of this makes perfect advertising sense for him. He thinks about confession as a kind of ritual that is really very interesting because it's kind of a weekly cleansing session. He admires the shrewdness in general of the church fathers who knew what they were doing. I don't think any of this is anti-Catholic, or even anti-religious, or anti-clerical. Rather, it's the kind of bristling, funny thinking of a man who takes a look at things and sizes them up for what he takes to be the kind of targeted nature of what they're up to, what it is they're really trying to get across. The fact that he does not understand the intricacies of Catholic ritual makes it all the more hilarious, the way he in fact interprets these matters.

Well, one form of lotus obviously in avoiding trouble and seeking some sort of narcotic evasion of it would be to avoid your ghosts. Bloom, like everybody else, me, you, everyone, has ghosts that he would like to avoid. His, in particular, have to do with the suicide of his father—not something that would be a lot of fun to think about, and the death of his son, Rudy, who died when he was 11 days old. I mention that because one of the oldest adages that we have in life is "Face up to things." How many times have people told you that? Face up to things. You can't keep ducking them. You can't keep evading them. You can't keep hiding from reality. Oh, no? Joyce has it the other way around. Anybody that's smart tries to duck things, to avoid things. Facing up to reality may be about the dumbest thing in life. He inspects that little adage, and he finds it quite wanting, quite quaint, quite inapplicable. So, Poppa's death worries Bloom, and he immediately tries to figure out ways not to think about that. Now, you can imagine what a boomerang that can be. Every time you try not to think about things, you often in fact think about them.

Likewise, he tries not to think about the fact that this fellow Blazes Boylan, who is the kind of stud, phallic figure of the novel, is slated to make love with his own wife, Molly, at four o'clock this afternoon. Can't think about that either, not my fun, and yet because this thing is on his mind, it creeps, sneaks, finds its way into the text—that is to say into Bloom's thoughts over, and over, and over. But I still want to say that avoiding trouble is one of the kinds of wisdom that this book puts out for us, and it's an everyday kind of wisdom. That's why to see *Ulysses* as an esoteric text that requires you to go to libraries or to go to specialists and experts to have it deciphered and explained, and I admit I'm doing a bit of that in these lectures, in a sense is kind of silly because this book is about absolutely elemental, basic things—avoiding trouble, or to use a term that Dickens used in *Oliver Twist*, becoming an "artful dodger," is something that really should be a kind of life wisdom for all of us. We all know that we don't want to get run over by a truck when we're walking across the street, but, of course, if you're willing to sort of make that a figurative remark, we also want to avoid the kinds of troubles that are coming at us. Life for most of us at some level consists of dodging bullets, of making sure that we don't think too much or end up in some terrible place in our minds thinking about the horrible things that are happening either in the world around us or could be happening to ourselves.

This, I think, is the kind of Odyssean wisdom that this book puts forth. I mean you should know that of Homer's two texts the *Iliad* is usually regarded as the great tragic text about the wrath of Achilles. But the *Odyssey* is thought to be the comic text that Homer wrote, the text about cunning, wiliness, survival, slithering through and moving around rather than direct confrontation, and that's the side of it that Joyce was interested in.

Life versus death—we've seen how much Stephen worried about those matters, about the death of his own mother, about the fate of the body when death arrives. These are things that haunt the intellectual young man of the book. Do they haunt Bloom? Well, they don't quite haunt him, but he's got lots of deaths. I just mentioned two of them. He's got the suicide of his father, and he's got the death of his son. They certainly bother him. They're certainly there permanently somewhere lodged in his memory and in his psyche, and it turns out in the day that this book is charting he is in fact going to a funeral—the funeral of his friend, Paddy Dignam. Well, this triggers some thoughts about what a cemetery is. One of the most splendid references for a cemetery is that it might be picnic grounds. How could a cemetery be picnic grounds?

Well, a cemetery is a funny place. It is, according to Bloom, a processing plant getting its daily ration of dead bodies. He thinks about all of the people who are picnicking at cemeteries like the rats that seem to help out. He thinks about the decomposing bodies. When I say "thinks about," Bloom invariably visualizes these things. He thinks about the black ooze that eventually exits the body. Contrast this to Stephen's own obsession with godsbody and dogsbody. There's something more material, pithy, and funny about the way Bloom looks at things. He also thinks about what it's like when people are dying, when they get the shove, and he figures that, well, wait a minute. They try to say no, no, no—you've got the wrong guy. Go next door. That's who is supposed to die, not me. Or he thinks about people on their deathbed right at the last minute where all of a sudden the doors can't be kept shut anymore so that you start becoming delirious. You rave, and all of the things that you had successfully repressed during your life become expressed at the point of dying.

There is a kind of vigorous imagination of these things. At the ceremony, as Bloom is leaving, one of his friends comes up and cites the biblical phrase, "I am the Resurrection and the Life." That's what Mr. Kernan says, and Mr. Kernan also says, "That touches a man's inmost heart." This is the way Joyce writes Bloom's response to this. To me this is one of the most perfect passages in the book. "I am the resurrection and the life. That touches a man's inmost heart. It does, Mr. Bloom said." That's what he said. Now, in the next paragraph without signaling it, he takes us into Bloom's own mind, "Your heart perhaps," it touches a man's inmost heart, "but what price the fellow in the six feet by two with his toes to the daisies? No touching that. Seat of the affections. Broken heart." That's the language we use, a broken heart. What does Bloom say? "A pump after all, pumping thousands of gallons of blood every day. One fine day it gets bunged

64

up: and there you are. Lots of them lying around here." This is how he begins to think of the cemetery as a place that's got tons of organs lying around. Hearts that have become—pumps that have become bunged up and that's why the guy died. "Lots of them lying around here: lungs, hearts, livers. Old rusty pumps: damn the thing else. The resurrection and the life," that's what was quoted. I am the resurrection and the life. "The resurrection and the life. Once you are dead, you are dead," Bloom says. "That last day idea," the idea of the last day being an idea, sounds like an ad-man. People are trying out the last day notion. What would the last day look like to a man like Bloom? "Knocking them all up out of their graves. Come forth, Lazarus! And he came fifth and lost the job." I think all of Joyce is in that kind of gross pun. Come forth, Lazarus, and he lost the job. Here is an imagination that pokes fun at everything, that takes "I am the Resurrection and the Life," this very solemn, high-toned, spiritual formula again about the exalted afterlife of the body, and instead gives us a rigorously materialist view as a response. Your heart is touched, but what price the fellow in the six feet by two?

The passage about pumps—your pump gets bunged. That's when your heart doesn't work anymore, but that pump pumps thousands of gallons of blood every day and that's pretty impressive. There's a kind of awe in front of the material, physiological equipment that the body possesses in this novel.

Well, that's the Bloom signature—to puncture these high-sounding, high-falutin' phrases about some afterlife, about some life beyond the flesh, and to instead celebrate the flesh as what is truly miraculous, grand, and us.

This book has much appetite in it. One of its chapters called "Lestrygonian" follows Bloom into a restaurant in which he looks at people eating. I don't know how much time you've ever spent looking at people eating, but it's usually not a very pretty sight as they shovel it in and the gristle comes out of their mouth and they spit little pieces of bone onto the plate. That's what happens here, or God-forbid you should ever put a mirror in front of yourself as you eat. That doesn't happen in this book, but I suggest that you try it once. It will take a lot of the romance out of eating. All of those lovely French menus don't quite look the same if you actually watch your mouth ingesting food and chewing it—not real pretty. Yet, in this chapter where you would say God knows there can't be much poetry in a chapter that is looking at people eating, in this chapter as Bloom is drinking a little bit of his burgundy wine, all of a sudden we get one of the most remarkable memories of the novel. It's a memory of Bloom's really rich, full-blooded passional life with Molly, a life that he doesn't have anymore. Their life is now sexless. Every since the death of Rudy they have not had sexual relations, and so this is a memory of a kind of splendor and plenitude that he no longer has. He remembers the first time they made love together, and he remembers lying with her. He remembers that she was lying on his coat, that there were earwigs nearby. I'll quote a part of this to see the kind of lyricism that Joyce is capable of. Lyrical is not a word I've used for this book.

> O wonder! Coolsoft with ointments her hand touched me, caressed: her eyes upon me did not turn away. Ravished over her I lay, full lips full open, kissed her mouth. Yum. Softly she gave me in my mouth the seedcake warm and chewed.

She's been chewing the seedcake, and she passes it on to him. It's an exquisite scene of kind of fleshly commerce, fleshly interaction, nurturing, sustenance, one body becoming another, entering another.

> Mawkish pulp her mouth had mumbled sweetsour of her spittle. Joy: I ate it: joy. Young life, her lips that gave me pouting. Soft warm sticky gumjelly lips. Flowers her eyes were, take me, willing eyes.

It's an absolutely from my point of view a splendid sensual description of two bodies that are lusting after each other, that are accepting each other, embracing each other. There they are, "Pebbles fell," is later written, and of course these are the goats that are walking by dropping their little droppings. Molly laughs. I quote again:

> Wildly I lay on her, kissed her: eyes, her lips, her stretched neck beating, woman's breasts full in her blouse of nun's veiling, fat nipples upright. Hot I tongued her. She kissed me, I was kissed. All yielding she tossed my hair. Kissed, she kissed me.

The last lines of this are, "Me. And me now." It is one of the richest evocations in the novel, and there are not many of them. It is squeezed, sandwiched to keep with my restaurant language into this passage where otherwise we are just looking at people eating. All of a sudden, Bloom has this extraordinary sensual memory of the kind of passionate past that he no longer has, of the kind of relationship with his wife that is no longer there—me and me now.

This is the economy of Joyce's novel that you realize; that there are moments of lyricism and grandeur in this book, but they are squeezed in. They are bites among all of the other bric-a-brac and flotsam and jetsam of this book. Again, I think Joyce is telling us— that's the way it is. We do not in fact say I'll spend the next 30 minutes and I'll use my watch to time it thinking about what was ecstatic in my life. Instead, it bleeds through. You're sitting in a restaurant watching people eat, and all of the sudden the taste of the burgundy triggers, or he actually sees two flies going at it on a window, and it triggers this memory of him and Molly going at it on Howth Hill with this lovely moment of exchange, the seedcake going from mouth to mouth. Well, that passage employs a kind of lyrical Joyce that we see so little of, and yet three pages after that passage, Bloom who seems often to be a roving camera sees on the street a dog. This dog chokes up and vomits some disgusting blob onto the cobblestones and then it laps it up. You've all seen dogs do this. It vomits up the stuff and then laps the same blob back with renewed appetite, and the text writes, "First sweet then savoury." It's one of the most delicious remarks in the book. "First sweet then savoury," sounds almost like a kind of gastronomical injunction. That's how you orchestrate your meals, sweet then savory, and yet you realize it's being applied now, this restaurateur's phrase, to the dog that has thrown up its food and the re-ingesting it again. Then it strikes you— well, wait a minute. This is a kind of weird post scriptum of the beautiful seedcake passage that I just read to you about Bloom and Molly exchanging the seedcake from one mouth to the next. That was the sweet, and the episode with the dog is the savory.

Have I not said that Joyce is contrapuntal? That's what I mean, sweet and savory, "sweet then savory" is not just a formula for restaurants or for food. It's a formula for life. It's how moments that we experience or remember as lyrical may then be followed by something that is much more pungent and cynical. That is the Joycean roller coaster. That's the Joycean directionality. Well, Joyce has a huge bag of tricks. I use the term "interior monologue," as one of the terms that is used to describe what *Ulysses* is. Many people, who particularly have never read *Ulysses*, that's the one thing they could probably say—oh, yeah, *Ulysses*, it's a book with lots of stream of consciousness in it, and it is. There's no question about it, and there's a lot of it. But that is only a partial feature of *Ulysses*, and really after about the first six chapters of the book it starts to really roll up its sleeves and flex its muscles as a verbal artifact so that stream of consciousness stops being what's happening and instead these chapters start to become the wildest, craziest, zaniest, unpredictable things that you've ever read. There will be a chapter called "Aeolus," who is the god of winds in Greek mythology, and that's a chapter that takes place in the newspaper room. It's written with a lot of headlines that are on newspapers. It's just the god of winds who then becomes the god of words, and we also have the notion, which will be important for Joyce that in fact words can be windy. Certain kinds of words can be hot air, in fact, so hot that they become flatulent.

So, that will be one chapter. It's certainly not stream of consciousness. Another chapter, "Wandering Rocks," is almost like a bird's-eye view of the characters of this book making their way across Dublin. They become like little bitty ants in an anthill, or like vectors in a large field. It's as if the humanity and depth of what we think of as literary characters is completely lost, as indeed it would be if you were looking at it from a bird's eye view. I don't think that those pigeons who said it was thrilling from the air were terribly interested in the psychology of their targets. Joyce is able to write from any perspective that he chooses. In fact, that's what you begin to understand in this book. When you ask, well, why is he doing it this way? The best answer is because I can, because it's fun, because why not, and this, I think, is inebriating. This opens our eyes because it doesn't just make the material more trivialized or just more the target of an exploratory. It's as if, yes, life can be perceived from countless different vantage points and angles. If we live in the city, it makes sense to see us as ants in an anthill as well.

Probably the most infamous chapter in the book is called, "Oxen of the Sun," and it is weird because it is focused on an event that is not important in the plot, which is Mina Purefoy, one of the ladies in the book whom we never really meet, who is giving birth to a baby in a maternity hospital. Joyce writes that chapter in terms of the birth of the English language. He writes it in terms of the evolving styles of

English from Anglo-Saxon all the way up to the English of his own day. So, it's a lot of plagiarism. He tries art pastiche. He tries out the styles of various kinds of novelists and writers from Malory in the Middle Ages to Dickens and Carlisle, and he has Sterne from the 18th century, writers whom we have in fact looked at in this course. He tells the story of Stephen and his friends in the hospital carousing, and he tells the story of the birth of this child through the birth and the evolution of languages. Most readers say this is insane. What connection really is there between the birth of a child and the birth of the language? You can imagine there are loads of professors who have given us tons of very erudite explanations, but I still think that Joyce had his tongue firmly lodged in his cheek when he wrote this.

One of the things that I don't think, however, is tongue in cheek is that by writing this chapter in terms of the languages that evolved from the Middle Ages to the present Joyce makes us realize how storied, how historical, how layered language is, and not just the language of literature. We often use words that have a provenance that goes back centuries. When we curse, we use terms that go back forever. We tend naively and wrongly to think that the words that come out of our mouth are words that we ourselves made. Well, if you think about it for a moment that's impossible. The words, the vocabulary, pre-exists us. So, in a sense this chapter that is so erudite in terms of his command of the English tradition, is also a chapter about the kind of daily miracle that happens, daily history lesson that happens when you open your mouth.

Other chapters get even wilder. One chapter is called "Sirens." That's, of course, the episode in the *Odyssey* when the sirens come and taunt Odysseus with their siren song, and he, of course, has tied himself to the mast so he won't yield. Well, "Sirens" for Joyce means a world that becomes entirely a world just of sound. What would a world just of sound be? Well, we have Bloom sitting in the bar thinking about the fact, trying not to, but thinking nonetheless that his wife is getting ready to fornicate with Blazes Boylan. He sits there, and he has his hands in his pockets. We have liquids that come into the text, "warm jamjam lickitup secretness," as he listens to the music that's being played. He thinks about things such as, "Tipping her tepping her tapping her topping her." We clearly know that his wife is on his mind, and he thinks as well about, "Flood, gush, flow, joygush, tupthrob." This is what it would be if it were just music.

This is taking words that we know and putting them together in different ways. This is closer to music, to song, to dance, and Joyce has opened up his own sort of register as a writer. Why should I just use ordinary dictionary words to describe what this character is thinking about? Here he is thinking about the fact that his wife is going to cheat, and he doesn't just think it in those moral terms. He then thinks about, well, what is it really going to be like between Molly and Boylan, "Flood, gush, flow, joygush, tupthrob."

He also thinks about the ravages of his own life, because what would happen if our own life were just words. So, one of the phrases that we read is, "Hate. Love. Those are names. Rudy. Soon I am old." Our first reaction is that's the story of his life. Does he hate Boylan? Does he love Molly? Those are names. Rudy, the name of his dead son—soon I am old. Is that just a series of monosyllabic terms—soon I am old. Well, what Joyce I think is getting at is these are words that perhaps signal his life, but they are just words also.

What if you could imagine that hate and love were just words? There's something strategic here. It would rob them of the kind of despotic power they have on your life. What if your life were just nominal—Rudy? What if you could reduce the pain of your dead son to just a four-letter word, if you could, if you could? Soon I am old— heaven knows that's a phrase that haunts many of us. It haunts me. What if I could just transform it only into words? What I'm getting at is in "Sirens," and in all of these chapters, what looks esoteric, what looks like it's a kind of showmanship, has a kind of profound, basic wisdom to it. I'll get further into that next time.

Thank you.

Lecture Twenty-Nine
Joyce—*Ulysses*, Part 3

Scope:

In this final lecture on Joyce, we tackle the three magisterial late chapters of *Ulysses*. "Circe," located in a brothel, is the theatrical highpoint of the novel; Joyce has now endowed everything with voice, so that what was only thought or desired now speaks. The hiding places of private thought and interior monologue disappear. Metamorphosis is the rule here, and Bloom's sexual fantasies and worries spiral into a spellbinding sadomasochist performance.

"Ithaca" depicts homecoming for Bloom and Stephen, but its narrative despotism—a voice hectors Bloom with catechism-like questions—makes us see that Bloom is the text's toy; this same distant voice makes us see the absurdity of any man's concern about his wife's sexual behavior (or anything else). In "Penelope," the novel closes, finally and richly, inside Molly Bloom's mind, as she reflects on her lovers past and present and on her life. We exit this book with an incomparable sense of discovery and vitality.

Outline

I. *Ulysses* is often mischaracterized as stream-of-consciousness fiction, but after chapter 6, it begins to narrate from different vantage points.

   A. Stream of consciousness is the subjective realm, our own interior monologues, which offer us a kind of freedom vis-à-vis circumstances and events that are otherwise coercive and determinant.

   B. "Circe," the brothel chapter in *Ulysses*, takes up one-third of the novel and is written in theatrical form. Why would Joyce abandon narrative for drama?

      1. In drama, everything is given a voice. In Shakespeare, for example, Hamlet speaks, as do Polonius, Laertes, and Gertrude. In Joyce, bars of soap, bedsprings, chimes, handbills, sins of the past, and waterfalls speak, along with all the characters.

2. If everything is voiced, then the inner sanctum of the individual is no longer private. The interior monologue is brought to language and goes public, telling all about the person whose monologue it is.

3. In the "Circe" chapter, Bloom is on trial not so much for something he has done but for what he has been thinking and feeling. The author Beaufoy appears to chastise Bloom for reading his story in the outhouse, as Bloom had done earlier in the novel. A group of women from the "horsey set" command him to lower his pants so that he can be whipped for ogling them. Nothing can be hidden here.

4. Bloom's meliorist reformist fantasies also appear in this chapter, telling us something about the intellectual climate of the 1920s.

C. Above all, Bloom is a target in the "Circe" chapter. All characters are manipulated by their authors, but in *Ulysses*, the puppet strings are visible.

D. "Circe" is also the chapter where we begin to dig deep into the substrata of Bloom's psyche, and as we've already seen, we find a good bit of sadomasochism.

E. Because "Circe" is a surreal chapter, we see metamorphosis here. Bella Cohen, the madam of the brothel where the chapter takes place, becomes a man, Bello, and Bloom becomes a woman.

1. In becoming a woman, Bloom is subject to extreme sexual aggression and humiliation on the part of the madam.

2. Bello impels Bloom to witness the fornication of his wife with Blazes Boylan, denigrating Bloom's sexual prowess in comparison to Boylan's.

3. Bloom watches Molly and Boylan through a keyhole, and his reaction is one of extraordinary sexual excitement.

4. The other chapters of the novel have Bloom trying to repress this event, but here, Joyce suggests that this is what Bloom wants at some deep level. Joyce tells us that sexual desire is a strange thing, not easily labeled.

F. Before returning to reality, the "Circe" chapter gives us two remarkable epiphanies. Stephen has a vision of his dead mother urging him to pray, and Bloom has a vision of his dead son, Rudy, reading Hebrew.

G. As Bloom and Stephen exit the brothel, Stephen taunts two British soldiers, who then lay him out. Bloom takes care of Stephen, who has clearly become a substitute for the dead Rudy.

II. We next turn to "Ithaca," which of course stands for homecoming, both for Homer and for Joyce, but the modern text pulls out the stops for delineating just where we keep house, inwardly as well as outwardly. This chapter is about taking measures; both Bloom and Stephen become toys to be measured by Joyce.

A. Scholars and critics have worked diligently to impose a humanistic interpretation on *Ulysses*. Despite the book's pyrotechnics, they claim that the great human themes of husbands and wives and fathers and sons are at its core.

    1. With Stephen and Bloom now together in the apartment, Joyce begins by exploring Bloom's name. He makes anagrams of it—Elpodbomool, Molldopeloob, and so on—opening up a series of possibilities for Bloom's identity.

    2. Next, Joyce blends the characters, calling them Blephen and Stoom, as their educational backgrounds are recited. He seems to treat his characters as an assemblage of letters and words, not the three-dimensional, living creatures that we expect a book to give us.

    3. Joyce is also interested in the difference of 16 years between the ages of Bloom and Stephen. He plays a multiplication game with the ages until Stephen is 1,190 years old and Bloom is 83,300.

    4. All these games lend a kind of hilarity and freedom to the emotion-laden issue of the father/son relationship.

B. Stephen leaves, and Bloom finally makes his way to the bedroom; there, he sees his wife's body and the traces of her lover's form. The novel transforms this discovery into something richly philosophical:

If he [Bloom] had smiled, why would he have smiled? To reflect that each one who enters imagines himself to be the first to enter whereas he is always the last term of a preceding series even if the first term of a succeeding one, each imagining himself to be first, last, only and alone whereas he is neither first nor last nor only nor alone in a series originating in and repeated to infinity.

1. The great fantasy of life from birth to death is that we are bounded individuals, that we have integrity, our lives have a shape, and we have a destiny. But this passage tells us that life is nothing but a serial process into which we are born and which will continue after we die.

2. At birth, we are initiated into a generic dance. We try to personalize it, but how much originality do we really have? We're not free, for example, to invent the gestures of lovemaking.

3. This seems to be one of the central points of the book: "I" is something of a fiction; it exists in an ecosystem that always dwarfs it, contextualizes it, and contains it.

4. Now, Bloom wonders, what would be the significance of a man and a woman fornicating, if seen from Mars? The text tells us that he registers the "lethargy of nescient matter: the apathy of the stars." The affairs that are so critical to us in our lives seem almost absurdly insignificant when viewed from a great distance.

III. The book closes with Molly, who offers us a shrewd, carnal, wise picture of the events we have read about from the vantage point of Stephen and Bloom.

A. Molly is the great priestess of desire. She remembers her past lovers and closes the book with a remembrance of her life in Gibraltar when Bloom met and proposed to her, and she gave herself to him.

B. Joyce knew that his book was quite possibly too theoretical, too abstract, and too overorganized, and he said that Molly's chapter would be the way the book would be "countersigned into eternity." Molly's voice, both of flesh and of spirit allied to flesh, complements the voices of Bloom and Stephen. Together, they give us one of the richest anthems of human life, of spirit and body, found in literature.

Essential Reading:

James Joyce, *Ulysses*.

Supplementary Reading:

Harry Blamires, *The New Bloomsday Book: A Guide Through Ulysses*.

Frank Budgen, *James Joyce and the Making of Ulysses*.

Clive Hart and David Hayman, eds. *James Joyce's Ulysses: Critical Essays*.

Hugh Kenner, *Ulysses*.

Arnold Weinstein, *Recovering Your Story: Proust, Joyce, Woolf, Faulkner, Morrison*.

Questions to Consider:

1. Circe is the sorceress who (in Homer) transforms men into swine; Joyce enlists the metamorphic principle in writing his brothel chapter, "Circe." Among the things that shift shape are Bloom's private thoughts and secrets: They now assume public form. Does this procedure wreck the earlier narrative of "interior monologue"? Can you imagine your thoughts taking public form? How would you feel?

2. Feminist critics have rarely been happy with Joyce's rendition of Molly Bloom in the final chapter, "Penelope." They claim that Joyce stays with a stereotype of the female—body, instinct, emotion—but offers little in the way of reason and discipline. How do you feel about approaching the novel in this way?

Lecture Twenty-Nine—Transcript
Joyce—*Ulysses*, Part 3

I've said that *Ulysses* is mischaracterized as a stream-of-consciousness fiction because after chapter six it really starts to flex its muscles, and it starts to narrate from the oddest possible vantage points. It privileges language. It privileges space. It privileges a parade of styles. We've talked about those models, and there are still more. But the reason that this matters is not just because Joyce has packed everything possible into his book. It's important to realize that stream of consciousness does not dominate the novel, because what is stream of consciousness? Stream of consciousness, and I love it, and you'll see that when we get to Faulkner and Wolfe I'll talk more about it, is our private, inside running story. It's what goes on inside the mind. It's the subjective realm that I think in terms of looking at literature, Proust begins to bring to the novel, even though he writes in a straightforward way.

Yet, in *Ulysses*, in two of the very greatest chapters of the novel, stream of consciousness or the notion of the subjective realm is blown sky-high. I really mean what I'm saying when I put it in these military terms. The interior monologue is your own private song and dance. It's not just a question of eavesdropping on what it's like on the inside of us. Of course, the meter is always on in the inside of us. It's rather the peculiar freedom we have vis-à-vis circumstances and events that are otherwise coercive and determinant. Our own consciousness, our own interior monologue, is our small way, our sometimes feisty, sometimes tragic way, of talking back to life. We don't have to say it aloud. How many times have you in your mind said dreadful things to people around you speaking to you that you would never voice? It's in that sense that it is a kind of modality of freedom, and it's critical that it not be voiced. It's voiced in literature, but we rarely utter these things in life. Nobody really wants to hear it.

Well, Joyce is going to annihilate this in some of these chapters and in particular the chapter, "Circe," or the chapter that takes place in a brothel, takes up one-third of the novel. It's written in theatrical form. It's written as if it were a drama instead of a novel. Why would Joyce avoid the narrative sort of discourse that he had had for dramatic form? Well, in drama everything speaks. Drama is where everything is given voice. We say everything. You think of the plays that you read, and you know that there's a whole cast of characters. Hamlet speaks but so too does Polonius, Laertes, and Gertrude. And this is James Joyce, folks. Hey, welcome. Here's what speaks: talking soap bars, bedsprings, chimes, caps, moths, fly bills, fans, sins of the past, waterfalls, paintings, and of course all of the characters. Living and dead, fantasized and real, all come in to have their little say. So, it's quite a chorus of folks.

However, if everything is voiced, then there is also one crucial thing that then disappears, which is your private inner sanctum, because it ain't private no more. It also is brought to language, and so now interior monologue, as it were, goes public, and does worse. It goes public, and it rats on the person whose monologue it is. So, "Circe" is the Kafka chapter of the novel. It's when Bloom is on trial for not what he's done but for what he's been thinking and feeling, which of course is one of the chief delights of the novel. The greatness of this book is the fun in hearing what this interesting man thinks and feels about what happens to him, or has happened to him, or might happen to him. In this chapter, all of that now acquires public voice. For example, in an early, not terribly important scene in the book, although it was shocking when it was first published, Bloom goes to the outhouse, and he rolls down his pants and starts reading in this outhouse. Among the things he reads in the newspaper is this serialized short story by this writer, Beaufoy. No reader thinks much about it. However, in "Circe," the author, Beaufoy, appears out of nowhere, enraged that his grand fiction has been sullied and tarnished in that way in an outhouse by Bloom. There are no hiding places left in this particular book in this chapter. For example, as well, Bloom, we are told—we don't see this happening, but we are told that Bloom has always enjoyed looking at female flesh. I gave you one instance of it earlier, but in particular he is drawn to what the text sort of conceives of as "horsey" women—women who are frequently rich, society women who go to the polo matches, who themselves ride horses, who are often dressed in furs, and who frequently have whips. There's a real sort of sadomasochism, an SM dimension to *Ulysses*, and you'll hear more of it in this lecture. Well, he's probably been ogling, and desiring, and arguably masturbating with the image of these women for a long time. In this chapter, they appear, and they go after him. They're going to punish him for the lusting after them that he has been doing, and so they command him.

They're going to horsewhip him, and they command him to lower his pants so he can be properly horsewhipped. Okay? Well, he does it tremblingly, and what you begin to realize is he wants nothing more than for these women to horsewhip him. This is going to be the great pleasure of his moment there.

What does he say? Now, in another kind of writer he would say, thank God, would you actually whip me? No, in *Ulysses*, he says as he takes down his pants, "The weather has been so warm." Like, oh, it's true I'm taking down my pants, but you realize it's only because it's been so warm today. You could write an entire page of Freud and not achieve, I think, the pith here of the kind of pathetic little covers and facades that we hide behind when actually desire or libido is at work. So, nothing can be hidden even there. The weather has been so warm—we see right through it. Bloom's fantasies are played out in this chapter in the brothel. Some of those fantasies are kind of meliorist, reformist fantasies that tell us something about the intellectual climate in the 1920s. For example, Bloom would like— because Bloom is now going to be the king of the world; that's one of his fantasies, to rid the world of tuberculosis and insanity. He will banish war and mendicancy, and these fantasies absolutely mix, as you would expect in the kind of contrapuntalism of Joyce's book, with other scenes, which are more interesting, that I'm going to get into, of degradation and humiliation, because Bloom is more often than not in this chapter a target. Bloom is a target.

Let me say this. Have you ever considered that when a character in a novel dies that it is also a murder—that the author has offed the character? Bloom is a target in a sense in a way that all characters are targets. Characters don't have their own integral, independent life. They're all being manipulated by their author. Usually this is done in such a way as it connotes a kind of realistic life, and we don't even ask the question about are they actually marionettes or puppets being moved around? We don't see the strings. In *Ulysses*, you see the strings. You see the author manipulating his character. You see this character en route to becoming some kind of a marionette, or a puppet, or even a Frisbee that can be just thrown at will. I'll talk more about that as I go.

This is the chapter as well where we begin to dig deep into the substrata of Bloom's own psyche and of his own pulsions and needs, and what we find, and I've already hinted at this, is a lot of

©2007 The Teaching Company.

sadomasochism. It takes place, after all, in a brothel. Moreover, because it's the kind of surreal chapter of the novel, it's also a chapter where there is a great deal of metamorphosis, where things can change shape. I've already told you about all of the weird things that come into the novel to speak in this chapter, but also the madame of the brothel, Bella Cohen, becomes Bello. She becomes a man, and of course the counterpart to that is that Leopold Bloom becomes a woman. Now, you have to ask yourself, why is this happening? Is this because Joyce is able simply to transform his characters, or if you push the psychological line is it conceivable that at some level this is what Bloom has always wanted, to be a woman, to become a woman? Well, he becomes a woman, and therefore he is subject, it seems, to extraordinary sexual aggression on the part of the madame who is now a man, Bello Cohen, who sexually humiliates Bloom further, and further, and further—thrusts his arm, "elbowdeep into Bloom's vulva," after already having ridden Bloom like a cock horse. It sort of mimics fornication as he is riding on Bloom, and this continues to move. You wonder how far it can go. Well, it goes further than you might expect because soon enough we realize that Bello is going to make Bloom witness the fornication of his wife with Blazes Boylan in their apartment at 4 p.m. All the stuff that Bloom has been trying to keep off his mind is now going to be a kind of theatrical spectacle that he is going to witness. Further, Bello makes certain to humiliate and insult Bloom along sexual lines. He looks at his limp organ and says, can you do a man's job? He explains to Bloom that there now is a fellow of brawn at work with his wife, a fellow who has a kind of weapon that has "knobs and lumps and warts," Bloom is going to have his nose rubbed in it. He is going to get graphic detail of what's happening in his apartment room, or the bedroom of his wife with her lover, and initially, predictably, logically, he is horrified.

But, of course, Joyce isn't prepared to stop there. His horror is going to be transformed into something further. I told you this is the SM chapter of the book. Maybe this man likes to be hurt. Maybe to humiliate and injure him sexually or to have his wife ploughed by her lover is in fact a kind of remarkably arousing thing for him. So, now he is going to be invited into the actual bedroom and allowed to watch, or at least invited to the doorway to watch. He will put his eye to the keyhole, and of course Joyce being Joyce, Bloom will also ask if he might bring two male friends to watch with him as his wife fornicates with her lover. He even suggests that he might be able to bring some Vaseline to hand it on to Boylan if in case, perhaps, he needs it. He is going to see the full show, and Joyce being the sound man that he is, as we learn from the "Sirens" chapter, lets us know what it sounds like when these two, Boylan and Molly, go at it. This is what Boylan sounds like, "Ah! Godblazegrukbrukarchkhrasht!" and Bloom listens as well to Molly who is fully engaged in this, "O! Weeshwashtkissinapooisthnapoohuck!" Bloom's reaction to all of this is that of extraordinary sexual excitement. He's got his eyes dilated. He's got his hands on his genitals. He's looking through the door at this event, and he explodes with passion. I quote, "Show! Hide! Show! Plough her! More! Shoot!" How do you assess this? What kind of label could you possibly put on this? What sense does it make that a man is going to get his most ultimate jollies in watching his wife fornicate with the lover?

The other chapters of the book have him trying to repress this event, but this chapter, which digs quite deep, suggests that maybe at some remarkably deep level this is what he wants. Joyce challenges us to put a label on this, to put a tag on this. I mean I know what the easy tag is—he's a pervert. These are always our little one-liners that make us essentially duck what's happening. That's the lotus answer to this. I think Joyce is saying sexual desire is a really twisted thing. It's kind of strange. We get our jollies in odd ways. We don't like to admit it, but this chapter in the brothel, the surreal chapter, is the chapter that allows Joyce to dig deepest and to show something about the actual equipment at work here, and I'm not talking about Boylan's equipment as he goes at it with Molly but the psychic equipment in Bloom about what in fact arouses a man.

Now, whatever label you have is yours, but I'm just telling you what Joyce puts out here for us to see. The brothel chapter, "Circe," does not close that way. It gets back to reality, but before that it treats us to two remarkable epiphanies. Stephen has one more vision of his mother, the dead made deadless, who comes in with her crab-like fingers and wants him once again to pray as he refused to. And then Bloom has this extraordinary vision, a very sugary vision that I think this book has earned, of his dead son, Rudy, brought back to life, walking across the scene, reading Hebrew. It's a remarkable sequence. It doesn't last very long. Then they exit the brothel, and they get back to reality. Stephen taunts two British soldiers who were standing outside of the brothel. One of them decks him, lays him out, and Bloom takes care of him. This is where we get close to the father/son theme of the novel. Bloom is solicitous. Bloom has been in the brothel in order to watch over Stephen. It's clear that Stephen is some kind of a substitution, ersatz son, for the dead Rudy.

So, Bloom invites Stephen to go home with him, and I now go to the chapter, "Ithaca," which is the penultimate chapter of the book. Ithaca, of course, for Homer, is the return home. It's where Penelope is. It's where Odysseus is trying so hard to get back to. Well, Ithaca will be the homecoming chapter, but this chapter explodes any notions that we might have of what home is or could be at least for James Joyce. Where do we keep house? Taking measures is what this chapter is about, and so Bloom and Stephen are going to become the kind of toys whose measure James Joyce wants to take. He's going to explore the father/son thesis of this book, the relationship thesis of this book in every way he can, and I want to make a slight digression here.

For generations, critics, professors in particular, have read *Ulysses* and said, Well, of course, it's a remake of the *Odyssey*. Hence, it's a remake of the relationships between a husband and a wife, and a father and a son, and a son and a father. Therefore, they have worked very, very valiantly to take Joyce's extraordinarily pyrotechnical book and give it a kind of humanistic interpretation—to say, well, all of the stuff, yeah, there's a lot of crazy somersaults happening on the page. But actually, actually if you bend over backwards, you can see that it's really about the great human themes of husbands and wives and fathers and sons.

I had a professor who once said, have you ever thought about what it looks like to bend over backwards? It's not a very attractive posture, and you have to sort of bend a long way to sort of yoke this book into a kind of nice, warm, cuddly, human theme. That's part of what I have in mind when I'm going to tell you about the way in which Joyce now explores the father/son theme, because this is his moment. He's got Bloom and Stephen together at Bloom's apartment, and so he wants to look at their characters. He first looks at Bloom's name. Most characters have a name in a book. In Russian novels this can be funny because they have all of these other nicknames, and patronymics and everything else. In this book, in English literature, usually it's just one name. That's what they get at the beginning, and they still have it at the end. Joyce wants to play with Bloom's name because Bloom, it appears, Joyce says had made anagrams in his youth. And so I'll treat you to these anagrams. Leopold Bloom— well, that's what we know him by. Here comes another one, Elpodbomool, Molldopeloob, Bollopedoom, and Old Ollebo, M.P. These are all anagrams of the words "Leopold Bloom," and for me this is just like walking into a hall of mirrors. It's like taking the words "Leopold Bloom" and opening it up into a series of other possibilities.

"Elpodbomool" seems like a new kind of animal species. "Molldopeloob"—you think, his wife's name is Molly. "Moll" sounds like it's his married life that's in play. "Bollopedoom" seems to have a mix of both farce and fatalism, and "Old Ollebo, M.P.," well, that's our hero the ad-man now become M.P., "public servant."

Well, that's one of the little liberties, one of the kind of manic, crazy, comic things, farcical things that this book does. Joyce also considers when he's thinking now about what the relationship between these two people, Bloom and Stephen, might be, thinks about their education. We know, for example, that Stephen is a graduate of the university, whereas Bloom has not gone nearly that far. So, Joyce is going to walk them through their various educational stages, except that he's going to shift them. He's going to make Bloom go through Stephen's and Stephen go through Bloom's. What does he call them? "Blephen" and "Stoom" instead of "Stephen" and "Bloom." Well, that's one way of bringing your characters together. After all, what is a character? I've just told you Leopold Bloom could also be Elpodbomool, Molldopeloob, Bollopedoom, and Old Ollebo, M.P. Why not Blephen and Stoom? You're beginning to see that this book takes its characters as just a kind of assemblage of letters and words, not the kind of fully flesh, three-dimensional, living creatures that we often want to believe that a book gives us. Heaven knows I want to believe it. I wouldn't be teaching this course otherwise. That's the greatness of literature—that the words on the page send us to life itself, pulsating life, richly endowed people, and that is a marvelous voyage for us. Joyce enjoys just as much making the return trip to say, wait a minute. You may think these are real people. They're just words on a page, and because they're letters that make up words, I can reassemble them if I like. I can recombine them, and he does. He puts them however he wants.

82

He is also interested in the age difference between Bloom and Stephen. As the novel plays out, it takes place in 1904, even though it was published in 1922; Stephen is 22 and Bloom is 38. There is a 16-year difference between their ages. Joyce is interested in that ratio of 16 years, and what he decides because he is the author, the God-like figure who can do what he wants—he plays with their letters, why not play with the ages as well, with the numbers—why not take that ratio of one to sixteen and turn it into a kind of multiplication game? Okay, how would you do that? Now, you know you can do this with numbers. You can do this with a computer. Can you do this with flesh? I don't think so. But this is what it would sound like. In 1920, the text tells us, Stephen would then be 38. Ah, but for Bloom we're going to use a factor of 16. Bloom would be 646. Okay, let's fast forward further to 1952. Now, Joyce published this book in 1922. Joyce died in 1941. We fast forward nonetheless because the mind is capable of doing this and the page is capable of receiving this. We fast forward to 1952. Stephen would be 70. How old would Bloom be? Remember, multiplying by a factor of 16, Bloom would be 1,190. That's pretty venerable.

Well, Joyce being who he is thinks, well, wait a minute—why should we stop at that? Why not give that age of 1,190 to Stephen? Now, that could be fun. Stephen is 1,190. That makes Bloom 83,300 years old, which, of course, requires, the text explains this to us, that he has to have been born at 81,396 B.C. Well, I would say that this isn't really serious, but it is hysterical. This takes the fiction of relationship, the father/son relationship, which we think of in oh-so-heavy terms as an emotional issue, and it turns it into a kind of arithmetic fantasy. That's the kind of freedom—that's the flexing of muscles that the author has in this text. Bloom is the text's cipher.

Then Bloom makes his way finally, predictably, crucially into the bedroom of his wife after Stephen leaves—Ithaca, homecoming, into that bedroom, and what does he see in that bedroom? He sees on his own marital bed two forms. One of them is the presence of his wife's body, and the other is the trace of his wife's lover. Now, you may remember in the *Odyssey* Odysseus slays all of the would-be portended suitors, portended lovers of Penelope. Well, this is a modern story. There's not going to be any killing in this. How is Bloom going to take care of all of these rivals, and in particular that form that is in the bed? What is he going to do? Well, it's one of the most famous passages in *Ulysses*, and it goes like this:

> If he had smiled, why would he have smiled? To reflect that each one who enters imagines himself to be the first to enter whereas he is always the last term of a preceding series, even if the first term of a succeeding one, each imagining himself to be first, last, only and alone whereas he is neither first nor last nor only nor alone in a series originating in and repeated to infinity.

It's a spellbinding passage from so many points of view. Joyce doesn't say that Bloom smiled. He says if he had smiled, why would he have smiled? If you think about it, is there really a lot to smile about when you walk into your bedroom and you see the remaining imprint of your wife's lover on the bed? Yet, nonetheless, this book is going to transform that into something richly philosophical. This is why he would have smiled if he had smiled, and what we then learn is that life is nothing but a serial process. The great fantasy of life that we subscribe to from the moment of our birth and probably don't let go of until the moment of our death is that we are bounded individuals, that we have our integrity, that we are an eye that makes its way through the world, that the things that happen to us are our adventures or misadventures, that we have a shape, that we have a destiny, that we have a life, that we have a biography, that we are real, and I'm saying "we" but let's say "I." What this passage does is it blows it to smithereens. It says, now wait a minutes, that's not the case. You're part of a long serial operation that began before you were born and will continue after you're dead. Your life is simply entering into the dance, the dance of the species. You remember the memory that the text gives us in "Lestrygonian" of Bloom and Molly making love on Howth Hill that I read to you, and now we see the imprint of her lover who has made love to her in the apartment. It's not Bloom, but the dance is the same.

We are initiated into a dance that is generic. We try to first-personalize it. We try to domesticate it. We try to say this is my form, my destiny, my action, and my life. How much originality do we have? Are any of us free, for example, to invent the gestures of lovemaking? How much in our life, in fact, is generic? And so therefore there is a kind of remarkable wisdom it seems to me in this, and it seems to me as well that this is what the book has been talking about all along—that "I" is something of a fiction, that I exist in an ecosystem or field picture that always dwarfs it, contextualizes it, and contains it. That is equally true for one's marriage, it would appear in this novel.

We get a sense here that this is not the way Homer would have written it, but this is consistent with the way Joyce is looking at things. We are free, of course, to say what a wimp Bloom is, what a coward he is. Here is a man who should be enraged—that's how Homer would have seen it, that his wife has cheated on him, and instead—I'm saying "instead," you can say "and as evasion," or you could say "as wisdom." It's up to us to figure out what sort of "valoration" we want to give to this, how we want to valorize it, valuation. Instead, Joyce lets us know that he sees it entirely as a kind of serial proposition, which then gives rise to thoughts about what could it really mean if my wife has fornicated with her lover? He thinks about relative ways—I've told you this is about Ithaca that challenges our notion of what home is, and the vantage point begins to move out of the earth itself to the stars.

What would a man and a woman fornicating on a bed look like from Mars, as if you could see it? But what would it mean on Mars? Joyce points out that, well, adultery or fornication isn't really worse than other things such as natural disaster, child abuse, arson, treason or homicide. Can it really matter that much? At one point the text actually says that what Bloom registers is "the lethargy of nescient matter: the apathy of the stars." It's a kind of brilliant, lethal perception about the affairs of our lives—that if you could possibly extract yourself from your life and ask what it might look like from far away—the things that seem so critical to you ranging, as I said, from making your bus to having sex with your wife or husband, how important can those things be if the distance is sufficiently increased from which you look at these things—the apathy of the stars. How much does any single life mean? How much does the sexual behavior of two people mean in the largest possible terms?

What I think Joyce is saying is that at a certain distance all of the things that we most value begin to look whimsical, private. How endowed with importance can they be—weightless, absurd? Well, that's the wisdom of Bloom, and the book closes famously, finally, at last, with Molly Bloom. Mercurial Molly, Molly who seems to have views that go all over the map, Molly who finally will tell us what it was like to have sex with Blazes Boylan, who performed quite effectively, thank you. He has this huge engine, and he used it. At the same time, she thinks that her husband, Poldy—how she refers to him—has more spunk, knows more what women want, knows better how to take a woman. Molly is the person who offers us a kind of shrewd, carnal, wise picture of the things that we have been reading about through the vantage point of Stephen and Bloom up until now. She is the great priestess of desire. She is the woman who remembers her past lovers and in an extraordinarily lovely sequence she is the woman who closes this book with a remembrance of her life and Gibraltar when Bloom met her and proposed to her. She is also having her period. Boylan has not impregnated her, and she thinks about her period and she also thinks of growing up in Gibraltar.

> O that awful deepdown torrent. O and the sea the sea crimson [and we don't know whether she is talking about her own menstrual flow or the wine-dark sea that she remembers at Gibraltar] sometimes like fire and the glorious sunsets … Gibraltar as a girl where I was a Flower of the mountain yes when I put the rose in my hair like the Andalusian girls used or shall I wear a red yes and how he kissed me under the Moorish wall and I thought well as well him as another and then I asked him with my eyes to ask again yes and then he asked me would I yes to say yes my mountain flower and first I put my arms around him yes and drew him down to me so he could feel my breasts all perfume yes and his heart was going like mad and yes I said yes I will Yes.

Joyce knew that his book was arguably too theoretical, too abstract and too overorganized, and he therefore said that the Molly Bloom final chapter would be the way that the book would be countersigned into eternity. Here then is the voice of flesh as well as the voice of the spirit that is allied to flesh—that is Molly, and that is what complements the voices of Bloom and Stephen. It gives us together one of the richest anthems of human life, of spirit/body, that I have ever seen. I hope that you can see it that way, too. Thank you.

Lecture Thirty
Woolf—*To the Lighthouse*

Scope:

In the central protagonists of *To the Lighthouse*, Virginia Woolf seeks both to represent and (somehow) to get clear of her own famous parents, Leslie and Julia Stephen. Are either of these projects possible (for anyone)? What all readers most remember about the book is the magnificent perspectival portrait of the mother, Mrs. Ramsay, seen as earth mother, priestess of marriage, and player in a violent Freudian drama.

By contrast, Mr. Ramsay is angular, hungry for praise, a tad caricatural; he, like his wife, is a quester. Woolf is unrivaled in her success at delivering this pair *as couple*, and the stream-of-consciousness narrative beautifully delivers the impossible (and absurd) balancing act between inner self and outer world, between "me" and "you" that goes by the name of marriage but rarely makes it into literature.

Outline

I. *To the Lighthouse* (1927), written by Virginia Woolf (1882–1941), is the most personal and, probably, the most beautiful novel in this course.

    A. One of the novel's central questions is, How can one write marriage? Can you imagine writing the marriage of your own parents? Could you show them in the round, as the adults they are, not just as your parents?

    B. A corollary question is, What kind of language could be used for depicting our tumultuous human feelings? Could you use straightforward, denotative language, or would a new kind of script be required?

    C. Woolf's parents, Leslie and Julia Stephen, were well known in British intellectual circles at the end of the 19th century and the beginning of the 20th century. Julia died when her daughter was quite young, leaving a wound that Woolf experienced all her life. Her father exerted a stranglehold on Woolf, nearly suffocating her. *To the Lighthouse* is the book in which Woolf attempts to exorcise her dead parents from her life.

1. In her diary, Woolf wrote that had her father lived, she would have been unable to produce books.

2. The response of Vanessa, Woolf's sister, to the portrait of their mother in the novel speaks volumes about what the author wrought: "It was like meeting her [mother] again with one's self grown up and on equal terms, and it seems to me the most astonishing feat of creation to have been able to see her in such a way."

3. Can you know your parents? This is the echoing question that underlies the novel, and it is not easy to answer, given that all children remain (no matter their ages) children to their parents. Could you write them as adults?

II. What most readers see in this book is the remarkable portrait of the mother, Mrs. Ramsay. Her beauty and presence strike everyone who knows her.

A. A hard-headed scientist friend of the Ramsays, William Bankes, pays tribute to Mrs. Ramsay, envisioning her as a Greek goddess. He is struck by her radiance, grace, and creative energy.

B. Charles Tansley, the mean-spirited, insecure, awkward student of Mr. Ramsay, finds in Mrs. Ramsay the most beautiful woman he has ever seen:

> What nonsense was he thinking? She was fifty at least; she had eight children. Stepping through fields of flowers and taking to her breast buds that had broken and lambs that had fallen; with the stars in her eyes and the wind in her hair—He took her bag.

1. Through such descriptions, Woolf makes lyricism possible in a realistic framework. In her language and her writing, Woolf shows us something of the splendor of the world that lives in our feelings.

2. Taking Mrs. Ramsay's bag may seem like a small thing, but for Tansley, it is momentous; it is his encounter with grace and beauty.

©2007 The Teaching Company.

C. Mrs. Ramsay is also the book's love apostle in her constant cheerleading for marriage. But inside the cheerleader is another Mrs. Ramsay, a sterner, darker, and more fascinating figure: the connoisseur of chaos.

   1. Mr. Ramsay is a philosopher with a range of principles, theorems, and ideas about man's fate in the world. Unlike her husband, however, Mrs. Ramsay has an intuitive sense that nature is brutal, that the world is inhospitable to human beings, and that her children will never again be as happy as they are at this moment in their lives.

   2. She is a magnetically beautiful woman with an absolutely lucid, unflinching view of the contest between us and the forces of life and fate.

D. The formidable Mr. Ramsay represents the noted intellectual Leslie Stephen, but he seems something of a joke in the novel.

   1. His son Andrew characterizes his father's philosophy as almost Platonic, relating to eternal forms that have little to do with the phenomenal world.

   2. One of the book's most famous and satiric passages depicts the exertions of Mr. Ramsay in his quest to get from Q to R. This gently mocking episode suggests that perhaps he can't even achieve full self-knowledge.

   3. Mr. Ramsay needs constant praise, a need that is fulfilled by his wife.

      a. In the first chapter of the book, "Madonna," Mrs. Ramsay sits with her son James enfolded in her arms. When Mr. Ramsay enters, needing his daily ration of support, she "braced herself, and half turning, seemed to raise herself with an effort and at once to pour erect into the air a rain of energy."

      b. Our traditional sexual images are all transformed here. Mrs. Ramsay, the goddess figure who essentially represents life, receives the male, giving him what he needs to sustain his own life. Her gift makes his life fertile.

      c. At the same time, James views the scene from an Oedipal standpoint, his father storming his mother.

  d. The language depicting relations between a husband and a wife here is quite different from any kind of sociological or realistic description.

III. Woolf is interested, in this novel, in the multiple subjectivities that make up relationships between two people in a marriage. She sees, in fact, the impossibility of marriage.

 A. Each partner must be himself or herself. Where is the middle ground? How can these two selves fuse?

 B. Woolf also sees the humor and the reality of marriage. She doesn't say that marriage is a façade or a fraud—it's real even if it is impossible to actualize.

  1. Focusing on the mundane, Woolf finds great riches in the simplest habits and behavior of husbands and wives.

  2. We see her perspectival genius in the scene in which Mr. and Mrs. Ramsay are walking together and discussing Charles Tansley as a prospect for their daughter.

  3. Mrs. Ramsay stops to look at some flowers, and Mr. Ramsay interrupts his own thoughts to try to share her interest. All he can say, however, is "These flowers seemed creditable."

  4. We get the same scene from Mrs. Ramsay's perspective. As she walks, she thinks that it is good for young men to simply hear her husband, the great philosopher, lecture; at the same time, she wonders whether she is seeing evidence of moles or rabbits on the property. The two subjects are deliciously scrambled in Woolf's prose.

  5. Woolf shows us how bizarre it is that we actually make sense to others, given that our minds are constantly flitting, moving, and dodging. Her depiction of the charming anarchy of human thought restores us to ourselves.

IV. As most people know, Woolf was one of the first great 20th-century feminists.

 A. We might think of Rousseau's famous term "social contract" to characterize the work that women have always done and have rarely gotten credit for: Women provide the glue for human connectedness.

1. Mrs. Ramsay surveys a dinner scene at the summerhouse with horror. All those gathered at the table are distracted and uncommunicative. She knows that it is her role to create a connection, a living exchange among the diners.
2. "Speaking French" is Woolf's metaphor for the effort required to bring life and harmony to social discourse.

B. At the dinner, Mrs. Ramsay serves *boeuf en daube*, an exquisite French stew that the cook has been preparing for three days. She takes great pleasure in seeing her guests partake of the stew; she inhales the fragrance of the stew that seems to hold these people together as a human community against the elements. Woolf writes: "Of such moments, she thought, the thing is made that endures."

Essential Reading:

Virginia Woolf, *To the Lighthouse*.

Supplementary Reading:

Rachel Bowlby, *Virginia Woolf: Feminist Destinations*.

Hermione Lee, *Virginia Woolf*.

Anna Snaith, *Virginia Woolf: Public and Private Negotiations*.

Arnold Weinstein, *Recovering Your Story: Proust, Joyce, Woolf, Faulkner, Morrison*.

Questions to Consider:

1. Woolf's style is famous for its lyrical and metaphorical splendor. Aside from the aesthetic virtues of such writing, do you think that image and metaphor might provide a unique way of bringing our "interior" to language? Woolf seems to do this in her rendition of the Ramsay family, as we see in the violent images at the beginning of the novel. How much figurative language would you use in representing your own emotions?

2. A famous scene in *To the Lighthouse* focuses on people sitting around a table eating dinner. Do you know of many novels that do this? Could eating together be at once pedestrian and philosophical? I used the term "social contract" when referring to this scene; do you sense that you are under contract at such moments? How significant is gender in these matters?

Lecture Thirty—Transcript
Woolf—*To the Lighthouse*

Virginia Woolf's *To the Lighthouse* is really the most personal novel of the course. It's probably the most beautiful novel of the course, too. One of its central questions, at least for me, is how could you write marriage? Let me complicate that. Could you imagine writing the marriage of your own parents, and, in this case particularly, if Mother died when you were a child, and if Father almost suffocated you with his needs? Can you know them in the round, as the adults that they were, not just as your parents?

Secondly, what kind of language could there be for depicting our tumultuous human feelings? Would it just be the straightforward, denotative language that we all know about that exists in dictionaries, or would there be some new kind of script that might convey this? It seems to me that Virginia Woolf is unforgettable on all of these fronts. Her parents were very famous people in British intellectual culture at the end of the 19th century and early 20th. Her father, Leslie Stephen, and her mother, Julia Stephen, are known to critics of English society. As I said, the mother died early when Virginia was quite young, and this was a wound that she experienced all of her life. She never really got over it, and her father, who was a prominent Victorian intellectual historian, exerted a stranglehold on her. He had a kind of insatiable need for praise; she almost suffocated under him. I say this because, therefore, *To the Lighthouse* is really an exorcist book. She is trying to exorcise these dead people out of her life, or trying to somehow come to terms with them. I'll quote you what she said in her own diary in 1928.

> Father's birthday. He would have been 1832 [that's when he was born] 96, yes, 96 today; and could have been 96, like other people one has known; but mercifully was not. His life would have entirely ended mine. What would have happened? No writing, no books;—inconceivable.

So this was a kind of exorcism. Their death was, in more ways than one, her birth. They birthed her while they were living, but they birthed her in some sense also by dying. This is her effort, in some sense, to right the record as well, to do her part. Her sister, Vanessa, who was a very talented and distinguished painter, was stunned by the book *To the Lighthouse* and told Virginia that she couldn't believe what had been accomplished in it. She said that the portrait of Mother "is more like her to me than anything I could ever have conceived possible. It is almost painful to have her so raised from the dead." Vanessa actually says it just right, because there's a kind of Orpheus/Eurydice feeling here that this woman has been resurrected from the dead. I want you to listen to the way Vanessa put it: "It was like meeting her again with oneself grown up and on equal terms and it seems to me the most astonishing feat of creation to have been able to see her such a way."

Can you know your parents? This is a question that sort of underlies this novel, because children, even when they grow up, are always children to their parents, and their parents are always parents to them. Could you write them as adults? And particularly, as we mature and lead our lives and our parents grow old and perhaps infirm and die, could we tell their story? Have we taken their measure? I think it's a kind of problem that life metes out to all of us. It's a kind of generational handicap: that we remain children and therefore in a sense locked out of what could have been the actual lives of our parents but that we can't see. We're blindfolded, blinded. I think this is a remarkable book to try to access that, to try to create that. They're not there to tell her. She had to make it herself.

What most readers most see in this book is the portrait of the mother, and that's, of course, what Vanessa saw, miraculous Mrs. Ramsay, one of the most remarkable portraits in British literature. This is a woman whose beauty struck everyone who knew her, everyone. People, who didn't want to like her in particular, were nonetheless struck, awed, and moved by this woman's beauty, and her presence, and her magic.

One of their friends, the Ramsay's friends, William Bankes, who was a scientist and very hard-headed, very level-headed, nonetheless is stunned by this woman's beauty and remembers thinking of her as a kind of Greek goddess. It was strange to him because there she was living in London. At one point he was speaking to her on the phone about which subway to take, when to get out of the tube, and at the same time thinking, "How is this possible that I'm talking about subways with this woman who is like a goddess?" She has in her beauty a kind of quivering quality, which is what Bankes is struck by, a kind of radiance, a kind of grace, a kind of life, a kind of creative energy. All the figures of the book are drawn to her. This story takes place at their summer house on the Isle of Skye—the Ramsays'—where there are many guests coming to dinner, and in particular Mr. Ramsay, who was a philosopher, a professor of philosophy, has invited one of his graduate students, Charles Tansley, who is a very mean-spirited, insecure, awkward young man, laughed at by the children—a rather stunted figure. He is invited one morning to accompany Mrs. Ramsay on an errand. She takes lots of walks, goes on errands, comes to visit people who are sick, to bring them comfort, solace, and gifts, and as he is walking with her, he is awed when she comes out of the house. They have had this wonderful conversation. She has this exquisite touch for people.

At first she has thought that Tansley is sort of a silly young man, awkward, insecure, ill at ease, and then she realizes that he is kind of stunted—that he has never had the opportunities that her children have got. In particular she knows that he was never taken to circuses. It's rather funny, and she tries to tell him about circuses. She thinks, "Well, maybe I'll tell my children not to tease him because the poor boy was never taken to circuses." Anyway, as she comes out of this house after having visited the sick woman, Tansley looks at her and has this realization that he has never seen anybody so beautiful. She's in her fifties, and this is the way Woolf writes it:

> With stars in her eyes and veils in her hair, with cyclamen and wild violets—[this is Tansley's mind] what nonsense was he thinking? She was fifty at least; she had eight children. Stepping through fields of flowers and taking to her breast buds that had broken and lambs that had fallen; with the stars in her eyes and the wind in her hair—He took her bag.

He takes her purse, and they walk together. This is the Woolf breakthrough—what I just read to you. It is this lyrical, almost classical evocation, pastoral, of this woman with stars in her eyes and veils in her hair, with cyclamen and wild violets and yet the reality that a photograph would tell you is that she is fifty. The reality that a historian would tell you is that she's got eight children, and yet she seems to step right out of Greek pastoral, "Stepping through fields of flowers and taking to her breast buds that had broken and lambs that had fallen," and he takes her bag. What Virginia Woolf is doing is making lyricism possible in a realistic framework. Now think for a moment. Make yourself the fly on the wall. You were there. You had

94   ©2007 The Teaching Company.

a photograph and you watched. You saw a woman come out of a house, and you saw a younger man take her bag. That is all you would have seen. You would not have seen stars in her eyes, veils in her hair, cyclamen, buds that had broken, or lambs that had fallen. Woolf is trying to show us through her language and her writing something of the splendor of the world that lives in our feelings, in our exalted feelings, when this young man, who has been, as I said, insecure and stunted, all of a sudden realizes that this radiant woman is the woman that he has the great good fortune to be accompanying on her errands, and he takes her bag. You may think, well, taking a woman's bag is really small beer. I mean how important is that? Well, I think Woolf makes us think again it's momentous. It's the great moment of his day. It's his encounter with beauty. It's perhaps his encounter with grace.

That's how Woolf re-writes our daily routines and invests them with a kind of exquisite sort of—I don't know the right word for this—it's a kind of moving, coursing sense of their life, and their radiance, and their beauty that no camera could possibly capture. It's because we project that onto the world, but we do this all the time. That's what our feelings are for. That is what they do. We can't even stop it. There's nothing volitional here.

So Mrs. Ramsay is the book's love apostle, not merely that others love her, but that she constantly preaches marriage. "Marry, marry," is how people remember her speaking, and, in fact, in the course of the novel there will be a couple that is also visiting them at their summer house that they're renting—it's not theirs—who will, in fact, become married. She's the cheerleader for marriage, and that is the easy way to see her. It's the way that people, who are a little bit dismissive of her, do see her, but what we also learn about Mrs. Ramsay is that she has also a kind of much more severe picture of life. She is not at all the kind of giddy person that some might think her to be. She is a kind of connoisseur of chaos in this sense. Her husband is a philosopher. Her husband has all kinds of principles, theorems, and notions about man's fate in the world, but, unlike her husband, she has an intuitive sense that nature is brutal, that the world is inhospitable to human beings, that her children will never again be as happy and spontaneous as they are at this moment in their lives, and life, she knows, is "terrible, hostile, and quick to pounce on you if you [give] it a chance." So we begin to realize the roundedness of this character. Yes, the love apostle; yes, the kind of magnetically beautiful woman, and at the same time the absolutely lucid, unflinching, clear-eyed figure of the book, who sees the unfair contest between us and the forces of life and fate.

What about her husband? He represents, as I said, Virginia's famous father, Leslie Stephen, and he is something of a joke in the novel. There are some readers who continue to think of him as a joke. I think you'll see that I don't. He is very easy to caricature. In fact, his son Andrew tells Lily Briscoe, who is one of the important guests of the novel (and I'll talk about Lily later), when Lily tries to get Andrew to explain what kind of philosophy teacher he is; what is his philosophy? Andrew's answer is, "Think of a kitchen table … when you're not there." It's a deliciously ironic line: that this is the man, who seems to devote his entire life to imagining these kinds of, really, almost mirage-like things that have nothing to do with the here and now, or with the life that our retina takes in, or our human relations are involved with. Instead, almost in a kind of platonic way, he is the man who envisions these eternal forms and has little to do with the phenomenal world, the world of matter that we see in front of us.

One of the most famous and satiric passages of the novel depicts the exertions of Mr. Ramsay, who is trying to move forward. He is the great quester of the book. Don't forget the title of this book is *To the Lighthouse*. It's about quests of different sorts. Mr. Ramsay's quest, because he is a philosopher, is a quest for truth, not merely a quest for truth though. It's also the quest of can he, Ramsay, achieve this vision of truth? Can he hold his own in the great tradition of philosophers? Woolf writes this almost alphabetically. He wants to get to Q. Very few people in the whole of England ever reach Q, and so this is Ramsay meditating. How on earth do you get to Q?

> But after Q? What comes next? After Q there are a number of letters, the last of which is scarcely visible to mortal eyes, but glimmers red in the distance. Z is reached once by one man in a generation. Still, if he could reach R it would be something. Here at least was Q. He dug his heels in at Q. Q he was sure of. Q he could demonstrate. If Q then is Q—R— here he knocked his pipe out, with two or three resonant taps on the handle of the urn, and proceeded. "Then R …" He braced himself. He clenched himself.

You almost feel like it's someone who is constipated, who is trying to somehow produce R. And, of course, we know that R is also the letter that is Ramsay. It suggests that maybe he can't even get to some fully achieved self-knowledge as well, but it's a kind of mocking, gently mocking, passage about the philosophical pursuit. It's also true that Ramsay is presented over and over as needing constant praise, and in particular he needs it from his wife, who gives it to him. In the passages that Woolf writes about how that transpires, we see, once again, the breakthrough of Woolf as a remarkable writer. How can this woman satisfy this man, who seems to be insatiable?

One of the sequences is she is sitting there. The first whole part of the book, the first chapter, the first long chapter—it's only got three chapters—is called "Madonna," and she is like the earth mother, the Madonna, with her children, her child James, in particular, who is there with her. She is folding him into her arm, and Mr. Ramsay comes to her, needing his daily ration of support:

> Mrs. Ramsay, who had been sitting loosely, folding her son in her arm, braced herself, and, half turning, seemed to raise herself with an effort, and at once to pour [listen to these metaphors] erect into the air a rain of energy, a column of spray, looking at the same time animated and alive as if all her energies were being fused into force, burning and illuminating (quietly though she sat, taking up her stocking again), and into this delicious fecundity, [the] fountain and spray of life, the fatal sterility of the male plunged itself, like a beak of brass, barren and bare.

It's an astonishing passage. It's an exotic passage. It's a passage that reminds me of the mating habits of peacocks and strange animals. It's a mating dance, a ritual, and yet, once again, if you'd been there watching, you would see a woman sitting there with her son folded in her arms and her husband approaching. He doesn't even touch her, and yet what Woolf is trying to graph for us, to illuminate for us, is the actual exchange of energies that are taking place there. Notice how our traditional sexual images are all being, in a sense, transformed here. The beak, which is phallic ordinarily, the plunging beak that the male puts into this great sort of fertile spray, that the beak is sterile. It is barren, and the woman is the goddess figure, who essentially represents all of life. She receives the male. She also gives him what he needs, which is support, sustenance, and love, enabling him to go back to his own life. Woolf also writes that her gift makes his own life fertile. It makes an entire world for him. It fills up the kitchen, and the drawing room, and the bedrooms for him. It's almost like Genesis. She is creating life out of nothing for this man, and yet James, the son, who is standing between her knees, cannot bear it. For him, this is his mother being stormed by his father. This book has a very strong sort of Oedipal dimension to it. James can't bear all of this, and what I want to stress here is the wildly figurative metaphoric, operatic language that Woolf has used to describe this encounter between a husband, a wife, and a child. After it's over, she writes:

> Immediately, Mrs. Ramsay seemed to fold herself together, one petal closed in another, and the whole fabric fell in exhaustion upon itself, so … she had only strength enough to move her finger, in exquisite abandonment to exhaustion, across the page of Grimm's fairy story, [that's what she's been reading to her son] while there throbbed through her, like a pulse in a spring which has expanded to its full width and now gently ceases to beat, the rapture of successful creation.

So this is the splendor of life that our eyes cannot possibly take in because this is the inside story of human feeling. Maybe this is a language for depicting relations between a husband and a wife that is very different from any kind of sociological, realistic, or photographic take that we could imagine.

Well, as I said, it's an Oedipal story as well. Hating the father is as important to this story as loving the mother. The father is the stern lawgiver. The book opens with the question, Will we go to the lighthouse? Mrs. Ramsay says to James they will if it is fine, the weather being fine. The father immediately says, no, but it won't be fine, and you sort of get the stage set for what's going to happen.

Woolf is very interested in depicting marriage itself, and that's not such an obvious issue. How could you depict marriage? How could you depict the kind of multiple subjectivities that relationships between two people have to consist of? Woolf is interested in the impossibility of marriage. I have to be I; you have to be you. Where is the middle ground, which is so-called marriage? How can we blend or fuse? Is it even conceivable? She's also interested in the humor and in the reality. She doesn't say that marriage is a façade, or a fraud, or a fantasy. It's real, even if it's almost impossible to actualize, and so we get some of the remarkable passages of this book that are devoted to husband and wife in the simplest kinds of settings. They are taking a walk together. They're walking together, and they're talking about Charles Tansley. They think about the poor possibility that maybe their daughter would be sought by Tansley in marriage. That would be a big joke. It wouldn't possibly work, and then they come to some flowers. Mrs. Ramsay loves gardening, and loves flowers, and looks at the flowers and spends a lot of time thinking about the nursery, and the flowers, and things like that, whereas Mr. Ramsay is interested in these eternal forms.

So we read that he didn't really quite look at the flowers. In fact he's thinking about Charles Tansley, who is one of the few graduate students who still respects Ramsay, and he's about to tell his wife, "Don't make fun of Tansley. After all he's one of the people who really"—and then he realizes—"Wait—no, no. My wife is looking at these flowers," and so he's going to choke back what he wants to talk about, which is this young man, who still idolizes him. Instead he tries to focus on the flowers. Woolf writes, 'These flowers seemed creditable, Mr. Ramsay said, lowering his gaze and noticing something red, something brown." Mind you, too, we've already read in this passage that his wife was looking at the flowers. He's not. He's looking about a foot or so above them. I want to say that it's a sweet passage. It's the kind of passage that the Woolf critics never talk about. It's a sweet passage of a husband trying to make his way to the wife. She looks at flowers; he will look at flowers. She cares about flowers; he'll talk about them instead of talking about this graduate student, who still respects him. Can he help it that he only looks a foot above them? Can he help it that all he can say about these flowers is that they're "creditable"? Can he help it that all he can see is that something is red and something is brown? This to me is very touching. It's also very profound in its homely way about the blindness that is endemic to the human species, and yet the very lovely efforts that we make to reach the one we love.

We also get a passage from the wife as they walk together, and it's an equally fascinating passage, where we see that these two people are going together and she has her arm on his shoulder. They're going up a hill, and she puts a little pressure on it not to go so fast. She's noticing that there are molehills, and she's wondering if they really do have moles. Are they molehills, or maybe are they rabbits? Then, of course, at the same time, she's not talking about that. She's talking to her husband about their life together and about the fact that he's preparing his lectures for going back to the university. She has great admiration for her husband. She senses that his mind is different from other people's minds. So I want to quote this passage here, and I want you to hear just how promiscuous and amphibian this passage is.

> All the great men she had ever known, she thought, deciding that a rabbit must have got in, were like that, and it was good for young men (though the atmosphere of lecture-rooms was stuffy and depressing to her beyond endurance almost) simply to hear him, simply to look at him. But without shooting rabbits, how was one to keep them down? she wondered. It might be a rabbit; it might be a mole.

And again, this one is never cited either by the critics, and I love it. This is what's going through her mind. She's talking to her husband. She thinks he is a great professor, but she is also interested in these holes in the ground, whether they are rabbits or whether they are moles, and all of this gets deliciously scrambled together in Woolf's prose. Why? Because that's the way the mind works. That's the way the mind works. We tend to think, well, it's either going to be great men and professors on the one hand—lecture halls—or it's going to be rabbits or moles on the other. No, the mind is far too agile a performer for that. It moves in and out of all of these topics instead. The mind is promiscuous. I said it's amphibian. I think Woolf helps us to understand how bizarre it is that we actually make sense to one another, because our minds are flirting all over the place, flirting, flitting, moving, and dodging.

What Woolf gives us is something of the charming anarchy of human thought, and it makes me think, as someone who is a teacher, that we tell our students to always organize their thinking, to write very clearly, to put down their subject, and then their argument, and then their conclusion. Huh? That's not the way the brain works. Eavesdrop for two seconds on your own mind and you'll hear it's a completely mishmash of things. That's the way Woolf writes it, and to me this restores to us ourselves. It restores to us the actual noise, babble, charm, and interest that we are—that we have inside of us, going on, pulsating, bubbling all the time. So it's in that sense that this book makes visible and audible to us, through Woolf's remarkable metaphors in some cases and in other instances just through the kind of human wit and wisdom, the way we actually live, the way we actually sound.

Well, Woolf, as you doubtless know, is a great heroine for feminists. She is one of the first great 20th-century feminists, and I want to use Rousseau's famous term, *The Social Contract*, in order to characterize what I take to be the work that women have always done and rarely gotten credit for and still continue to do in my view. Women provide the glue for human connectedness, and so one of the major scenes in this book, which you will find in very few other books, is dinner—people sitting down at a table at this summerhouse, eating together. Mrs. Ramsay comes in and she looks at that table, and she looks at all of those people sitting here, and she is struck with a kind of horror—they are all limp, inert, dead figures. They're not saying a thing. They're looking at their plates. They look distracted. There is no current, no connection, no life between these people, and she knows that if they are ever to be brought together, if this is to become a dinner instead of a series of isolated mannequins, she's got to do it. This is what women's work is about. It's what women always do.

Woolf writes that, "As always, she feels the sterility of men." It's her job to bring this to some kind of living exchange, and so she gives herself "a little shake like one gives a watch that has stopped"— that's the way Woolf puts it. The old familiar pulse begins beating. The watch ticks. This is the ticking watch, the ticking pulse of human social life, and that's what this book wants to achieve. The watch ticks. The pulse beats. What happens when watches stop ticking? Isn't there a time when the pulse stops beating? That will be the subject for my next lecture, but I want to stay with the social contract that's at work here. Woolf beautifully puts it that when people are seated around a table together what they have to do is "Speak French." She is speaking figuratively here. She says they have to find topics that everybody can get into. It makes no difference if you're an expert in these things or not. She says that perhaps it's bad French. Perhaps French won't quite convey your thoughts, but still some order is achieved. At this dinner table, there is also this young couple, the Rayleys, Paul and Minta, and we know that Mrs. Ramsay wants to encourage their courtship. We hear about the fact that they've been down to the beach and that Minta has lost her brooch there on the beach. Mrs. Ramsay is going to work it out through her powers that Paul will actually propose to Minta. But at this dinner table, we see these people sitting together, and the great *pièce de résistance*, the great dish, is a *boeuf en daube*, which is a recipe from Mrs. Ramsay's grandmother. It has taken the cook three days to make this exquisite French stew, and I want you to read the way Woolf describes this as Mrs. Ramsay takes great pleasure in seeing her guests partake of the stew.

> She hovered like a hawk suspended; like a flag floated in an element of joy … [and I go on] all of which was rising in this profound stillness (she was helping William Bankes to one very small piece more, and peered into the depths of the earthenware pot) seemed now for no special reason to stay there like a smoke, like a fume rising upwards, [it's the fragrance from the stew, but it's a larger kind of smoke, and fume, and air that is coming] holding them safe together.

People at a dinner table, in a cottage, on an island, surrounded by the sea, sharing a meal. This is both mundane, primitive, and epic. It's the human community against the elements, and there is the earth goddess, the earth mother, serving this *boeuf en daube*, and, as she hands a piece to Mr. Bankes, Woolf writes it like this, "It partook, she felt, carefully helping Mr. Bankes to a specially tender piece, of eternity. … Of such moments, she thought, the thing is made that endures." Vintage Woolf, signature Woolf—what we think of as the most trivial, ephemeral thing in the world, people sitting there breaking bread and eating stew, is elevated here to eternity, as this woman dips into this earthenware pot, hands him this tender piece of meat and realizes that of such moments the thing is made that endures. These are the human bonds and threads. This is the great jewel of life. These rich, evanescent pleasures of food and talk, they are the real treasure in life, not the brooch that was lost on the beach. Of course, the thing that endures, as well, is Virginia Woolf's language that creates this.

Thank you.

Lecture Thirty-One
Woolf—*To the Lighthouse*, Part 2

Scope:

The most famous passage of this novel depicts Mrs. Ramsay (a figure richly particularized and present) as, in fact, "an inward core of darkness," suggesting that our outer form is a façade, that we extend inwardly in time and space in ways that no one sees. With stunning brutality, scarcely halfway in, this beautiful woman is "killed" by the plot, as Woolf pays tribute to "the reign of night," the forces of death and war that decimate the human family. Can anything be saved?

Then, 10 years later, the family reassembles, including the book's spinster-artist and figurative daughter, Lily Brisco, who seeks to make sense of all this: the life and death of Mrs. Ramsay, the mystery of human relationship, the possibility of retrieving one's dead via memory and art. Can we go to the lighthouse? Woolf offers two exquisite final versions of just that.

Outline

I. Woolf rivals Proust as our premiere writer about love, death, and memory. Mrs. Ramsay is one of literature's greatest creations, which makes her death—depicted as an aside, in parentheses—all the more shocking and brutal.

   A. In the last lecture, we spoke about the inevitable miscommunication between people who live together. Indeed, we might easily see the fate of all human relationships as the impossibility of two subjectivities ever coming together perfectly. Of course, the true fate of human relationships is death, and that's what this novel seems to be about: what happens to loving people when time exerts its terrible power.

   B. In Proust, the grandmother must be re-captured and re-felt by the boy long after she has died in order for him to fully understand the horror of her loss. With that in mind, let's begin this lecture by returning to Mrs. Ramsay to see what is so wonderful and what is lost in her.

II. In Mrs. Ramsay, Woolf offers her most profound depiction of human reaches and multiplicity, of the self we are, beyond the obvious roles we play.

A. Mrs. Ramsay is an exquisitely sensitive mother, attuned to the needs and wants of her children, her demanding husband, and her guests. She is a well-endowed woman, yet she can surprise us.

1. In a famous passage, Woolf writes about Mrs. Ramsay's musings after she has put her son to bed:

> For now, she need not think about anybody. She could be herself, by herself. … All the being and the doing, expansive, glittering, vocal, evaporated; and one shrunk, with a sense of solemnity, to being one's self, a wedge-shaped core of darkness.

2. A witness to the scene would see only a woman knitting, but she is somewhere else entirely, inwardly. This "wedge-shaped core of darkness" is, in some sense, moving. Paradoxically, when Mrs. Ramsay sits alone for a few moments, she feels "free for the strangest adventures."

3. Woolf writes: "Beneath it is all dark, it is all spreading, it is unfathomably deep; but now and again we rise to the surface and that is what you see us by." Woolf is not just saying that there is more to us on the inside than what we show others, but that we are mobile, untrackable creatures—what's on the inside is also elsewhere.

4. This idea radically changes our sense of a bounded form of identity. One's apparently cogent and identifiable self is really just an illusion, an appearance for the benefit of others.

5. Thus, any kind of realistic art form, such as a traditional novel that describes its characters, can't get at what matters, because it can't possibly track the voyage that takes place inside human beings.

6. The 16th-century philosopher Montaigne used the word *ondoyant*, meaning "wave-like," to try to describe the human psyche, and scholars since have connected Montaigne's view to Shakespeare's, seen particularly in

Hamlet. The bottom line is that we are "other" even unto ourselves. We move, shift, and re-form.

7. Woolf seems to say that we have far more possibilities within ourselves than what we show to the world. It's even conceivable that self can be a prison, something that people try to alter through various means.

8. We see the fuller extensions of this idea in a scene in which Mrs. Ramsay awakens in the night and seems to experience orgasm. Whereas we customarily think of great pleasure as a deeply private experience, Woolf suggests that ecstasy is a rupture of the self; it comes when we let go of our contours and experience otherness.

B. The death of Mrs. Ramsay stuns us: Scarcely more than halfway into the novel, its almost mythic heroine dies. Most readers are shocked by the severity of this move.

1. Killing off your heroine means breaking all the rules of fiction; why would an author do it? Moreover, the death comes almost as an aside. Woolf writes of Mr. Ramsay reaching out his arms, "but Mrs. Ramsay having died rather suddenly the night before … [t]hey remained empty."

2. This sets the stage for the great questions of this novel: Does anything survive? What's left when someone of this beauty and vitality dies?

III. The middle section of the novel is about the reign of night; it seeks ways to depict chaos.

A. Chaos doesn't come only because Mrs. Ramsay dies. The wedge-shaped core of darkness, which was Mrs. Ramsay's expression for the freedom and mobility of the human mind as the self exits its contours, has changed from a description of human subjectivity to a description of the terrible darkness of the world and of life itself.

B. Earlier, we saw that Mrs. Ramsay was a connoisseur of chaos. She knows that life is brutal and that her children will never be as happy later as they seem to be in childhood. This darkness spreads over the novel in the middle section, signaling to us the darkness that spread over Europe with World War I. Remarkably, Woolf has found a way to write this dark night of civilization into her story of a particular family.

C. We come to understand that chaos takes not just a single endowed, beautiful person, but many people. It dismantles the summerhouse itself and the people who have lived in it.

1. The dinner party scene highlights a small group of people sharing a meal at a house on an island, surrounded by the sea, by the elements. We realize how disproportionate those forces are—the elements versus a fragile human family sharing a ritual of food, wine, talk, and love.

2. The water, the wind, and the darkness rule here. The "little airs" (Woolf's term for the damage and deterioration meted out to the summerhouse) yield their unstoppable results, invading even the bedroom.

3. These forces of destruction and entropy cannot be denied, bringing the deaths of Mrs. Ramsay and others, again brought to us in parentheses.

4. Nothing can stop these brutal forces of nature. The inward core of darkness is no longer inward; it has become an outward tempest. We are reminded of the horrible forces of destruction that we see on the heath in *King Lear*—forces of turmoil and war that will destroy the human family.

D. The third phase of the novel depicts the return to the summerhouse 10 years later of those who have survived. Lily Brisco has played the role of Mrs. Ramsay's figurative daughter, yet she feels nothing on her return. How can feeling be reborn? Time not only destroys people, but it erases what we felt for them.

1. Lily's love for Mrs. Ramsay, one of the most poignant elements of the early part of the novel, is expressed in a stunning passage about the urgency and impossibility of "reaching" the one you love. As Lily presses against Mrs. Ramsay's knees, she imagines that inside the woman's heart and mind are tablets that bear sacred inscriptions. Are such inscriptions readable?

2. As the passage continues, the inscriptions become urns, then waters that are poured from one container to

another. Lily asks, could you press into another's secret chambers? How do you become the same as the person you love?" These are the great questions of human relationships.

3. In this light, these inscriptions become far more intimate and somatic, concerned not so much with knowledge as with unity, fusion with the other. This is what must be reborn in Lily 10 years later: She must resurrect those feelings of tenderness and desire that she felt for Mrs. Ramsay.

4. The spinster Lily also remembers Mrs. Ramsay's cheerleading for marriage as an institution, and now, in hindsight, she can see how much the great lady got wrong, especially in connection with Paul and Minta Rayley, whose marriage "came apart."

5. But the Rayleys' connection—dead or not—nonetheless explodes into Lily's awareness as evidence of passion's strange imperviousness to time. Does feeling live forever?

IV. Resurrection is the question of the final chapter. "The lighthouse" is not only about what remains but about what can be brought back to life.

A. Human feeling is now seen as the ultimate motor force that animates these survivors in the old house.

B. Here, we realize how much the title of the novel means. The great unanswered question at the beginning of the book—to go or not go to the lighthouse—is actualized in the final scenes.

1. Mr. Ramsay and two of his grown children will go to the lighthouse and bring gifts, parcels for the lighthouse men.

2. The imagery picks up John Donne's famous line "No man is an island." This fragile human family will go into the watery element to make a bridge to the lighthouse, itself an emblem of human isolation.

3. The children have forgotten nothing of their father's bullying, but at the same time, they want to please him, to receive his love and benediction.

C. Complementing the narrative of the trip to the lighthouse is Lily's emblematic reprise of her unfinished painting of Mrs. Ramsay. Both of these actions are tributes to the great lady. In fact, Lily's completion of the painting seems nothing less than an effort to bring Mrs. Ramsay back to life. Art, we see, is akin to what Walt Whitman called "retrievements out of the night."

1. The painting is meant to keep Mrs. Ramsay alive through memory, through Lily's tribute. But how does one paint a picture in such a way that one's love for the deceased reappears, shows itself as part of the picture, keeping the subject alive?

2. Lily knows that this is a great challenge, but she tries to meet it. Woolf writes that her painting is an act of tunneling into the past. The way Lily will make the painting is by re-immersing herself in her loving, pulsing memory of Mrs. Ramsay.

3. When Lily first returned to the empty house, she felt empty herself. Only when her feeling is rekindled can the painting be completed. Lily is surprised to find that when her feeling for Mrs. Ramsay is reborn, she is hurt, but the rebirth of Mrs. Ramsay takes place through Lily's tears.

4. Lily finishes the painting just as Mr. Ramsay and the children arrive at the lighthouse. Mr. Ramsay looks back at the island and sees a "plate of gold." He steps off the boat like a young man, giving us a sense that the past and love can, indeed, be recaptured.

Essential Reading:

Virginia Woolf, *To the Lighthouse*.

Supplementary Reading:

Rachel Bowlby, *Virginia Woolf: Feminist Destinations*.

Hermione Lee, *Virginia Woolf*.

Anna Snaith, *Virginia Woolf: Public and Private Negotiations*.

Arnold Weinstein, *Recovering Your Story: Proust, Joyce, Woolf, Faulkner, Morrison*.

Questions to Consider:

1. Mrs. Ramsay is characterized as a "wedge-shaped core of darkness" in the famous sequence when she "voyages" out of herself and into the world. This would appear to be the end of "self." Is it possible that our deepest feelings lead us out of personality and into something else? What else?

2. Mrs. Ramsay dies in the middle of the book. The last chapter is about measuring, 10 years later, what is left or what might be retrieved and how it might be done. What answers does Woolf give? Do you find this credible or not?

Lecture Thirty-One—Transcript
Woolf—*To the Lighthouse,* Part 2

Virginia Woolf rivals Marcel Proust as our premiere writer, it seems to me, about love, death, and memory. I've said that because I believe that Mrs. Ramsay is one of literature's greatest creations, and for that reason it's all the more shocking and seems all the more brutal to see what her fate is. She is simply felled in this novel not as a beast on a bed, which was the fate of the grandmother in Proust, but a death that is depicted essentially as an aside, in brackets, not even narrated. It's awful. I spent some time in the last lecture on *To the Lighthouse* talking about the charming but inevitable gap and miscommunication between people who live together, husband and wife, and it's easy to imagine the impossibility of two subjectivities ever coming together perfectly as the kind of fate of marriage or the fate of human relationships. But, of course, if you think about it, the true fate of human relationships, the most awful thing that happens to human relationships is death. Death is what can dismantle, what will dismantle, the human family. So, this book has a kind of gravity in that regard—that it's about what happens to loving people when time, of course, exerts its terrible power.

You may remember in Proust the grandmother must essentially be re-captured, re-acknowledged, re-felt by the boy long after she's died in order for him to fully understand and fully feel the gravity, weight, and horror of her loss. In somewhat of that spirit I'd like to return to Mrs. Ramsay and take a closer look at what it is that is so wonderful and that is going to die because in Mrs. Ramey I think Woolf gives us her most profound depiction of human reaches, of what sort of extension, what kind of dimensionality a self might have. I was rather brief in my last lecture about her. There's more to her. We see her in this book as a very sensitive, exquisitely sensitive, mother attuned to the needs and wants, the unexpressed, unstated wants of her children, their natures, also the rather complex wants of her demanding husband, and the needs and whims of the guests who comes to her house. She is a well-endowed woman, and yet she can surprise us.

I want to read a passage that's one of the most famous passages in Woolf about Mrs. Ramsay's musings after she has put her son,

James, to bed and she is gathering the pictures that he has been cutting out but she is alone now. Woolf writes it like this:

> For now she need not think about anybody. She could be herself, by herself. And that was what now she often felt the need of—to think; well, not even to think. To be silent; to be alone. All the being and the doing, expansive, glittering, vocal, evaporated; and one shrunk, with a sense of solemnity, to being oneself, a wedge-shaped core of darkness, [it's a very striking phrase, "a wedge-shaped core of darkness," and I'll talk more about it] something invisible to others.

The woman is continuing to knit, and once again, had you been there watching the scene, been the fly on the wall, all you'd have seen is a woman knitting. You couldn't have known what she's thinking about, but in this case what she is thinking about is so germane because she is thinking about where she really is. This "wedge-shaped core of darkness," is nothing less than something that is vehicular. It's something that is a journey, a voyage, and so that's how Woolf continues to write it. "It was thus that she felt herself; and this self having shed its attachments was free for the strangest adventures. When life sank down for a moment, the range of experience seemed limitless." It's interesting. We think of when life sinks down, when the people that we know leave the room and we sit on a sofa by ourselves. We rarely think of this as a moment of extraordinary exploration and expansion, but that's what it is. She feels that everyone she knows has these same resources, and probably secretly, unknowably, is taking the same kinds of trips. She finally says: "Beneath it is all dark," and she means beneath the surface, beneath the flesh, beneath what we can see about people, inside, "it is all spreading. It is unfathomably deep; but now and again we rise to the surface and that is what you see us by."

That, she says, is what you see us by. To me it's an astonishing passage. It's an extraordinarily rich, exploratory passage about the whereabouts of self, about the mobility of self, and what you see us by, which is in other words what you see me as when you look at me, what I see you as when I look at you, what you see when you look in the mirror, what you see when you look at others, all of that is the tip of the iceberg, as the old cliché has it. Most is underneath, but even that won't begin to take the measure of what Woolf is saying because it's not just underneath. It's on the move. These strange adventures are taking place. We are mobile, untrackable creatures, fluid creatures. It's not just that there is more to us on the inside, but what is on the inside is also elsewhere and other. This, of course, radically challenges our sense of a bounded form of identity. This is me. You can see my shape, my contours. No, Woolf, would say. All we can see is the sort of tip of it. All we can see is the illusory shell of things, of people, and that our apparently cogent and identifiable self is something of an illusion. It's an illusion for other people's benefit.

Therefore, any kind of realistic art form, like a traditional novel that just describes (and some of them describe in great detail) what a person looks like, how tall they are, what their hair looks like, what their features look like, but the implicit response here in Woolf is, well, that's fine. There's nothing wrong with that, but it just doesn't get what matters because it can't possibly track that voyage that's taking place on the inside, which is the true promiscuity, the true dimensionality, the true mobility of every human being.

The self in Woolf goes out for adventures. It goes out, as we might say today, on wildings, outings. In the 16th century the French philosopher, Montaigne, used the wonderful word *ondoyant*, which means "wave-like," to try to describe the human psyche—that it's wave-like. People have I think persuasively connected Montaigne's view of the human psyche to Shakespeare's and in particular Hamlet. Hamlet's personality is thought of also as *ondoyant*. What does all of that mean? Well, it means that we are "other" unto ourselves even. We move, and shift, and reform. How many times have people told you—you're not yourself today? What do you think they mean by that—you're not yourself today? If you're not yourself today, who are you when they tell you that? For the most part I think what we come up with is that they themselves have a fixed, bounded sense of who we are but that for whatever reason, for mood or whatever else, we are acting out a different self today—one that they know nothing about, one that seems out of character as far as they're concerned— you're not yourself today.

I think that Woolf is pointing at something quite fascinating. How much bookkeeping, how many sort of strings do you have to tie on your fingers to maintain a stable, recognizable self? It's as if when we get out of bed we recompose the self that everybody knows, and we trot that self off to work or whatever, or to the breakfast table. But I think what Woolf is saying is that actually things are far more anarchic than that. We have far more possibilities in ourselves. Could self itself be a kind of restrictive frame, a prison even? I want you to reflect on that. Can self be a prison? I think at times it is, and I think that's true for many people's lives. I'm going to go further and probably make a fool of myself by saying that people do drugs, and change mates, and do all kinds of things in their lives in order to re-create their self, in order to somehow find another self because they are so dreadfully fatigued, or hurt, or whatever by the self that they've got. Self really could be something asphyxiating and suffocating. It seems to me Woolf's passage about that inward core of darkness points to all of these matters.

One of the most surprising moments where we see the fuller extensions of this, it seems to me, is where Woolf tries to depict in this novel a scene of pleasure. Now, Virginia Woolf is well known for being extremely scrupulous about depicting scenes of pleasure—in fact perhaps even a little bit hemmed in. Friends of hers like Lytton Strachey said, "Where's the copulation in your books?" I mean, if you're looking for sex in novels, you don't read Virginia Woolf, although Woolf's biographers read her work with great prurience, it seems to me, to find out about her own possible lesbian interest. But there is a moment in *To the Lighthouse* which is really one of the most sexually exquisite things that I know in literature, and it's where the self seems to flow out not really as a hemorrhage but as again an adventure. Mrs. Ramsay awakens at night, and the steady, pitiless, remorseless light of the lighthouse bends across the floor in their summerhouse. It bends across the bed as if it were stroking her. Woolf writes of it, "As silvery fingers stroking a sealed vessel in her brain making it burst with pleasure," and the sea is described as, "rolling in waves of pure lemon that curve, and swell, and break on the beach." This is a version of ecstasy, of bursting these vessels. How can you not think that it's also a description of orgasm? It's a description of the entire organism being flooded with pleasure. This is how sexuality gets written in Woolf. "Ecstasy," as you doubtless know, etymologically means "ex-stasis," to be moved from the place that you are.

I think what Woolf is getting at, and it's surprising it seems to me, is that our moments of greatest pleasure are strangely impersonal and anonymous. They may be just the moments when we escape the confines of self, let go of our contours, and encounter and experience otherness. All of that I think is what's in play with that passage about the core of darkness, the inward core of darkness. All of that tells us again something about the gravity and tragedy of the loss that occurs when this woman dies or is felled by Virginia Woolf.

The death of Mrs. Ramsay stuns us partly because it comes slightly more than halfway into the novel, which again seems to break all the rules of fiction. Many readers are shocked by this, and moreover it comes in brackets, as I said. It's not even a beast on a bed. It's almost like an aside. We read about Mr. Ramsay in brackets. It's bracketed in the text—stumbling along a passage on a dark morning, and he reaches out his arms. And then Woolf actually writes, "but Mrs. Ramsay having died rather suddenly the night before, his arms remained … empty." Well, that sets the stage for the great questions of this novel that I want to think about as we work through the end of this lecture. What survives? What's left when someone of this kind of beauty and vitality dies because those are life's and biology's laws?

The way the book is structured is that the middle section of it is about the reign of night. In this sequence, the novel seeks ways to depict chaos. There's a marvelous line, which many people know from Othello, when Othello remarks that, "if he no longer loves Desdemona, if that should ever happen, chaos is come again," and I think that's what happens in this text. But it doesn't just come because Mrs. Ramsay dies. It's as if that wedge-shaped core of darkness, which was her expression for the freedom and mobility of the human mind as the self exits the contours that we know ourselves by and goes on these strange adventures—as if that darkness moved from being a term for human subjectivity and becomes a term for the terrible darkness of the world and of life itself.

Earlier I called Mrs. Ramsay a connoisseur of chaos who knows that life is brutal, who knows that life will pounce on you if you give it a chance, who knows that life will erase you, who knows that her children themselves will never be as happy later as they seem to be now. And so that darkness spreads over the novel. It's like night enters the novel, and what it is doing in this text is that it is also operating it seems to me as a kind of code language for an event we know all too well, which is World War I. What Woolf is talking about is night that spreads over Europe, night that spreads over civilization, and she has found a way to write this as the story of a particular family where the loving mother dies and so too will some of the children.

And so we understand that chaos means not just death taking a single endowed, beautiful person but that it takes many people. It dismantles the summerhouse itself, and it dismantles the people who have lived in it. We remember again the scene, the exquisite, beautiful, simple, domestic scene of the dinner party, of people sitting around a table, in a house, on an island, surrounded by the sea, by the elements. As I have said, we have to realize how disproportionate those forces are, the elements have to win—the fragility of that human family, that human construct sharing this timeless ritual of food, wine, talk, and love. Woolf has actually written that passage about looking out the window when they're seated together where "things wavered and vanished waterily." She invents that adverb, "waterily," and it's as if the water and the elements now take over and the wind itself and the night. Woolf calls that the "little airs." That's her term for the damage and the deterioration that is meted out to the summerhouse, and we watch these little airs. We watch them attack the house, which of course if you know anything about summer houses that are left unattended for years on end, or any house, we watch the deterioration, and the decay, and the dismantling of the house. They invade the cottage, these little airs. The wallpaper goes. Then Woolf writes, and it's really rather frightening—they make their way toward the bedroom. It almost is the language of rapists. They make their way to the bedroom. They're going to dismantle the bedroom too—the place where husband and wife have their nightlife together, the place where the lighthouse itself caresses the body of Mrs. Ramsay.

These are the forces of destruction and entropy that one cannot say no to, and so we have the deaths of many Ramsays, not only Mrs. Ramsay. But we read again in brackets, that first Pru Ramsay married with her father escorting her down the aisle, and then within one or two lines that she died in childbirth. We read in brackets as well that a shell exploded and some 20 or 30 soldiers are blown up in France, and the next sentence is, "Andrew Ramsay is one of them," one of the children. These are the brutal forces of nature that nothing can stop. This is the reign of night. This is the horrendous transformation of that inward core of darkness. It's not inward anymore at all. It's outward. It's something like the tempest. It's something like the horrible forces of destruction that we see in *Lear* on the heath. In fact, *Lear* is not a bad analogue to *To the Lighthouse* because it too is about the huge forces of turmoil and war that will destroy the human family. There's a wonderful domesticity in *Lear*, and we watch it be wrecked. We watch discord in a family. There's no discord in this text, but it's the same pathos about the family being taken apart.

So it is that the third phase of the novel depicts the return of those who have survived to the same summerhouse to see what is left. It's the great question. It's the great human question. What is left after our loved ones die, after some of them die? This is where the role of Lily Brisco becomes far more prominent. Lily is the kind of charming, rather shy spinster friend of the Ramsays who is in a sense the figurative daughter of Mrs. Ramsay. Many readers and critics have taken the view that in a sense, if Mrs. Ramsay represents Virginia Woolf's mother, to some extent Lily is a self-portrait of Virginia Woolf. I'm not sure how much I buy that, but nonetheless that's been said.

Lily comes to that house ten years later and feels nothing. How can feeling be reborn? Time not only destroys people, but it erases what we felt for them. Time destroys us who live as well as those who die. The book has spent time talking about Lily's really quite beautiful, tender feelings for Mrs. Ramsay. One wonders whether Mrs. Ramsay herself fully understands it, and there's one passage that's frequently cited where Lily is sitting next to Mrs. Ramsay and she has her arms around Mrs. Ramsay's knees. She is sort of pressing her knees, and she wonders whether Mrs. Ramsay can possibly feel what she is feeling. What she imagines inside of Mrs. Ramsay's heart and mind as she is sitting there with her arms lovingly around this woman's knees are tables—tables that bear sacred inscriptions. She asks herself, could you read these inscriptions? It's a very sweet, interesting image. Could you read these inscriptions that are located deep inside the inner sanctum of the person that you love? Are they readable? Are they knowable? But then we watch this evolve, this particular passage, and instead these sacred inscriptions become urns. They become waters that are poured from one to another, and when Lily seems to question, "Could you press into another's secret chambers?" Now, that's not a question of reading—could you press? It's almost a sexual image. Could you press into another's secret chambers? Then it goes further, "How do you become the same as the person that you love?" These are the great questions of human relationship. They're the great questions of marriage. I have said this is our premiere text about marriage, about what it means. Could you become the same as the one you love? In that light, these inscriptions about reading become something far more somatic, it seems to me, something far more about human flesh and desire—that what we seek is not so much knowledge as unity, fusion with the other. It's a lovely account of the language of desire, of the need to become the one that you love. That's what has to be reborn ten years later. Lily in some sense has to resurrect those feelings of tenderness and desire that she felt for Mrs. Ramsay.

Lily also remembers that Mrs. Ramsay's mantra about marry, marry, marry was in its own way rather quaint. I mean Lily is a spinster. She doesn't have at all the same belief in marriage. Moreover, she can see now in hindsight that the great lady got it wrong at times. In particular, I mentioned this young couple, the Rayleys, Paul and Minta. You remember that Minta has lost her brooch on the sand, and it turns out that they will become married. It also turns out that their marriage will fail, and Woolf will refer to it in some very striking passages about how the two of them were in love and then not in love. They still lived together. They still were friends, but love had died.

Lily knows this. We never know how she knows it, but she knows it and she thinks to herself, boy, did Mrs. Ramsay get it wrong. Woolf actually suggests that one of the few benefits of people that you love dying is that when they're dead you can finally gloat about how they got it wrong. It's not a very pretty perception, but it's an interesting perception. If they're not there anymore, you're no longer sort of afraid to ever say how fully you disagree with them. So, Lily is gloating. "You were wrong, wrong, wrong. Take a look at the Rayleys. They didn't last together." Then in a kind of really marvelous passage we have the words "in love" that come to Lily's mind. When those words come to her mind, there's a kind of explosion of a great pagan scene of fire and celebration on a beech, of roar and crackle, of a sea that has turned red and gold, and you realize this is the landscape of love. This is what Lily is being rocked by as she remembers Paul and Minta, and you actually get the sense that, well, it makes no difference that they're no longer in love because nonetheless, love lives. Love comes in and startles and brutalizes this spinster woman who is an artist. Her reaction to it is I think I will move a little bit the line and the color on my painting. It's the only way she knows how to respond. That's an interesting line about I will change something in my painting, and I used to think what a silly response that is, what an inadequate, incommensurate response that is to human love, which is the great drama that Lily has missed. First, I'm wrong on so many fronts here. Lily hasn't missed it. She has in fact loved Mrs. Ramsay, and that love we're going to see is inseparable from her art.

The final part of the book, in some sense, is about resurrection. It's about what still can be brought back to life—not just what remains but what can be brought back to life. Human feeling is going to come about as the fuel, the motor force for resurrection, for animating these survivors. That's when we realize how much this title means, going *To the Lighthouse*. As we said, that was the great question at the beginning of the book, will we go or will we not go—to go or not to go, it's almost Shakespearean. Mrs. Ramsay has said, yes, we will go if it's fine, and Mr. Ramsay says, no, it won't be fine.

But now in the third section of the book plans are made for a real visit to the lighthouse that Mr. Ramsay now, and it's never quite said— Woolf doesn't write this as a tribute to Ramsay's dead wife. But the reader can't help feeling that, yes, this is the great project that is now going to be actualized and completed. They will go. He will take two of his now grown-up children to the lighthouse, and they will bring gifts. During the early part of the novel we keep seeing Mrs. Ramsay knitting, and she is knitting socks for the son of the lighthouse keeper. These gifts will be brought to the lighthouse. The imagery is unmistakable. It picks up John Donne's famous lines that no man is an island. You once again realize that's the way this novel is written. This family, human family, a fragile family of people who love each other, at a summer house on an island in the sea, and they're going to go into the watery element in order to reach the lighthouse, which itself is a kind of structure in the midst of the sea as almost an emblem of human isolation. They're going to bridge to it. They're going to make the trip to it. That's the title, *To the Lighthouse*.

He will take the children with him, two of the surviving children, and there is nothing mushy and gooey about this. They remember what a tyrant he was. You remember the passage that I cited earlier about Mr. Ramsay storming his wife with his need for affection and James there huddled between her knees hating his father, wanting in fact to take a knife and pierce his father's breast. They will sit there in this boat with their father as they move toward the lighthouse, remember this, remembering what a bully he was, and at the same time wanting nothing more than to please this man who is their father, to do right by him, to receive his love and his benediction.

So, completing the narrative of the trip to the lighthouse, the literal trip to the lighthouse, is what I would call a figurative trip to the lighthouse. Not surprisingly, it comes to us as a work of art. Lily Brisco will reprise the painting that she never finished, which was a painting of Mrs. Ramsay, and she will try to complete it. We have to see these things as versions of each other—Lily completing the painting, Mr. Ramsay taking the children to the lighthouse. Both of these are in some sense grand tributes to Mrs. Ramsay. The second voyage, Lily's painting, I think is really nothing less than an effort to bring Mrs. Ramsay back to life. Whitman once in his great elegy to Lincoln talked about art as being "retrievements out of the night." Whitman was thinking about the death of the president, of Lincoln being assassinated, but "retrievements out of the night" is a lovely image, it seems to me, of our tribute to the dead, our memory of the dead, our way of in fact making it possible miraculously that the dead are not dead through our memory, through our tribute. So, this painting is meant to do exactly that. How do you paint a picture of someone who is dead? How do you paint a picture of someone whom you loved? How do you paint a picture in such a way that your love for this dead person reappears, shows, as part of the picture, and in that light the person is no longer dead? Isn't that what art is, one looks at a painting, a portrait of someone and they're there?

Their bones may be moldering in the earth, and yet they're there living in the picture. Anyone who has ever tried to paint knows this is no simple matter. Woolf expresses it, to exchange "the fluidity of life for the concentration of painting." Lily feels that her grand desire to be a painter is fraught with impossibility. "It's a contest," she says, "that you cannot win. You're fated to lose. Art can never match the kind of quicksilver nature of reality. It can't do it. It's not in the cards, and yet it is a gallant challenge. It's a grand challenge. It's the one that you don't duck—that you try to meet." And so she does try to meet it, and Woolf writes this as actually tunneling into the past, but the way she makes this painting is to sort of re-immerse herself in the actual substance of Mrs. Ramsay. It's very close to Proust here because the only way to capture Mrs. Ramsay on canvas is in fact to fully experience her death. You may remember I said Lily returns to this empty house and feels empty herself. The dead are dead. There's no feeling, and only when this feeling is rekindled, is reborn, can the painting take place. Of course, it hurts when the feeling is reborn, and Lily is stunned and shocked. It's ten years later, and she discovers to her surprise that these are salty tears coming out of her eyes. She says to herself, "Is it possible that we can still be hurt, that we can be hurt ten years later by the death of the people that we loved?" We feel like this is the very birth of Mrs. Ramsay again, the re-birth of her. It takes place through the tears of those who loved her. This is hunger—tears. I'm saying all of this partly because it's possible to read *To the Lighthouse* as a kind of work of art about art. It closes with Lily who is making a painting, but the aesthetics are secondary to the human feelings. It's feeling that makes art possible, and so at the end of this book Lily completes her painting just as Mr. Ramsay arrives at the lighthouse with the children.

As he gets off of that boat, he looks back and Woolf writes, "With his long-sighted eyes perhaps he could see the dwindled leaf-like shape standing on end of a plate of gold quite clearly. What could he see?" This is the thought of his children. What is he looking back for? The island he looks back towards is the island where that house is where his wife lived, and I think the plate of gold is just such a beautiful image because it is turned into something precious. As he gets off the boat, Woolf writes, "he sprang, lightly like young man," and it's a beautiful moment. It's like going back to the past, recapturing the past, recapturing his dead wife, recapturing human love. That's what Woolf has created in this book. Art is the outcome of love and desire, and it makes life.

Thank you.

Lecture Thirty-Two
Faulkner—*As I Lay Dying*

Scope

As I Lay Dying, a Faulknerian masterpiece in stream-of-consciousness writing, explores the nature of both death and art through the death of a mother and the trials and thoughts of her family. This metamorphic novel stuns us also with its grasp of natural forces outside the human scheme. Perhaps the most resonant figure of the novel is its coffin: What, this book of elements and fluids repeatedly asks, does it contain? What does it mean to contain something?

A key theme in the book is *encounter*: with others, with the coursing natural world. At a climactic moment, the family wagon (with its precious cargo of mother in the coffin) enters the floodwaters, and the Faulkner baptism takes place: the immersion into the elements. But it is a baptism in reverse, because *I* comes undone when subjected to such pressure. The book's title is its great (modern) question: Can *I* die? Is *I* a fiction?

Outline

I. *As I Lay Dying* (1930) was an early novel by William Faulkner (1897–1962) but, arguably, his greatest masterpiece in stream-of-consciousness writing. As different as the tonalities of the two writers may be, we can find many parallels between Woolf and Faulkner, including the subject matter of this book—what lives and what dies.

   A. The title, *As I Lay Dying*, tells us everything we need to know about the novel in terms of what Faulkner is getting at in modern thinking and modern life: the death of the notion of *I*.

   B. *The Sound and the Fury* was Faulkner's first breakthrough stream-of-consciousness text, but *As I Lay Dying* seems to take the technique even further, yielding perhaps the most philosophical text he ever wrote. We see perspectival narration with a vengeance in this novel, which is composed entirely of first-person vignettes, but the point-of-view technique is focused on great, unanswerable questions.

II. The novel has a seemingly simple theme—getting the coffin with the dead Addie Bundren from the farm to Jefferson for burial. This mission generates a complex set of responses, ranging from family members' diverse opinions to those of outsiders in the community.

   A. Faulkner reprises the plot-enabling dilemma of the *Antigone* of Sophocles: what to do with a dead body? This is scarcely a literary motif; how to manage dead bodies is a crucial element of all religious cultures.

   B. Whereas so much modern literature seems to be about the human psyche—and Faulkner ranks high here—this novel also gives us an unforgettable sense of the elements themselves, the nonhuman landscape and stage where the players go through their paces.

      1. Faulkner is one of the rare modern writers who does full justice to the priority, authority, and ferocity of our natural world. He manages to give us a rich sense of the incredible tumult inside human beings, as well as of the physical world we inhabit.

      2. In that light, Faulkner is one of our most pagan writers. The material world—the world of wind, water, earth, and sun—exists for him as something that dwarfs the human being.

   C. *As I Lay Dying* is justly renowned for its stream-of-consciousness narration, its vignette-like composition. We thus encounter a staggering spectrum of responses to Addie Bundren's death.

      1. Anse, the seemingly shiftless husband for whom everyone in the novel feels contempt, has an astonishing country wisdom; he also has his own design in going to Jefferson. Anse observes that horizontal things, roads and wagons, are for moving, but that God made men and trees upright for staying put. As we will see in this text, stability is a fiction; nothing can stay put.

      2. Jewel, the favored (illegitimate) son, is presented as the impassioned, almost nonverbal literalist whose feelings

for his mother are largely unavowable. He is the physical force in the family.

3. Cash, the carpenter, is the book's pragmatist, the man who expresses himself through artisanal means. He is the maker of the coffin, and his mother rightly sees this as an expression of love.

4. Darl, the philosopher, is the novel's most stunning and authoritative figure: capable of metaphysical flights, blessed/cursed with a kind of X-ray vision into others, and yet ungrounded. Darl's poetic and metaphysical flights constitute one of the high points of Faulknerian fiction.

    a. In one early scene, Darl remembers getting up in the night to get a drink of water. When he puts the dipper into the bucket, he "stirs the stars awake."

    b. Echoing Proust, Shakespeare, and others, Darl says, "In a strange room you must empty yourself for sleep. … When you are emptied for sleep, you are not. And when you are filled with sleep, you never were." In other words, if you are just a sleeping body, you have no consciousness; you are not.

    c. The same passage closes: "How often have I lain beneath a rain on a strange roof, thinking of home?" We realize just how homeless this character is, how the mind itself has exiled Darl from any sense of groundedness.

5. Dewey Dell is the unwed, pregnant daughter whose response to her mother's death is inseparable from her feelings about pregnancy. Faulkner's account of her sensations of carrying a living seed in her are compatible with her no less powerful sense of collapsing self.

6. Vardaman, the youngest child, is also the most unhinged figure of the novel, and his trauma is unforgettably conveyed by Faulknerian associative logic and startling metaphor.

    a. At the moment his mother is dying, Vardaman catches a huge fish. In his mind, the two become confused: His mother cannot be dead because she was still alive when the fish was flopping around.

    b. When the coffin bearing Addie is nailed shut, Vardaman drills holes in it so that she won't suffocate.

D. The family's responses to Addie's death are dramatically cut with the no less diverse reactions of the neighbors and townspeople to this death and this traveling coffin that begins to smell in the Mississippi heat.

    1. Peabody, the book's doctor, offers some of the most speculative ideas about the phenomenon of death:

> I can remember how when I was young I believed death to be a phenomenon of the body; now I know it to be merely a function of the mind and that of the minds of the ones who suffer the bereavement. The nihilists say it is the end; the fundamentalists, the beginning; when in reality it is no more than a single tenant or family moving out of a tenement or a town.

        a. The core imagery of the novel is contained in the idea of death as a tenant moving out of a tenement. Like a tenement, a coffin is a container, but what does it contain? A body? A soul? A single identity—an *I*?

        b. Later in the novel, we're forced to ask whether even language contains meaning.

    2. Tull, the neighbor, serves as a kind of barometric, common-sensical figure, but he also has moments of visionary insight. He says that sorrow and affliction are liable to strike anywhere, like lightning.

    3. Cora Tull, his wife, is one of Faulkner's splendid comic creations: opinionated but deliciously wrong in many of her judgments.

    4. And then there are those who are shocked by the sheer stench of this traveling coffin with its rotting cargo.

III. Faulkner sets up the human pilgrimage, then subjects it to inhuman trials. He hits his characters biblically with water and fire, lining up obstacles to complicate the Bundrens' trip with the coffin to the cemetery in Jefferson.

A. The first obstacle is the swollen flood waters and the strangeness of the river. Tull says, "It was thick like slush ice only it kind of lived." We get a sense that the water is animated, demonized.

1. Darl says of the river, "It talks up to us in a murmur, becomes ceaseless and myriad." The elements are not just alive, but they speak, cluck, and murmur.

2. When the Bundrens reach the point where they will cross, they feel as if they have come to the end of the earth, the place "where the motion of the wasted world accelerates just before the final precipice."

3. In the eyes of the mules, Darl sees "a wild, sad, profound, and despairing quality as if they had already seen in the thick water the shape of disaster, which they could not speak and we could not see." This takes us back to Tiresias, the blind seer of *Oedipus*.

B. "Leaving the road" comes to resonate as a notation about the tug between civilized pattern and elemental forces. In Faulkner's novels, we find that we might fall off the road, out of sanity or reality, and into the elements.

1. Darl and Cash share an encounter as they ready the wagon to cross the river, in which they see each other completely denuded and stripped. We see here a collision between human subjectivities, and between humans and the elements.

2. To see the Bundrens and their wagon entering the elements is to see the novel's primal encounter with nature's fury. The result is catastrophic; the wagon is overturned by the rushing waters, and the coffin simply flows out of it.

3. The Bundrens' efforts to retrieve the coffin function as a reverse baptism. As they are immersed in the elements, they become un-named, "undone." Darl says, "As though the clotting which is you had dissolved into the myriad original motion."

4. In Faulkner's world, all that we take for granted about the cogency, the unity, and the value of the self can come undone, as if, again from Darl, "you could just ravel out in time."

Essential Reading:

William Faulkner, *As I Lay Dying*.

Supplementary Reading:

André Bleikasten, *Faulkner's "As I Lay Dying."*

Linda Wagner-Martin, ed., *William Faulkner: Four Decades of Criticism*.

Arnold Weinstein, "Faulkner's *As I Lay Dying*: The Voice from the Coffin," in *Nobody's Home: Speech, Self and Place in American Fiction from Hawthorne to DeLillo*.

Philip Weinstein, *Faulkner's Subject: A Cosmos No One Owns*.

Questions to Consider:

1. Faulkner's world in this novel can seem at once entirely mental (the whole novel as a suite of interior monologues) and entirely physical (the presence and authority of land, water, air, flesh, and blood). Do you find there to be much communication between these two realms? Regarding your own condition, does this model appear to be viable?

2. What are the benefits Faulkner derives from writing *As I Lay Dying* as a series of vignettes? Is there a price to pay? Are you able to see the lineaments and outlines of the fuller story? Can you imagine your life inscribed in such a sequence of personal visions and voices?

Lecture Thirty-Two—Transcript
Faulkner—*As I Lay Dying*

As I Lay Dying is arguably William Faulkner's greatest masterpiece in the area of stream-of-consciousness. It's an early novel that Faulkner wrote. It has, I think, the verbal brilliance of *Ulysses*, and it also has some of the pathos of both Proust and Woolf. It too centers on the death of a mother. But Faulkner's account of the dead Addie Bundren and the "difficulties" (and that's, you'll see, a very modest word I'm using, given what happens in this book) of getting that body in a coffin to the cemetery, is in a league by itself. I should say up front I am a Faulkner fan. I'm a Faulkner fanatic. I have to admit that. I was born in the South. Faulkner, for me, occupies a unique place not only in American literature but somewhere in my brain and probably not just in my brain. This book is grotesque. It's metaphysical. It's hilarious. There's nothing quite like it even in Faulkner's particular oeuvre.

It's about what lives and about what dies, and of course I said that's exactly what Woolf was about. There are a lot of parallels as different as the tonalities might be between Woolf and Faulkner. But look—you will hear me saying this over and over, look at Faulkner's title, *As I Lay Dying*. As I understand it, this title is lifted from Homer, from *The Odyssey*. But the fact is that the title tells us everything about this novel, and it tells us everything about what Faulkner is getting at in modern thinking and in modern life—that *I* might die. I'm not talking about me, Arnold Weinstein, dying. I'm talking about the notion of *I* could die.

The Sound and the Fury was Faulkner's first great breakthrough text about stream-of-consciousness, and *As I Lay Dying* is the book that comes afterwards. I think it's the most philosophical book that he wrote. It's perspectival narration, stream-of-consciousness narration, interior monologue narration with a vengeance, because it is composed entirely along those lines. I'll say more about that. It has a seemingly simple theme, getting the coffin that has the dead Addie Bundren from the farm to the cemetery in Jefferson. It's a pledge that her husband, Anse, had made to her. At one point he says, "Her people is waitin' for her in Jefferson," and you get a sense that these are real people. They're not just bodies in the graveyard. These are people, dead people, waiting for Addie to join them, and that is a remarkable sort of plot device to get this coffin to the cemetery because it will generate a whole series of responses, not only among the Bundrens themselves as the sons reflect on the difficulties and the meaning of getting Mother, who is dead, to the grave, but it is also going to incite a number of different kinds of reactions in the community itself as this coffin travels across the land and across the water in the heat of Mississippi summer.

This is the plot-enabling dilemma of many literary texts, the most famous of which is the *Antigone* of Sophocles—what to do with a dead body. You might remember that Sophocles' plot has to do with the two brothers who are killed and which one is going to be offered burial rights and which body will lie on the ground. It's Antigone who says, "No, you are flouting God's law." She insists that both be buried, but of course the whole activity depends on what we know about the scandal of human flesh. As I have said before when talking about other writers, all cultures are strategic here—flowers and wreaths surround the dead body but very quickly one wants to get it into the ground. You may remember, as well, as far back as Dostoevsky, the notion of the odor of corruption; that the Elder Zosima, his body, starts to stink way too soon. So, these are issues that seem to me to resonate in literature, and they're issues given that the death of the mother or the death of the grandmother has been so much with us in these last texts. They're issues that seem to form something of a kind of thread in this course.

Now, so much of modern literature, and certainly you've seen this in this course, seems to be focused on the activity of the mind. It's not for nothing that Faulkner's most famous book is called *The Sound and the Fury*. *The Sound and the Fury* represent the nose inside the brain, the noise that's 24/7, and Faulkner is among our greatest writers for tapping into that noise and being able to render it.

Having said that, *The Sound and the Fury* also, as we well know, represents the convulsive life of the earth itself and of the heavens. When we have tornadoes, hurricanes and tsunamis we get a different sense of what "sound and fury" might mean. Faulkner is one of the rare modern writers who does, in my opinion, full justice to the priority, and I mean it temporally—it got there first—and authority, and ferocity of our natural world, so that he manages to do both things at once—to give us a sense of the incredible tumult inside of the human being as well as giving us a rich sense—Proust, for

©2007 The Teaching Company.

example does not do this—of the physical world that we inhabit. In that light, I think Faulkner is among our most pagan writers, but the real material world, the world of wind, water, earth and sun, exists for him. It exists in a sense as something that dwarfs the human being, the human player who "struts and frets his hour" on the stage. The elements are real in Faulkner. The elements are there on the inside and on the outside.

Now, *As I Lay Dying*, as I said, is renowned as being exclusively stream-of-consciousness narration. Therefore, it's a series of vignettes. Everything about it is first person, and as I have said so often in this course, one of my purposes in giving this course and in choosing the texts that we're looking at is to show you something of the astonishing scope and diversity that exists in literature—that there's so many different ways of telling the human story, of telling the life story. To tell it exclusively as a series of first-person vignettes is going to give us a particular purchase on what is sayable and, of course, what's not sayable—what he can't get out. So, let me talk about the various first persons that we're going to get in this text, people who respond to the death of Mother.

Let's start with the husband, Anse, who is a seemingly shiftless man for whom everyone in the novel has contempt. But he has some lines of astonishing country wisdom. He has also, as we will see at the end of this book, a design of his own for getting this body to Jefferson. People marvel at his shiftlessness, his genius for using other people. When I said he can be memorable himself—in some of his lines he comes across as a kind of country philosopher. He thinks, for example, that his luck has changed when the road came to his house, and he makes the observation, it's a pungent observation, that roads and wagons are for moving but that God made men and trees up and down for staying put. It's an interesting line in this text because we will see in this text that nothing can stay put. It's about the fiction of stability, the fiction, the fictiveness, the fantasy that anything can stay what you think it is. Things change, evolve, metamorphose. Death is one of those things.

Then there is the son, Jewel, who is the favored son and who is the illegitimate son. Not everyone knows it. His mother, of course, knows it, and one of his brothers senses it. He is the impassioned almost non-verbal literalist whose feelings for Mother are intense and almost unavowable. She can never acknowledge that she loves him more then the others because he is the illegitimate one, the son of a true love relationship. He is the physical force in the family. He wants Mother entirely to himself. At one point, he imagines, "Just me and her on a high hill rolling down rocks at the others." One of the other sons is named Cash, and he's the carpenter of the novel. He is the book's pragmatist. He is also the figure in the novel that will finally sum things up, and he expresses himself through artisanal means as a carpenter. You'll see how important I think that is as I continue to talk about this book.

As the book starts, he is making this coffin, and his mother—she is dying, looks out the window and sees her son making this coffin. Almost the first lines of the book are, "Chuck. Chuck. Chuck, of the adze that Cash is using to make this coffin." And she looks at it, and there is nothing horrifying about it. She knows that this is a labor of love. She knows this is his last act of filial love for her to make this box, which will be her last house. But Cash being the kind of person he is, the craftsman, he wastes no words. He is not metaphorical the way some of the other sons are, and one of his marvelous chapters is just a list of 13 reasons, and they're numbered one, two, thee, four, it goes right to thirteen, reasons why he made the coffin exactly the way he did.

The most I think memorable and significant of the sons is Darl, who is the philosopher of the novel. He is the one that in a sense Addie Bundren has denied her love to, and because of that, and I say because of that—it's a little simple. I'm not sure it's because of that, but I do believe that in Faulkner's world if the mother denies the love to the son, then the son is in some critical sense ungrounded, unmoored, unanchored.

However, in Faulkner if you're ungrounded or unmoored, it means you're in some weird way liberated and freed; because Darl is the figure whose thoughts simply stream out into the world and whose vision streams out into the world. At one point his vision is described as something like a water hose. He looks at you, and you feel like you're being knocked over by the power of this thing. So, you can imagine where I'm going with this or where Faulkner goes with it. His vision essentially penetrates other people. He can see what is otherwise hidden. He will tell us about Addie Bundren's death. He will narrate that death, and he is not there. He is somewhere else. So, he is the omniscient figure in some ways in this book even though he

©2007 The Teaching Company.

is ungrounded. Therefore, he is in some sense a figurative version of William Faulkner. To be omniscient in a book is to be a surrogate figure of the novelist, who is also omniscient.

He has the great poetic and metaphysical flights of the book, and I think, therefore, he really constitutes one of the high points in Faulknerian fiction. There is a lyricism about him. For example, one early scene that is not much emphasized by critics but I think it's just exquisite is that he remembers getting up and going to the cedar bucket where he would take his dipper and get water at night to slake his thirst. But what is lyrical and what is so fine is that he looks into the bucket. He takes the dipper and what he does is he says he stirs the stars awake. You have to think for just a moment of that. Here is the water that looks black at night in this cedar bucket. He looks at it and he stirs it because the black water reflects the stars in the sky. His dipper makes the stars themselves stir awake, and, of course, you begin to think Big Dipper, Little Dipper. This is sort of the economy in poetry of the way Faulkner writes.

He is also the most philosophical character in the book, and I'll read you one of the most famous passages in the book about Darl's problems with falling asleep. Proust's novel opens, *Longtemps je me suis couché de bonne heure*, "For a long time I used to go to bed early," and Marcel in the novel and Proust himself, they are both famously insomniacs. Well, Proust is writing it in his particular way. This is the way Faulkner writes it. "In a strange room you must empty yourself for sleep." You remember in Proust the difficulty of sleeping in a strange room. Watch how this one happens because notice the verb here—empty yourself for sleep. That's not what Proust said. Proust says you've got to drown out the noise that this strange altered room, this room that is not you, all the noise it's making and that it's going to crush you—not so in Faulkner. You have to empty yourself for sleep. "And before you are emptied for sleep, what are you. And when you are emptied for sleep, you are not." He is talking about consciousness and a body and how different they are, and the way to go to sleep is to gradually sort of drug consciousness out of play so that the body can turn off.

"When you are emptied for sleep, you are not." In other words, if you're just a sleeping body, consciousness is finally dulled away. You die figuratively. You're not there. "You are not." The *I* that you are is no longer there. He doesn't stop there. "And when you are filled with sleep, you never were. I don't know what I am." And this is where this Mississippi farm boy starts to sound little like Hamlet or Descartes. "I don't know what I am. I don't know if I am or not." Remember, Jewel is the literalist, the one who has no curiosity at all. "Jewel knows he is, because he does not know that he does not know whether he is or not." That's Shakespeare re-written in Faulkner's English. "Jewel knows he is, because he does not know that he does not know whether he is or not." It also sounds like Lacan, the French guru philosopher, linguistic philosopher, of the 20th century, talking about consciousness and subjectivity and rewriting Descartes for a generation of modern thinkers. And about Jewel, "He cannot empty himself for sleep because he is not what he is and he is what he is not." There again, that sounds like it's paradoxical, but if you think hard about it, it's not. "Is" and "is not" has to do again with the body versus consciousness, and that they have a very fitful coexistence in Faulkner. This kind of rather tortured language, like these are the exercises. Some of us do other exercises, we count sheep, we do other things—these are the exercises that Darl goes through before he falls asleep. The passage closes, "How often have I lain beneath rain on a strange roof, thinking of home." You realize, "home," how distant home is, how homeless this character is, how the mind itself has exiled this character from any sense of groundedness at all. These exercises he is going through, is and is not, being and not being—you feel like you're hearing Sartre. You feel like you're hearing Shakespeare. You feel like you're hearing Laclos.

Well, that's part of the repertoire of this book, and that's the sort of note that Darl sounds. There are other children too. Dewey Dell— that's the name of the single daughter that Addie has—is unwed and pregnant, and therefore her response to Mother's death is going to be different from the others because it's always going to involve her own anxiety, but also her own astonishment at carrying a fetus inside of her and not knowing what to do about it. People have said that Faulkner doesn't understand women, and at some conceptual level if you use the word "understanding" it's probably true. But he can write creatures. He can write creatures who live in bodies, and in a sense a pregnant woman is a woman who is having some astounding kinds of somatic sensations. He knows how to write that, oddly enough, and so there's one marvelous scene where she goes to the barn because she hears the cow moaning to be milked. Faulkner writes about the "dead air that lies flat and warm on her touching her naked through her clothes." That's the way he writes it—touching her naked through her clothes. You begin to wonder—is she just naked, or is the touching her making her naked through her clothes? Then she thinks about what she is carrying inside of herself. "I feel like a wet seed wild in the hot blind earth."

The youngest son, Vardaman, is the most unhinged figure of the novel, and his trauma is remarkably conveyed by Faulkner's associative logic and his metaphors. In particular, Vardaman at the moment as his mother is dying has caught this big, huge fish that is sort of flapping around. He's bringing it in for dinner, and it's bleeding and everything. In his young mind, the trauma and crisis of his mother lying on a bed dying and this bleeding fish that is flapping on the ground and then going to be put in a skillet, there is a kind of disassociation and reassociation. There is a kind of recombinant strategy. He confuses the two at some primitive level in his own mind, and so these are all strategies of denial. Mother cannot be dead. She was still alive when the fish was still flapping, and therefore, she must still be alive. He thinks the person in the coffin is not Mother. He calls that the "other one," and then when the coffin is nailed shut, he can't bear it because if she's in there and it's nailed shut, she's going to suffocate. He takes an auger, and he drills holes into the coffin so that Mother can breath. And he drills holes right into her face. I say this book is grotesque, and yet it is extraordinarily I think poignant—this boy trying to keep Mother alive because she can't be dead, and he has the most famous chapter in the novel. It has one brief phrase, "Mother is a fish." This is how scrambled it gets for him, the way in which these different moments have been juxtaposed, fused together. This is his way of both denying and expressing the reality of his mother's death. So, this is a family you don't quickly forget as they go on this pilgrimage, because that's what it is to take this coffin with this body to its final resting place.

But Faulkner, as I said, also gives us the response of the other people in the book, and some of these other people are quite remarkable. One of them is Dr. Peabody, who comes early to the book when Addie is not yet dead. Peabody reminisces and reflects on what he thinks death is, and it's important for Faulkner.

> I can remember how when I was young I believed death to be a phenomenon of the body; now I know it to be merely a function of the mind and that of the mind—and that of the

ones who suffer the bereavement. The nihilists say it is the end; the fundamentalists, the beginning; when in reality it is no more than a single tenant or family moving out of a tenement or a town.

You may not think that's an interesting definition, but I do. What is this tenement that death moves tenants out of? What I want to suggest to you is that the core imagery of the novel is somehow contained in that phrase, and it's contained in my language, and it's contained in the word that I've now pronounced three times, "contain," because that's what a tenement is, a container.

What kind of a container is this book interested in? There are several different kinds. One of them is a coffin. A coffin contains what? Is it Mother? Is it just a body? Is it rotting flesh? But another one would be a body itself. What does it contain? Does it contain a "tub of guts"? That's one of the phrases that's used in this book. Or does it contain a soul that is you? What is a self? We have a body on the one hand, but is there a single identity, an *I* that is contained? Finally, you will see later in this book language itself—what does it contain? It too might be a tenement. Does language contain meaning? Does it contain the meanings that we need in order to exchange words, values, and feelings with each other? All of that, I think, is implicit in this remarkable definition that Peabody gives.

Others also respond, as I said, to the pilgrimage of this body being taken to Jefferson. We get Tull, the neighbor, who responds. He thinks about sorrow and affliction and I think significantly says it's liable to strike anywhere like lightning. And we have the Dr. Peabody who remarks that here in Mississippi everything hangs on too long, "Like our rivers, our land: opaque, slow, violent; shaping and creating the life of man in its implacable and brooding image." There again, the pagan Faulkner, the correlation between our own thoughts and feelings and the larger scheme, the larger stage that we inhabit.

Then you have Cora Tull, who is really one of the delicious figures in the book, like Mrs. Malaprop in English drama. She gets everything wrong. She misconstrues every relationship in the book, and we have others who respond to the unbearably increasing stench of this coffin as it makes its way through the Mississippi heat. One of the characters, Samson, says, "a woman that's been dead in a box four days, the best way to respect her is to get her into the ground." And another one says, "It's an outrage. They should be lawed." In other words, the police should come after them. Some of the negroes who see this coffin being carried across, and then after they see it smell what's in it, "Great God, what they got in that wagon?" This constantly pushes the question—is that still Mother?

Well, I've suggested to you that the pilgrimage of this coffin is what's going to cause the trouble, and the reason it causes the trouble is that it's not so easy to get from this farm all the way to Jefferson. The reason it's not is that Faulkner has thrown everything he could at these people trying to get this coffin to the graveyard. He has hit them Biblically with water and with fire, and so it turns out that the river they are supposed to cross has flooded because of the rains, and here you have the classic Faulknerian scene. How are they going to get this wagon with its precious contents, once more a container, the wagon with its precious contents, which is Mother lying in the coffin—how are you going to get it across this swollen river, which is going over its banks? Faulkner writes this, I think, beautifully. He makes us understand how much is at stake here. Everybody looks at this river, and they understand something is strange. It's not just a river anymore. Even Tull looks at the water and says, "It was thick like slush ice only it kind of lived." And you get a sense that this water is sort of animated, demonized. We have the water described almost as a kind of god-like figure that has a will of its own.

I talked about the elements in Faulkner. Here they are, the raging waters, and we will see that the analogue to that will be the flowing blood. Darl, who comes to the water, and they've got to ford this river in order to get to Jefferson, looks at it and says, "It talks up to us in a murmur becomes ceaseless and myriad." Darl looks at it, and he thinks that something is coming alive in this water and waking up. He says as well, "It clucks and murmurs among the spokes." You get a sense that the elements speak in Faulkner. Even "pantheism" is too tame a word because the elements are not just alive, but they speak, cluck, murmur and talk, ceaseless and myriad.

Then they reach the part of the river where they have to go across, and they feel like they have come to the end of the earth. "We had reached the place where the motion of the wasted world accelerates just before the final precipice." Darl looks at the mules that are supposed to take this wagon across, and he gives one of the most exquisite, I think, references that I've ever read about the wisdom of animals and the benightedness of humans. He says that the mules are breathing now with:

> a deep groaning sound; [then he says] looking back once, their gaze sweeps across us within their eyes a wild, sad, profound and despairing quality as [if] they had already seen in the thick water the shape of the disaster which they could not speak and we could not see.

We are all the way back to Tiresias, the blind seer in the *Oedipus*, who can see what others can't, but this is William Faulkner. These are the mules that can see in the water the shape of the disaster that is coming. They can't speak it, and we can't see it.

What do you call this? Is this country wisdom? Is this prophecy? Is this poetry? It seems to me it's impossible to sort it out. They are trying to stay on the road, and you begin to realize that too is a metaphor because on the sides of the roads are the deep precipices. We're not talking about the obvious ones. You could fall off the road. You could fall out of sanity. You could fall out of reality. You could fall into the elements. This is the moment of encounter and the moment of baptism, this family that is going to enter the elements. Here is the encounter. There are Darl and Cash on the wagon trying to get this wagon across getting ready to enter the waters. They look at each other so that's why I call it "encounter."

> He and I look at [each other] with long probing looks, looks that plunge unimpeded through one another's eyes and into the ultimate secret place where for an instant Cash and Darl crouch flagrant and unabashed in all the old terror and the old foreboding, alert and secret and without shame.

It's as if they have been completely denuded, stripped. It almost goes back to the caveman status of things. They see each other naked and raw. That's the kind of moment of encounter and collision that takes place here. It's a collision between human subjectivities, and it's a collision between humans and the elements themselves. They are going to enter the elements. This is the Conradean baptism. He says this in *Lord Jim*, "Into the elements immerse yourself," and that is what is going to happen here. But it won't just be them.

It will be the wagon that contains the container that contains Mother. Is it still Mother? This thing is stinking so much, is it Mother? Can it be? And they're trying to bring it across.

Well, that is what is going to be the great question of this novel. Can you enter the elements and can you emerge from them? Can this coffin be put into the swollen waters and somehow also be salvaged from it? What will happen when that moment of great immersion takes place? The way Faulkner writes it, it is catastrophic. The wagon is overturned by the rushing, flowing waters, and the coffin simply flows out of the wagon. At that point, we will have the efforts of the Bundrens to retrieve this coffin. I called it a baptism. Baptism, of course, is a rite. It's one of the rituals in Christianity. It's also when we receive our name, and it is too an immersion into the water.

In Faulkner, what happens is that the immersion into the elements functions as a reverse baptism. It's when you are un-named. It's when words go out of business. It's when you are un-done, and so Darl reflects on this, and he gives what is to me one of the most memorable expressions of the fictiveness of identity, the fictiveness of *I* that I've ever seen. "As though the clotting, which is you had dissolved into the myriad original motion." What a phrase. "As though the clotting, which is you, had dissolved into the myriad original motion." The clotting that is you—who on earth has ever thought of themselves as a clotting? But in Faulkner's role it's as if what we take for granted as the cogency, the unity, the coherence, but also the value of a self. All of that can come "undone." It can dissolve. Faulkner actually writes as well that, again, from Darl's perspective, "if you could just ravel out in time." In the world of William Faulkner, you can ravel out in time and you don't choose to do it. You will ravel out in time. It will, in fact, be Darl's fate in this book. The clotting that is you—I tried to get at this even in Conrad, even in *Heart of Darkness* that as they go up the Congo to try to find Kurtz, they feel a sense of being utterly unmoored, unanchored, without directionality. But Faulkner takes it much, much further, that the self is dissolving. The clot is coming undone. *I* is dying. That's what his book is about.

Thank you.

Lecture Thirty-Three
Faulkner—*As I Lay Dying*, Part 2

Scope:

The philosophical heart of this novel is located in the dead mother's astonishing chapter, where she offers a withering critique of all language as mendacious, cowardly artifice, severed from the things it names. This grand modern theme of language-as-lie is expressed with pith and splendor. We may nonetheless ask: How can a writer not believe in language?

This novel registers the countercharge of art itself as a response to the fictiveness of both language and self. Faulkner has met the challenge of capturing in words the spectacle of a world of endless flux where no forms or containers can hold: body, coffin, identity, word. The writer possesses only his own tools, and they constitute a humanist creed. Writing itself withstands time and death; writing is to be understood as a "voice from the coffin."

Outline

I. As we've seen, in Faulkner's world, *I* can die if exposed to sufficient violence and pressure. Faulkner's language to depict this crisis is sharp-edged, but the novel also gives us an indictment of language as mendacious, as producing a "word world" that is incommensurate with the real flow of life. This is a basic dynamic in human life because, unlike animals, we are verbal creatures.

II. The richest, most astounding chapter in the novel presents the testimony of (the dead?) Addie Bundren. She—and her views—may be thought of as the core of this novel, its center.

   A. What kind of schoolteacher was this strange woman?

      1. How do we assess her desire to whip her students? We see here a pure enactment of will, to make herself real to her students, to penetrate them in some way.

      2. Addie's desire to enter her students in this way may be a metaphor for writing itself. At some level, every writer may desire his or her words to enter the flesh and bloodstream of the reader.

3. Faulkner is interested in the physiological, somatic, and even carnal dimensions of language. As speakers and writers, we experience some of the same primitive desire to penetrate our audience with the power of our language.

B. Addie Bundren's quintessential quality would seem to be pride.
   1. Faulkner characterizes her as a "private woman," "particular." He defines her pride as "that furious desire to hide the abject nakedness which we bring here with us, carry with us into operating rooms, carry stubbornly and furiously with us into the earth again."
   2. Above all, Addie Bundren displays a resistance to being seen or opened or altered. It is worth considering this "closedness" in the context of this novel's array of penetrating forces.
   3. Her son Darl is cast as the man with eyes that go right through you. Is this not the vision of the novelist? Yet Darl is also the figure who is coming apart, who, in fact, "unravels" at novel's end.
   4. Daughter Dewey Dell is afflicted with the same dissolution as Darl, the collapse of *I*. She tells of a nightmare in which she lost all sense of self: "*I couldn't even think of my name I couldn't even think I am a girl I couldn't even think I.*"

C. Addie, farm wife though she is, is the great theorist of these matters. She denounces the archetypal deceit in human life: language.
   1. Addie says, "That was when I learned that words are no good, that words don't ever fit even what they are trying to say at." Words are always approximate, groping, trying to get close to something that they don't ever quite match.
   2. Addie decides that all words are specious, evasive. They are not ways of dealing with reality but substitutes for reality. Words cover for experiences, but the experiences themselves are unspeakable. There is no way to make our experiences felt or understood by others.

3. Addie goes even further: "I would think how words go straight up in a thin line, quick and harmless, and how terribly doing goes along the earth." We seem to live on two axes, one of language and one of action, and in Addie's view they diverge because language itself is incommensurate with meaning or experience.

4. One of the crucial arguments in modern culture has to do with the rupture between language and reality. But unlike the arid propositions of linguistic theory, Addie's diatribe against the mendacity of words is stunningly metaphoric and beautiful.

5. In trying to describe the connection between words and deeds, Addie speaks of words as "coming down like the cries of the geese out of the wild darkness in the old terrible nights, fumbling at the deeds like orphans to whom are pointed out in a crowd two faces and told, That is your father, your mother."

    a. Because Addie is thinking of her lover in this passage, we associate the cries of the geese with the noises we make when we speak love.

    b. The final analogy of the orphan shows the tenuous relationship between language and meaning, between the gestures of love and love itself.

6. Writers, of course, can never get clear of language. Faulkner indicts language here as fallacious, erroneous, and incommensurate with meaning, but he does so using the most fiery, eloquent, remarkable words imaginable.

III. The great heroism of *As I Lay Dying* is its magnificent response to the crises of both language and self.

A. The world of this novel is a world of coursing elements, of flow and metamorphosis.

    1. The world *moves* in this book, and the job of writing is to capture that movement. It is also a book of voices—of wind, water, and people. Faulkner's world is one of elemental, primitive logic.

    2. From Vardaman's anguished cry, "Mother is a fish," to the stunning evocation of Jewel with the horse, Faulkner creates new amalgams, blends of human/animal.

3. Darl, unable to associate the stench of the body with his mother, sets the barn in which the coffin rests on fire, but Jewel, the literalist and the favorite son, saves it in a spectacular scene. Faulkner's language here reaches toward myth and surrealism to speak what is unavowable in Jewel's relation to his mother.

4. At the end of the novel, Darl goes mad. The last words we hear of him are, "Yes, yes, yes, yes, yes," as if he is dissolving into nothing more than a collection of noises.

B. "Coming apart" seems to be Faulkner's dark wisdom: If the self is subjected to sufficient stress, it will not hold. Language is severed from deed. What form of "doing," then, is still imaginable?

1. Recall the scene of immersion, of fateful baptism, when the Bundrens enter the floodwaters and are "undone." Immediately afterward, the Bundrens form a human chain and reenter the waters, searching for Cash's lost tools. In other words, they retrieve from the elements the tools of human measure.

2. We see here a saga of human civilization against the odds that beset it. Cash, too, becomes more visible to us after this scene. Faulkner seems to tell us that things made by humans may offset the anarchic forces of deterioration and death.

3. Faulkner exhibits a great artisanal pride here. Unlike Addie's pride, which is the desire not to be exposed, this is the pride we experience after we have made something fine. Perhaps that's what humans are here for—we cannot win over the elements, but we can make things.

4. The book opens with Cash making his mother's coffin, and Addie knows this is a labor of love. Perhaps labor is love. We saw a similar ethos in Conrad, where work is the only thing imaginable to offset chaos in humans.

5. The container in this novel—the coffin—is real, no matter the status of what's inside. And no matter what we call the container—coffin, tenement, body—it has its own integrity and beauty.

6. Humans are the species that builds forms; they are coffin-makers. Addie Bundren's coffin has pride of place in this tumultuous novel. It is the precious

container, and Faulkner treats it with the awe it deserves. After the coffin is retrieved from the river, Darl says it is "still yellow like gold seen through the water."

C. Ultimately, Darl tells us that he hears Addie talking from the coffin "in little trickling bursts of secret and murmurous bubbling."

  1. We might interpret this as the very voice of human decomposition and rot, but we might also read it as a human voice from a coffin, a perfect figure for literature.

  2. Yes, Addie is dead; so, too, are Homer and Chaucer and Shakespeare and Faulkner. Art—this novel, all novels—is itself understood as a voice from a coffin.

Essential Reading:

William Faulkner, *As I Lay Dying*.

Supplementary Reading:

André Bleikasten, *Faulkner's "As I Lay Dying."*

Linda Wagner-Martin, ed., *William Faulkner: Four Decades of Criticism*.

Arnold Weinstein, "Faulkner's *As I Lay Dying*: The Voice from the Coffin," in *Nobody's Home: Speech, Self and Place in American Fiction from Hawthorne to DeLillo*.

Philip Weinstein, *Faulkner's Subject: A Cosmos No One Owns*.

Questions to Consider:

1. Addie Bundren's posthumous monologue is a bravura piece in American fiction. In it, she lambastes language as mendacious, escapist, and severed from the truth. This indictment is roughly similar to the theory put forth by such linguists as Saussure at the time the novel was written, arguing that all language is *referential*, that is, a sign system that can never get beyond its network of words. What do you make of the fact that an uneducated Mississippi farm wife comes up with the same view as a professional linguist?

2. Faulkner's universe seems to be one of violent and penetrative forces, against which the frail enclosures of self cannot hold. Here would be also the meaning of the book's title. Do you find such a vision altogether too dark, or is there some dignity in it?

Lecture Thirty-Three—Transcript
Faulkner—*As I Lay Dying*, Part 2

As we've seen in Faulkner's world, *I* or the "clotting which is you" can die. At least it can if it's exposed to sufficient violence and pressure. You'd think that a novelist would need his own language to be as honed, chiseled, sharp-edged as possible to depict this crisis, and of course I think Faulkner's language is that. Yet, this novel has an equally devastating second shoe to drop, which is an indictment of language itself as mendacious, as producing a word-world unattuned, incommensurate with the real flow of life. Now, this may sound abstruse, like a kind of writerly problem, but it's actually a very central basic dynamic in human life since we are the verbal creatures, unlike the animals. Literature hinges on this, but so does human communication.

The richest, most astounding chapter in the novel represents the testimony of the presumably dead Addie Bundren, and in some sense this is the core of the novel. We learn a lot about Addie. It's the only chapter that gives us a kind of vertical picture of what this woman's life was like. In particular, she talks about her career as a schoolteacher, but it's not the way anybody else would describe his or her career. She tells us that she would look forward to the times when her students would fault—that's her word. Why? So that she could whip them, and she says, "When the switch fell and when the flesh ridged and welted, it was her blood as much as theirs that ran." In her mind she was thinking, now you are aware of me. Now, you know who I am. Now, I am inside of you. It is a forbidding image of penetration, of entering another, and I think we are meant to think of the flowing blood as the strict analogue to the flowing waters. Faulkner's world is irrigated by these powerful flowing forces that are not easy to contain, not easy to navigate.

Well, what does it mean, that scene—to whip the students in such a way as to force your entry into them that when their flesh ridges and welts, it's her blood as well as theirs? I'm going to take a step beyond that passage and suggest what I think its largest ramifications are, which is that I think it is an astonishing metaphor or figure for what writing itself is. Well, you may think, well, writing isn't violent. Writing doesn't have anything to do with blood, and it doesn't. But I think the notion of entering somebody else's flesh and entering their bloodstream is at some deep and doubtless denied, repressed level what every writer desires. In other words, let's say that you write a poem, and you publish it, and you want people to read it. At some level, and this is a very primitive, brutal image I'm going to give you. At some level, you want the words on your page to enter into the flesh of your reader and into their bloodstream. At some level, that is the violent nature of human communication, which we soften customarily as we think about it. We say, oh, it's just exchanging words, and I've mentioned Saussure before and other theorists, linguists, who talk about language is just words. Faulkner is interested in the physiological, somatic, and even carnal dimension of this. When I speak to you, I want my words to get into you. You heard what I just said—when I speak to you. It's not merely that writers desire this, professional people who want their words to penetrate, and penetrate is an ugly word in today's cultural climate because it has too much of a kind of male sexist sound to it. But I don't think I can avoid it here. Writers want their words to enter into the people who read them.

So, as I just said to speakers, when we speak to one another, it's not like we want to murder the people we're talking to, but we want our words to get through. When you think of all the times, in fact most of the time this happens, all of the times that you've had conversations with people where, particularly if you're talking to your children but frequently when you're talking to anybody that matters as well as people who don't matter, you feel like your words are not getting in. They're not getting inside. They're just sort of bouncing off the surface, or as we used to say, "in one ear and out the other." So, I think that in fact this rather brutal image of Addie Bundren's work as a teacher, whipping her students, saying now I am part of your secret life—that has something to do with the project of writing and speaking. It has something to do with the kind of violent, intrusive and invasive powers of language that at some level we desire.

Addie Bundren's essential quality in this novel would seem to be pride. Faulkner characterizes her over and over, and he doesn't accent this—it's just you have to see it in the book, as a "private woman." That's what her husband, Anse, says, "She was ever a private woman." That's when he asked if they maybe should take that coffin on somebody else's wagon to the cemetery because it turns out that Cash and Darl are somewhere else trying to fix that wagon. He says, "She want to go in ourn" our wagon, "ever a private woman." Later in a more thoughtful kind of language, Faulkner writes about her pride as "that furious desire to hide the abject nakedness which we bring here with us, carry with us into operating rooms, carry stubbornly and [furious] with us into the earth again." It's as if at some profound level we want to be covered and protected, and we call that pride. We do not want to be invaded. We do not want to be exposed. This is really a book about that dynamic. On the one hand, penetrating people either through words—and you remember I described Darl's vision as a water hose that when that man looks at you, you feel like he's gone right through you. He sees through you.

That on the one hand, and on the other hand what it feels like to be on the receiving end. That's where pride comes into the picture. To preserve your secrets, preserve your darkness, preserve your opaqueness, and preserve the thickness of your skin so that others cannot see into you or penetrate you. Faulkner seems to me to be working it both ways, and yet we see that his characters are very much described as people whose vision does go into others. Darl, as I said, is not just the vision like a water hose, but the man who can see into others. For example, Darl alone knows that Dewey Dell is pregnant. It's like he could see this fetus, and she knows he knows. At the end of the book she is going to pounce on him and beat him up as much as she can because she knows that he knows. Likewise, Darl alone knows that Jewel is illegitimate. He keeps taunting Jewel with that. How can he see that? But he does. He is the man for whom there can be no secrets. As I said, he pays a heavy price. He is ungrounded. He is not connected to the earth. He "unravels" at novel's end.

All of the characters seem to be afflicted with this problem. Dewey Dell has similar feelings. Even though she is carrying this seed inside of her, she tells us about a time when she had a nightmare:

> *I thought I was awake but I couldn't see and I couldn't feel I couldn't feel the bed under me and I couldn't think what I was I couldn't think of my name I couldn't even think I am a girl I couldn't even think I.*

It's one of those moments where all of your supports, all of the floors and platforms that we stand on to be who we are, name, body, gender, all of those things are disappearing. "I couldn't think what I was. I couldn't think of my name. I couldn't even think I'm a girl. I couldn't even think I." This is the kind of unraveling dissolution, which seems to be everywhere striking people in this book. Addie Bundren is the great theorist of these matters, both to dissolution of self and the problem of language. Her chapter is the great chapter where language itself is under attack. Now, again, by any realist standard this is totally improbable, really inconceivable. I mean how is a Mississippi farm woman going to speak the way she does? Well, how would you get a Mississippi farm woman to speak the way a sophisticated linguist would talk about the problems of language. This is what it sounds like. "That was when I learned that words are no good; that words don't ever fit even what they are trying to say at." Let me repeat that because it is just stunning. "Words don't ever fit even what they are trying to "say at." It's the "at." Not what words are trying to say—what they're trying to say at" Like, words are always approximate, groping, trying to get close to something but they can't ever match it, fit it, be it. Now, the linguist would have agreed with that, but she's going to take it a step further. She's going to decide that words as well are specious, evasive. They're ways of not dealing with reality. They are substitutes for reality. They are an ersatz for real experience. "I knew that fear was invented by someone that [had] never had the fear; pride who had never had the pride." It's as if either you have the thing or you have the word, and if you have the word, you don't have the thing. This is catastrophic for someone who writes or someone who speaks, but it's a very, very sharp distinction here. Heaven knows all of us know of people. I mean it's not just a question of people who lie. We all know that people tout words about. I've been doing it in tons of lectures in this course—tout words about, which may or may not be connected to reality. That is the kind of crisis that this woman is talking about— the words cover for the experiences and that the experiences themselves are probably unspeakable. But there are no words that are commensurate with them. There is no way to make them in fact understood or felt by others. This is a very dark picture of things. She goes further, and she is nothing if not consistent.

> I would think how words go straight up in a thin line, quick and harmless, and how terribly doing goes along the earth, clinging to it so that after a while the two lines are too far apart for the same person to straddle from one to the other.

It is as if we have these two axes that we live on, the axis of language and the axis of doing. In Addie Bundren's view, they become increasingly divided, and again it won't do just to say, well, that's because liars don't tell the truth. It's that language itself is in some systemic way incommensurate with meaning, incommensurate with experience, not connected to it. Well, this, as I said, is a death knell, it seems to me, in some ways, for writing itself.

She has views that parallel those of modern theory, but unlike the theorists who have written on these things her expression of it, this sort of country speak, this farm woman's writing, of course it's Faulkner writing, this farm woman's language has I think a kind of pith and eloquence that is astonishing. I'm going to read you one more that takes it even further. It takes it in a different direction. She is reminiscing now. Again, the woman is probably dead. We don't know where this whole chapter is coming from, and she's thinking about her love life, her sex life. I've already told you that Jewel is the illegitimate child that she had in fact with the preacher, the Preacher Whitfield.

So, she is talking about her relationship to Anse, her husband, and we know that Anse is a person of empty language at least in the eyes of his wife. She tells us that, "He died," and I don't think she means literally. But she means he died in terms of being meaningful, in terms of being authentic. "He did not know he was dead," she said, and then she talks about lying by him in the dark in bed at night. And then she talks about hearing the land and hearing about God's love and his beauty. Then you realize she's not talking about Anse. She's talking about her lover, Whitfield, the preacher, although it doesn't say that—hearing about his beauty and his sin, and then we hear about the voicelessness where the words are the deeds. That's the great gambit to make the words the deeds. Some words that are true are deeds, and other words are empty, lax, gaps. How does she describe that? Listen to this passage.

> Coming down like the cries of the geese out of the wild darkness in the old terrible nights, fumbling at the deeds like orphans to whom are pointed out in a crowd two faces and told, That is your father, your mother.

In a book that is filled with mind-boggling passages, this may be the most mind-boggling of all. What on earth is this saying? It's saying that all things that should be together are coming unglued and unhinged—that the words don't connect to the meaning. But think about the context—a woman lying in bed with a man, making love to him. The words that they speak are not connected to what they're doing—is that what she's saying? Is what they're doing not connected to what they feel or to any notion of true love itself? These are things that we don't want to be unglued, separated, and they're coming unglued here.

Then the exquisite, again mind-wrenching analogy of the cries of the geese out of the wild darkness and the old terrible nights—again, I think the nights of love-making, fumbling at the deeds. It's as if the noise we make when we speak love is like geese cries that are fumbling at deeds. Then the final analogy, "like orphans to whom are pointed out in a crowd two faces and told, that is your father, your mother." That would be the tenuous relationship between language and meaning, between the gestures of love and love itself, between what we say to one another and what we really feel. It's as tenuous as looking at two faces in a crowd and someone telling you, oh yeah, that's your mother and that's your father. This is philosophical. This is metaphysical. This is simply stunning, it seems to me—I mean stunning in the sense that you get knocked back when you think about what this writer is trying to get across here.

Okay, this is, we're supposed to believe, an enormous critique of language. I hope you have felt in everything I've just read to you that this is incredibly eloquent. How could any writer truly disbelieve in language and still write? Faulkner has it both ways here. He is going to indict language as fallacious, as erroneous, as incommensurate with meaning. How does he do it? He does it with the most fiery, eloquent, remarkable words imaginable. He has it both ways. No writer can get clear of language.

Well, the great heroism of this novel is its extraordinary response to the crises of language and of self. The world of this book is the world of coursing elements, whether it's the river, whether it's the blood, of flow and metamorphosis. The world *moves* in this book, and the job of writing is to capture that movement just as that body that is lying in that coffin traveling across the Mississippi land in the heat of the summer is moving too. This is a book of voices, of wind, of water, of people. It's as if human life takes place in a force field. It's as if human beings were filings caught in a magnetic field. You almost have to think pre-Socratic philosophers. Think Heraclitus. Think of a world of elements where all that exists is air, and fire, and water. In a world like that our polite word "psychology" doesn't even mean much. Here is the primitive, elemental logic of Faulkner's world, and it's in this world that you can say my "mother is a fish," because it's a world of elements. It's a world that almost precedes our cognitive distinctions. It's a world of new amalgams, a blend of animals and humans. You heard about the cries of the geese that are invoked to talk about the failures of language and even the failures of love.

The characters, therefore, are going to be described in terms that are almost surreal at times, terms that often also go back to the best sharing. So, with Vardaman we have, "My mother is a fish," but with Jewel, the illegitimate son, he can never say to his mother and she can never say to him that they have a special bond that the legitimate children do not have. And so he displaces all of that onto the horse that he buys with money that he makes by working all night long for weeks on end. Then he is with that horse. It's an extraordinarily violent, passionate, physical relationship. At one point, Jewel goes into the barn to get the horse, "Come her, Sir," he says, and Faulkner writes it this way, "Moving that quick his coat, bunching, tongues swirling like so many flames." It's not easy to see horse there, but Faulkner is trying to give us the kind of extraordinary movement of this beast as this man goes in. At another point:

> Jewel is enclosed by a glittering maze of hooves as [if] by an illusion of wings; [we get the sense that these are animal deities, like centaurs, horse-gods] among them, beneath the upreared chest he moves with the flashing limberness of a snake.

When Faulkner did his revisions on this book, he made the language all the more tight and fascinating, where he took discrete things and blended them, fused them, forced them together. That phrase I quoted, "Moving that quick his coat bunching, tongues swirling," we don't know what the subject is. We don't know what the object is. We don't know if "tongues" is a verb or a noun, "Tongues swirling like so many flames."

Well, Jewel is always allied to the horse, and at a late moment in the novel this coffin, which has been delayed over, and over, and over in this scalding heat starts to smell so much that when they visit one family, they are told to put this coffin in the barn. They put it in the barn, and its stench is so great that we will learn later the barn catches on fire and it is Darl who has set the barn on fire because for him this can no longer be Mother. This is some carrion that smells and reeks, and the only thing to do is to set it on fire. I told you the book is Biblical—to be subjected to water, to be subjected to fire.

Jewel, I said, is the literalist. For him, no matter what it smells like, it's Mother. It can't be anything but Mother, and so into the burning barn where the coffin with whatever is in it lies Jewel rushes in. Faulkner writes that we see him up in the coffin, and he slides it single-handedly from the sawhorses. The fire rains on Jewel. Sparks rain on the coffin, rain on "it" in "scattering bursts as though they engendered other sparks from the contact." And then the coffin sort of topples forward. Then one sees Jewel and:

> the sparks raining on him too in engendering gusts, [it's like he's catching on fire, he is becoming fire as he is trying to move this coffin] so that he appears to be enclosed in a thin nimbus of fire. [It's like he has now become the fire god.] Without stopping, it overends [this is the coffin] and rears [coffins don't rear, horses rear—watch what's happening] again, pauses, then crashes slowly forward and through the curtain. This time Jewel is riding upon it.

This is magnificent. Jewel is riding that coffin. He is riding the horse/coffin that is his Mother. This is the expression of the love that he experiences for her that he has never been able to speak. He is still not speaking it. He is doing it, and it's also like myth coming alive in front of our eyes as he rides that coffin out of the burning barn. It's as if this is his truth at last made visible—not just made visible, turned into flames, turned into an active myth.

Well, this is a book of many extreme events. As I've said, it's a book that has a view of "I," of the human self as something that could unravel in time. It does. Darl unravels in time. At the end of this book, Darl goes mad. It's as if he literally dissolves. Before that happens, Jewel and Dewey Dell, who cannot bear having their secrets invaded by this man, turn on him and beat him as hard as they can. He will be finally taken away because he set fire to someone else's barn. We know why he did it. No one else does. He will be taken away, and the last words we hear of him are, "Yes, yes, yes,

yes, yes." It's as if he were dissolving as if he were just kind of congeries of noises.

Coming apart then would appear to be Faulkner's dark wisdom. If the self is subjected to sufficient stress, it will not hold. Language is severed from deed. So, what form of doing is still imaginable? Do you remember, words go up thinly and quickly, but that doing goes terribly about the earth? And yet we have to believe that for a writer words also are a form of doing. Might there also be forms of doing that could offset, counteract these primordial forces that are anarchic and chaotic like the swollen river and the flowing blood?

I told you about the scene where the coffin goes into the swollen waters. It's the Faulknerian baptism of sorts where they are undone. *I* comes apart. The clotting that is you comes undone. But what happens after that scene is what I want now to speak of because what happens after that scene is that these Bundrens go into the water again. They rescue the coffin and put it onto the banks, but then they go back into the waters as a human chain—now, you've got to visualize this. These Bundrens holding hands together going into these rushing flood waters. What are they looking for? They're looking for Cash's tools, which have been lost in the water. These are tools are measure, and they retrieve—I hope you can hear that this is a myth almost—they retrieve from the elements the tools of human measure. They immerse themselves in the flow and bring up to the light and back into their possession the rule, the chalk line, the plane, and the saw. It is a little saga of human civilization against the huge odds that beset it. It is about making life again. This is where Cash starts to become visible to us, Cash the carpenter, the artisan, the maker of things. We begin to realize this is where Faulkner is trying to show us what might offset the anarchic forces of decomposition, of deterioration and of death. Maybe humans can make things that would somehow resist this.

There is a great artisanal pride in Faulkner. I spoke of pride in relation to Addie Bundren as the desire not to be exposed, not to be penetrated, not to have your secrets known, and now I want to redefine pride as the feeling that you get when you have made something fine. It may be at bottom—that's what humans are there for. They cannot win over the elements, but they can in fact make things. Once again, that is why this book opens with a man making a coffin in the very sight of his dying mother. She knows that this is a labor of love—a labor of love. Maybe labor is love. You remember that I spoke of the work ethos in Conrad as the only thing that could be imagined to offset the chaos of becoming wild and savage once again, of losing your way, of not having the policeman, in Conrad's view, to help sort of protect your behavior—not so here. There's no policeman in sight. Rather, it's people working together and trying to make things that will resist these pressures—making a container, making a tenement—a tenement that will contain a body that will contain meaning.

When you read this book, the question you always ask is, What's in the coffin? Because that's what the Bundrens are asking. Is this Mother, or is this rot? What does this smell mean? What do the responses of all these other people mean? Is this Mother? Is this still Mother? How long can this continue to be Mother? Remember what I said about Kafka—the drama that appears over and over in his work is to exit the human. Having said that, I want now, as you can see, to focus not on those grand existential questions, but to focus on the thing itself, the container itself, the novel's containers, whether we call them coffins, whether we call them bodies, whether we call them words—to focus on them as having their own integrity and their own gallant beauty.

Humans are the people that build forms. Humans are coffin-makers. Addie Bundren's coffin has pride of place in this novel. It is the previous container, and Faulkner treats it with the awe that it deserves. Before Addie is even put into it, it is described as light, but they carry it slowly. It is described as empty, but they carry it carefully. It is described as lifeless, but yet something that slumbers lightly alive.

The finest touches of awe are those when we hear about the view of the coffin, and this is very discreet in this book. "Between the shadow spaces," this is the coffin that Cash is making, "they [he's talking about the boards that are going together] are yellow as gold, like soft gold." In another sequence, this is Darl speaking, "the long pale planks hushed a little with wetting … still yellow,"—this is when the coffin has been retrieved from the river—"like gold seen through water." It's a very, very sweet phrase, "gold seen through water." We cannot escape the view that this coffin is of precious value. In the barn when the stench of Addie Bundren is so great, Darl tells us this:

The breeze was setting up from the barn, so we put her under the apple tree, where the moonlight could dapple the apple tree upon the long-slumbering flanks within which now and then she [this is Addie] talks in little trickling bursts of secret and murmurous bubbling.

That's the voice that comes from a coffin. They stand there in the barn, and between the flanks of this wood she speaks in little, trickling bursts of secret and murmurous bubbling. The most obvious interpretation is this is the very voice of human decomposition and of rot, and they can hear it. But the other way of looking at this is this is the human voice from a coffin. This is the voice coming out of a coffin, and so what I want to say is that the voice coming from a coffin is about the most perfect figure I know for what literature is. It's not just Addie Bundren—Homer, Shakespeare, and Faulkner. What are they if not a voice from a coffin? That's what literature is. That is its own permanence.

Thank you.

Lecture Thirty-Four
García Márquez—*One Hundred Years of Solitude*

Scope:

Called a triumph of Magic Realism, *One Hundred Years of Solitude* is an appropriate close to this course because it challenges the essential laws that seem to govern both reality and fiction. At issue are the dictates of time and space, as well the taboo against incest and the social constraints on desire. The story of Macondo and the Buendía clan centralizes such tensions as passion/punishment, war/peace, self/other, and history/text, always asking: What rules apply?

Magic Realism claims that things have a life of their own, and this novel is studded with fantastic events, ranging from natural miracles to the ascension into heaven and the reprieve from death. Spirits abound. The love life of this family is front and center. We also witness the evolution of Macondo from Edenic beginnings to the acquisition of language and the inroads of technology and "progress": railroads, the telephone, a banana plantation, gringos, a workers' revolt, a massacre, and denial. Magic? Or a history we know all too well?

Outline

I. *One Hundred Years of Solitude* (1967), written by Gabriel García Márquez (1927–), is an appropriate conclusion to this course because it rings a change on everything we have read up to now. Rather than exploring the abyss, it rises into the air.

   A. This novel takes us full circle, returning to the sense of exploration and play evident in *Tristram Shandy*, but it also marks a turning point in the history of fiction. García Márquez acknowledged the critical influence of such writers as Kafka and Faulkner, but he transforms their doom-oriented narratives into something rich and strange, known in literary terms as Magic Realism.

   B. It's easy to see this kind of fiction as escapist, but perhaps it makes more sense to view it as a bid for freedom, a new way of imagining time, space, desire, the course of a novel, and the course of our lives.

1. In Tolstoy's *War and Peace*, we saw lives lived with the illusion of freedom, but from our vantage point of knowing the entire novel, we realize the extent to which the characters' lives are coerced by the fates of history.

2. Consider, too, the story of Oedipus, the preeminent text that shapes Western thinking. Oedipus lives his life blindly under the illusion of freedom, not knowing that it is utterly determined by past transgressions of parricide and incest.

3. Could we reshuffle this deck? Could we flout the laws that seem to coerce and constrain human freedom? What might there be on the other side of history, fate, and moral injunction ("thou shalt not")? More drastically, can we imagine or re-imagine Eden?

4. Macondo, the mythic community at the core of *One Hundred Years of Solitude*, is an Eden, a place "before the Fall."

C. Like Rome, Macondo is founded on a murder and a curse. José Arcadio murders Prudencio Aguilar, who taunts him about his unconsummated marriage with his cousin Úrsula and introduces the possibility of a curse: The union of José and Úrsula could result in the birth of an iguana or a child with a pig's tail. After murdering Prudencio, José tells his wife that there will be no more killings; they will take their chances with their offspring.

1. When the story of Oedipus opens, Thebes has already been afflicted with plague. Retribution for the crime he committed unknowingly has been enacted. There is no maneuvering room or freedom.

2. García Márquez's book is different, however; sexual desire has its play here, and desire is not the same as incest. We have no idea whether Oedipus desired Jocasta, but in this text, we are treated to expressions of the characters' desire.

3. Aureliano José, for example, is infatuated with his Aunt Amaranta, and she feels the same tug. José Arcadio (the fabulously-endowed son) leaps into marriage with Rebeca, thought to be his sister. These encounters are

narrated in the language of the earth and nature. We feel here a natural force field of sexuality that fuels these lives.

4. The book will close with a magnificent tribute to liberated desire: Aureliano (the great-great grandson of the founder of Macondo) has an ecstatic sexual relationship with his Aunt Amaranta Úrsula. This time, fate is enacted; their coupling terminates in the birth of a child with a pig's tail and, worse still, the deaths of the mother and the child and, finally, the extinction of Macondo.

5. Nonetheless, the moral verdict here is not an easy one. The relationship between Aureliano and his aunt is ecstatic, playful, and free. They know that they're risking a curse and punishment, yet there is an Edenic feeling to their union. Repeatedly, the book measures sexual freedom/excess against its opposite number: coldness of heart. Which is worse?

6. At one point, Úrsula tells her son, Aureliano the warrior, "If you execute your best friend out of political necessity [which he is poised to do], it is the same as if you had been born with the tail of a pig." There are many ways to lose one's position in the human family—incest, as well as coldness of heart.

7. García Márquez understood from Kafka what it takes to leave the human realm.

II. The story of Macondo, like that of much of Latin America, takes place under the sign of war, and at one point, the assertion is made that the community is fighting so that a man can marry his mother. This is not an endorsement of incest but a challenge to the prohibitions of law and denial.

A. For the most part, these wars highlight the "usual suspects": the liberals versus the conservatives, the atheists versus the Church. One of the chief characters, Aureliano Buendía, commits his life to the liberal cause.

B. In *War and Peace*, Tolstoy showed us the battlefields with startling immediacy, but García Márquez writes war as an endless, repeating, interminable backdrop, like a plague that never diminishes. No amount of magic can overcome this kind of death, and it is the death that Latin America has known for a century.

C. Yet one could argue that the greatest war in the novel is the war against logic as we know it, the logic that rules our everyday thinking, as well as our notion of what a novel is supposed to be. We may think, for example, that time moves forward in an unstoppable course, but this novel asks us to think again. Inwardly, in our memories or our feelings, we can be in many places at once. The book also tells us that people can return from the dead.

III. Magic Realism gives us a new fix on all these crucial terms. What might the world look like if the laws of time and space and desire were overcome? Remembering Kafka's story of the man turned insect as well as his own grandmother's tales that mixed fact and fantasy, García Márquez reinvents fiction.

A. As mentioned at the beginning of the lecture, Macondo was created as a place that has parallels with the Garden of Eden.

  1. No one has ever died there, and there is no need for either priests or government. It lives in tune with the Creation. As Melquíades, the philosopher of the novel, says, "Things have a life of their own … It's simply a matter of waking up their souls."

  2. There are deaths in *One Hundred Years of Solitude*, but they are not like the deaths we've seen in Proust, or Woolf, or Faulkner. Imagine, again, overturning this curse on our species.

  3. In this book, when the patriarch dies, yellow flowers appear. The girl Meme is in love, and yellow butterflies fill the room. Prudencio Aguilar's ghost returns because death is too lonely. Melquíades comes back frequently from death in new forms. The beautiful girl Remedios ascends, in front of our eyes, to heaven without truly dying. The afterlife here is, in fact, life.

B. Even the writing style is a cunning mixture of present, past, and future. The book opens with a line that already sends us into the future: "Many years later, as he faced the firing squad, Colonel Aureliano Buendía was to remember the distant afternoon when his father took him to discover ice."

1. The novel reconceives familiar issues and concerns. The child Rebeca arrives, bearing her dead parents' bones in a sack. What kind of allegory is this? The image is much more pithy and material than our words "mourning" or "grieving."

2. This same child experiences a voracious, ungratifiable hunger and devours earth itself, giving weight and density to the idea of yearning. García Márquez refuses abstractions, presenting his characters' feelings in terms of blood, bone, nerve, and sinew.

C. We witness, in this novel, the "evolution" of Macondo from Eden as it enters history.

1. Macondo experiences the "insomnia plague," which entails a universal loss of memory. From this loss of memory (and culture), we arrive at the creation of language, enlisted as our only means of retrieval.

2. Founded as Eden before the Fall, Macondo also experiences the inevitable inroads of "progress." Mr. Herbert comes to Macondo and discovers bananas; he is followed by engineers, Mr. Brown, the gringos, and ultimately, the banana plantation. In parallel, we see other forms of progress: the railroad, film, and the telephone.

3. This history seems eerily familiar, and it proceeds apace with its own hideous logic. Predictably, the banana workers protest their conditions and are massacred. The massacre is flatly, publicly denied: It never happened; 3,000 "satisfied workers" simply returned to their families.

4. Is this magic? Or is this, indeed, the dirty history of our time? Have we not seen this before, in many Latin American countries, in the Balkans, and elsewhere?

5. José Arcadio Segundo witnesses the massacre, and his entire subsequent life is cued to this event. García Márquez asks us: How do we bear witness to disaster? How long do we remember? Is it sufficient, as the priest is told, that we exist at this moment, or do we have a greater duty?

Essential Reading:

Gabriel García Márquez, *One Hundred Years of Solitude*.

Supplementary Reading:

Michael Bell, "The Cervantean Turn: *One Hundred Years of Solitude*," in *Gabriel García Márquez: Solitude and Solidarity*.

Eduardo Posada-Carbó, "Fiction as History: The Bananeras and Gabriel García Marquez's *One Hundred Years of Solitude*," *Journal of Latin American Studies* 30.2 (May 1998): 395–414.

Michael Wood, *One Hundred Years of Solitude*.

Questions to Consider:

1. Magic Realism—with its fuller play of fantasy and desire—is revered by some, despised by others. What arguments would you present for it? Against it?

2. In what senses do you feel that *One Hundred Years of Solitude* bears witness to the earlier work of Kafka and Faulkner, both of whom García Márquez saluted as precursors for his work? How does it alter their vision and their logic?

Lecture Thirty-Four—Transcript
García Márquez—*One Hundred Years of Solitude*

One Hundred Years of Solitude is the right way to conclude this course because it rings a change on everything that we have read up to now. For starters, it's fun and it's easy. It seems to be asking why should great literature, great writing, be difficult? because I don't think it has escaped your notice that Conrad, Proust, Joyce, Faulkner, and Woolf are not easy. They are difficult. They're writing about one crisis or another, whether it's in their stories or in their language, in their material. Could there ever be a literature of ease, of pleasure, of fantasy and freedom? Could you ever get clear of the anguish of modern Europe and modern America? What about death? Think of the very poignant deaths that we've seen in this course, the grandmother's death in Proust, or Mrs. Ramsay in Woolf, or Addie Bundren in Faulkner. Could death be reconceived? Have we ever learned to celebrate life rather than exploring its problems and abysses? Could you do this without evasion into some sort of never-never land? Could a literature of desire actually tell you something about history and about your own daily life? So much great literature dives into the wreck; *One Hundred Years of Solitude* rises into the air.

This book, published in 1967, takes us full circle. It returns to the sense of exploration and play that we saw in Sterne's *Tristram Shandy*, but it also, as I have suggested, marks a turning point in fiction. García Márquez acknowledged the critical impact of writers like Kafka and Faulkner, but he transforms what I want to call the doom-oriented nature of their narratives into something very, very different. The only literary term we have for this is "Magic Realism." Magic Realism is what I'm going to be talking about in different ways throughout these two lectures. I think it's easy to misconstrue it. It's easy to see it. I found this when I first began to think about Magic Realism. It's easy to see it as evasive, as escapist, as facile, and as a way of ducking reality, but perhaps it makes more sense to see it as a bid for freedom, a new way of imaging time, space, desire, what a novel might be, and what our lives might be. Is it possible that the dark stories have it wrong—that they only tell what they tell and that there's so much more in what we want to do and experience that hasn't gotten onto the record?

In this light, let me evoke some of the text that we've talked about, in particular Tolstoy's *War and Peace*. In particular, I want to mention the fact that in Tolstoy what we have brilliantly done over many, many pages is lives lived with the illusion of freedom, but lives that we with our vantage point of seeing the entire book, the container that contains these lives, realize the extent to which these people are coerced by the fates of history—as they come to realize as it happens to them. Freedom is an illusion. One's own maneuvering room is illusory in Tolstoy, or to go further back in the past with the preeminent sort of text that I think shapes Western thinking, again the *Oedipus*, about a man who thinks that he is free and then comes to learn that an act of violence was, in fact, parricide, and that the woman he shares his bed with is in fact his mother.

Could you reshuffle this, imagine a kind of openness and maneuvering room? Could you flout the laws that seem to coerce and constrain human freedom? Might there be something on the far side of history, fate, and even moral injunction—"thou shalt not"? In its most drastic way, could you imagine Eden? Could you re-imagine Eden? What would it look like? I think that's what Macondo is, Macondo being the kind of mythic community that is at the core of this book. Macondo is "before the Fall." Now, it is true that Macondo, like Rome, is founded on a murder and on a curse. I don't want to minimize that. The founder, Jose Arcadio Buendía, murders Prudencio Aguilar because he is taunted about the unconsummated marriage that he has with his cousin Úrsula, and there has been the threat that if these cousins marry there may be a curse, which would be the birth of an iguana or a child born with a pig's tail. But José Arcadio, after murdering this man who has taunted him, tells his wife there will be no more killings. He does want to have sex with her. He loves her. She loves him. They will take their chances, but there will be no more killings.

I want to contrast this once again with the more familiar stories like the *Oedipus* where there is a curse as well by the Oracle. In the *Oedipus*, for example, the story opens with bodies around the place, dead bodies, cadavers, because plague has hit Thebes. That is what triggers the plot—that Oedipus the king must solve this problem, this medical problem, this political problem. It's all done. The damage is done. Whatever you have committed without knowing it, we're seeing the dead bodies pile up. It's evident that this has happened.

There is no maneuvering room here, no play, no freedom. The first of fate is shown.

Well, in this book it's different. Sexual desire has its play, and sexual desire is not the same thing as incest. We have no idea whether Oedipus desired Jocasta. We do know that his coupling with her is going to be incest and fate, but how he felt about her beforehand we have no knowledge in that text. In this text, we are treated to sort of an expression of what these people felt. Aureliano José, for example, is infatuated with his Aunt Amaranta, and she feels the same tug. García Márquez writes their own sort of sexual experiment with each other. It doesn't go all that far. "He felt Amaranta's fingers searching across his stomach like warm and anxious little caterpillars," just vintage language for this book. This isn't prurient language. This is the language of the earth, the language of insects, the language of nature. Or even about José Arcadio, who is the grand, sort of overly endowed figure of this book, fabulously endowed, who leaps into a marriage with Rebeca, whom people believe to be his sister. It turns out she is not.

"She had to make a supernatural effort not to die when a startlingly regulated cyclonic power lifted her up by the waist." Cyclonic power—this is the power of the elements. It's the power of the earth. It's the force field of sexuality that fuels these lives and this book. It's a life force. It's not pornographic. It's not titillating. They are behaving according to the law of the species. The novel closes with a magnificent tribute to liberated desire. Aureliano, who is the great, great grandson of the founder, of the patriarch, has an ecstatic sexual relationship with his Aunt Amaranta Úrsula. This time fate does come about. This will eventuate in the birth of a child with a pig's tail and, worse still, I think it's worse, the death of the mother, the death of this child, and finally the death and extinction of Macondo. This happens at the end of the book. Harsh results, bad news, and yet it's hard to say what the moral take on all of this is, how deserved this is, how this feels, how this sits with you as a reader. That relationship between Aureliano and his aunt is an astonishing thing even in this book of remarkable sensual generosity because it seems to be ecstatic, playful, and free. They do sense that they're related. They know that they're risking a curse and punishment, and yet there is an Edenic feeling to their union.

In one of the really most, I think, remarkable passages, García Márquez writes that after their lovemaking they become creative artists with each other's bodies. He rubs her breasts with egg whites and her stomach with cocoa butter, and he puts clown's eyes on his member, even bow ties and little hats. What I want to say is that this is procreative and creative at the same time. It's almost a poem of the earth and of its bounty, and there is no guilt in it. Repeatedly, this book measures sexual freedom, even sexual excess, against its opposite number, which is coldness of heart. Which is worse, it wants us to ask. At one point Úrsula tells her son, Aureliano the warrior—she says to him, "If you execute your best friend out of political necessity," which he is poised to do, "it is the same as if you had been born with the tail of a pig." It, I think, is an absolutely clear statement that there are many ways to lose your position in the human family. Yes, incest may produce a child with a pig's tail or an iguana, but coldness of heart also casts you out, makes you an outlaw. We have seen with Kafka the persistent theme of exiting the human, and we know that García Márquez read Kafka with great interest and thought of Kafka as a kind of pivotal figure for him. In particular García Márquez said that of "The Metamorphosis," you could start a book with a man transformed into a bug; this, in a sense, opened the door for him about the kind of liberties he could take in his own writing. But he also understood from Kafka what it takes to leave the human realm, what Kafka called the frozen sea that art is supposed to chop into like an ax.

Coldness of heart is a way also of leaving the human realm, of exiting the human. The story of Macondo, like so much of Latin America's history, takes place under the sign of war. At one point, the seemingly mad assertion is made, "we're fighting so that a man can marry his mother." I don't think that this is at all an endorsement of incest. It's rather a challenge to the prohibitions of law and denial. It's a call for freedom, not a call for orgy. These wars, for the most part, highlight the "usual suspects," the liberals versus the conservatives, the atheists versus the Church, and as I said, one of the chief characters of the book, the son of the patriarch, Aureliano Buendía, commits his life to the liberal cause. He is the great warrior of the book.

Tolstoy in *War and Peace* takes us to the battlefields themselves. We have Austerlitz. We have Borodino. We see up front, close up in a kind of startling immediacy, what it feels like to hear the mortars, to see the carnage. That's not at all what García Márquez does. Instead, he writes war as the endless, repeating, interminable backdrop to a story like a plague that is never over—always taking victims. This would be a kind of death that no amount of magic can overcome, and this is the death that Latin America has known for a long time—a century of war. How limited is this to Latin America? Look around you today, and you will find revolution and counter-revolution going through their hundred years of dance still.

But as I suggested, the greatest war in this book might be the war against logic—logic that governs our everyday thinking as well as our notion of what a novel is. One of the challenges that he faces head on is that of time moving forward in a linear fashion. We all know that subjective time doesn't go that way. Inwardly, with our memory or with our feelings, we can be in many places at once, in our past, in a might-be, in a might-have-been. In this novel, time can be frozen. It can be broken into segments. It can repeat. It can be postponed. It can be twisted. It can be re-figured. Folks return from death. That surprises us. We don't think that happens usually, but living in the present can also be future-haunting, so that your death could be present even though it's not there.

Magic Realism undertakes to give us a new fix on all of these crucial items. What would the world look like if time, space, and desire were reconfigured? As I said, García Márquez was much impacted by Kafka, by the liberties he took, but it's fair to say that he was as much influenced by his own grandmother who used to tell him stories. In particular, he noted that she told him stories with a kind of brick face. She would make the most outrageous, crazy assertions that absolutely flouted the laws of logic, and you would never know it looking at her. Her voice didn't change. Her face didn't change. Her expression didn't change, and he figured that's the way to write. That's what he decided to do in this book, and so he gives us Macondo.

As I've said, it's his bid for re-creating Eden, and I alluded to the ecstatic lovemaking at the end of the book as an effort also to have passion and love without guilt. That might be one form of Eden. There are other forms as well, we learn—that the very founding nature of Macondo is such that it seems to be a place where no one has ever died. Macondo is a place where they have no need of priests or of government. For many people, this might sound quite Edenic, and in Latin America it hasn't happened very often. In fact, maybe no place is where it's happened.

Macondo is a place that lives in tune with the creation. As the philosopher of the novel, Melquíades, says, "Things have a life of their own … It's simply a matter of waking up their souls." These are prodigious claims. How do you wake up the souls of things? How could you have a place where there is no death? There are deaths in *One Hundred Years of Solitude*, but they're not like the ones that we're accustomed to. I've already referenced the poignant, hard-to-forget, hard-to-come-to-terms-with deaths in Proust—the grandmother who was just "a beast lying on a bed," or the extraordinarily warm and endowed Mrs. Ramsay, whose death is depicted in brackets, it's so brutal—we just learned that she died in her sleep one night, or Addie Bundren whose body rots during *As I Lay Dying*. Could you overturn this? Could you get clear of this curse on our species? Could you rewrite these rules? Waking up the souls of things—things have a life of their own. What kind of life would things have? Well, in this book, for example, the patriarch dies and yellow flowers appear out of nowhere. The girl, Meme, is in love, and yellow butterflies appear out of nowhere and fill all the rooms. Prudencio Aguilar's ghost returns because death is too lonely. Melquíades returns frequently from death in new forms.

The beautiful girl, Remedios, dies, and then ascends to heaven in front of our eyes. Let me re-state that. We usually think, don't we, that to ascend to heaven you've got to die. I mean that's the ordinary sequencing of it. She doesn't die despite what I said. Instead, she is simply out in the garden folding sheets, and then she rises into heaven waving good-bye. This is one way of re-writing the rules. What rules are being re-written? Well, one of them is gravity— gravity that makes our bodies weigh what they do. We don't rise into heaven. We can maybe jump a few feet off the earth, but we don't rise into heaven. Well, she does, and as I said, she rises into heaven alive, not as the spirit or soul of Remedios but as Remedios. She goes into heaven body and all, no transcendence required. This is not an afterlife. This is life.

Even the writing style is a cunning mixture of present, past and future. The first line of this book is memorable. "Many years later, as he faced the firing squad, Colonel Aureliano Buendía was to

166 ©2007 The Teaching Company.

remember that distant afternoon when his father took him to discover ice." Already, it sends us to a future many years later as he faced the firing squad. Everyone who opens this book has to believe that Aureliano will die his death at a firing squad—no, not going to be the case. Won't happen at all. In fact, that's not what's most relevant here. What's most relevant is ice. He's going to die of ice. He's going to become ice, and yet the passage has it all there. It's in plain sight if we know how to sort of put it back together again.

This book takes issues, problems and concerns that we're familiar with in our own conventional language and reconceives them. The child, Rebeca, arrives bearing her dead parents' bones in a sack. What kind of an allegory is that? We have our word "mourning," "grieving." He gives us something so much more pithy and material—a child with her parents' dead bones in a sack. She also eats the earth, and it makes me think that our little term such as "yearning" or "hunger" all of the sudden acquires a kind of density and weight when you actually see someone putting the earth in their mouth because of some craving.

We think of characters in literature. We read about characters in literature, and the novelist tells us he or she felt sad, happy or despair. But in this book García Márquez presents our feelings in terms of blood, bone, nerve and sinew. He refuses abstractions. In the book we watch the "evolution" of Macondo from Eden where it begins, no one has ever died, no priests, no government, and we watch it enter into history.

It experiences an "insomnia plague," and this is followed by universal loss of memory—an insomnia plague. I mean other books tell us about bubonic plagues, smallpox plagues, influenza plagues, but this is an insomnia plague. What about what it is followed by— universal loss of memory? Loss of memory is loss of self. It's loss of the human culture. Could we be erased? We certainly know something about that in our own lives with the aged, those who have senility or those, worse still, who have Alzheimer's, who are erased. Could this happen on a collective scale? What is the antidote to being erased, to losing your memory? One antidote that this book offers us is language, and they start putting tags on the things because they no longer remember them. The tags will tell you by words what they are. Language is an act of retrieval. I want you to think about that, and it will come up more than once in this discussion. When all else is dead, language remains our umbilical cord to reality. Surely, many of the books read in this course were written by authors who are long dead, but their language still lives.

Macondo moves from Eden into history. I'm old enough to remember going to the movies where the short that came on first in black and white was called the "March of Time." In some usually funereal voice-over, it would give us the usually dreadful events that were taking place, the "March of Time." This book registers the march of time. I said that Macondo is founded as Eden "before the Fall." So, what is "the Fall?" The Fall is what we call progress. I think the Fall is progress much more than sexual excess. What kind of progress is this? It's progress that we also give a very benign term to when we call it technological progress. Let me be more precise. Mr. Herbert comes to Macondo and discovers bananas, and he eats several bananas. He weighs the bananas, and he uses calipers to calculate their dimensions. He checks the temperature, humidity and light, and he then brings in engineers who do further research. The engineers are then followed by Mr. Brown and the gringos. The banana plantation finally is established by American interests. Parallel to that we see other forms of progress—railroad, film and telephone. These are, we are told, all the ways in which the world moves forward.

Well, that first history of Mr. Herbert, Mr. Brown, engineers, gringos, and the banana plantation seems to me to be a story that we may know all too well. As we read about this, we have this kind of queasy feeling that we've been there before. We've seen this. We know that this could entail a curse—this could be future-haunted, and so things continue apace with their own terrible logic. The banana workers predictably at some point protest their conditions, and they are massacred. This massacre is utterly denied by the forces of order—denied. It never happened. Three thousand people simply disappear. It's a remarkable event. It's the grand political event of this novel. "Yet, the authorities say that there were no dead, that the satisfied workers had gone back to their families." We are told that instead, "All is fine." García Márquez also writes that at night there was a search for people who were causing trouble, and they were exterminated, the hoodlums, he says, the murderers, all of the people that the government said, these are the undesirables. At night they're picked up, but if you ask about it the next day, why is it that X or Y is not here? the answer was "You must have been dreaming. Nothing has happened in Macondo. Nothing has ever happened, and nothing ever will happen. This is a happy town. Macondo is a happy town."

Three thousand people disappear, and I want to say, is this magic? Is this Magic Realism? We're not in the circus here. We're not talking about yellow flowers or yellow butterflies, and yet this is a disappearing act. It is a terrible political magic show, and it's a magic show that we have seen in many Latin American countries with their "disappeared," and in the Balkans, and elsewhere.

José Arcadio Segundo witnesses the massacre, and his entire subsequent life is cued to this event. I think García Márquez wants to ask not only how he witnesses it but how we witness it. How long do we remember? At one point, the priest is asked, "You don't believe it, that the army machine-gunned 3,000 workers and put their bodies on a train with 200 cars, and carried them off to the sea and threw them in?" And the reply is, "My son, it is sufficient to be certain that you and I exist at this moment." Is this sufficient? Are we not "interpolated"? The insomnia plague gave rise to a loss of memory, and so I want to close this by saying, who are the amnesiacs here? Is it not us? Do we not see on our TV screens the relatives of the murdered and the disappeared everywhere? Do we not often perform our little act of Magic Realism by simply flicking a button or changing a channel? Might there be more asked of us? Thank you.

Lecture Thirty-Five
One Hundred Years of Solitude, Part 2

Scope:

One Hundred Years of Solitude has a splendor and zest and impudence that seem unique in the Western tradition of the novel. It plays tricks with time and space; it flouts the laws we have thought to be real; it explores the power of desire. Yet its darkest truth is in the title: solitude. In the figures of Colonel Aureliano Buendía, Amaranta, Rebeca, and Fernanda, we see the threat of living death, of hollowness at the core, of mummification. What can oppose emptiness and repression? Lust for life.

Melquíades, the gypsy-philosopher, presides over a mysterious script, kept locked up in the recesses of the Buendía house, and with rabbinical fervor, each generation of Buendía (men) tries its hand at deciphering this book. Not unlike the Book of Revelation, this "intertext" contains the fate of the family, but can the austere, solitary task of "reading" coexist with the vibrancy of flesh and life? Is this not literature's grand query? The novel's ecstatic but tragic ending leaves the question open—for us to decide.

Outline

I. We've seen repeatedly in this course that literature gives us unique access to the inner life, what Hamlet called "that which passes show." *Hamlet* is one of the great texts about the inner realm that others are in the dark about, while a book like *The Brothers Karamazov* shows us, in the person of Ivan, the self as a tomb.

    A. What about the drama of death in life, which is another way of saying "solitude"? How do we take the measure of solitude, given that we live and die in ourselves? Further, isn't reading itself an act of solitude? In some sense, this issue, the attempt to gauge the meaning of solitude, relates to the whole project of reading literature.

    B. The gaiety, zest, and sheer chutzpah of *One Hundred Years of Solitude* may constitute its strongest claim on our interest. The great contribution of Magic Realism to Western fiction is its widened grasp of what reality entails, enabling dreams, desire, and imagination to coexist with the contingent world of facts and laws. One risk that García Márquez runs is that we will see his book as "touristic," as a kind of facile, make-believe world in which fantasy rules.

C. As we have noted, the grisly world of historical fact—colonial exploitation, cruelty, and abuse—is not elided in this novel, but emerges powerfully and, perhaps, as a direct result of the discourse of magic and play. Conrad's news of racism and ideological warfare, along with Faulkner's sense of family doom, can be glimpsed behind García Márquez's humorous and surreal rendition of life.

II. However, the richer, still darker quarry of this novel is advertised in its title: solitude. Few writers have sketched a grimmer picture of the incurable loneliness of being alive, of the incessant risk of being emotionally buried alive.

A. Amaranta, a woman of deep passions, nonetheless turns down numerous suitors; burns her hand black; spends her last days sewing her own shroud; sees herself as a messenger for, and enters willingly into, death.

1. Amaranta acquires a carton of letters to take with her to the other side. This is an image of death as continuation of, literally, commerce, an exchange between life and death.

2. Often, the deaths of characters in this novel are other dimensions of their own beings, a different view from our Western notion of death. In García Márquez, death is part of what one is.

B. Rebeca seems to satisfy her primordial hunger, evidenced by her habit of eating earth, through marriage with the sexually powerful José Arcadio (the son), yet after his death, she literally exits the commerce of the living to bury herself alive in her house, forgotten by all.

C. Perhaps the most intriguing figure of solitude is Fernanda, the devout and pretentious wife of Aureliano Segundo.

1. Fernanda constantly refers to her distinguished father, who sends the family a yearly Christmas gift. One year, the gift is the father's dead body, with the skin broken out in festering sores.

2. This scene makes it clear that Fernanda represents the tradition of death, which is the denial of life and pleasure—solitude in the sense of literally being buried alive.

D. Even the great matriarch of the book, Úrsula, who lives to 145 and has brought up countless generations of children, emerges in her old age as a figure negotiating the world via touch and smell, entering into solitude as the last truth.

E. But the master portrait here is of Colonel Aureliano Buendía, the younger son of the patriarch. Aureliano is García Márquez's candidate for war hero, the man who spent his entire life fighting for the liberal cause and paying the supreme price for this career: an increasing coldness of heart, a solitude that cannot be breached.

1. Aureliano is the man whose fate is not to die at the hands of a firing squad but to die by becoming ice.

2. On his return home from war, he declares that "no human being, not even Úrsula, his mother, could come closer to him than ten feet."

3. One of the most moving passages in the book is the moment when Aureliano realizes that Úrsula fully understands and is saddened by what he has become. She is the only person who penetrates his misery.

4. Aureliano looks at his mother and sees how old she has become, yet he feels no pity: "He made one last effort to search in his heart for the place where his affection [for her] had rotted away, and he could not find it."

5. Aureliano is the dark conscience of the novel. Perhaps we are all enclosed by 10-foot circles. Perhaps we cannot feel, but only see, the scars that life has given to those we love.

6. Aureliano is the figure who lives, as it were, the 100-year history of war in the novel. This history has corroded him, and he knows that he is living death.

7. How does Aureliano die? He watches a circus going by, a woman on an elephant, a camel, a dancing bear, and clowns, and through it all, he sees his own solitude. He puts his forehead against a tree and dies.

III. What, one asks, can counter solitude, mummification? The book's reply is: lust for life, human appetite, and desire.

A. As we've seen, the novel seems to celebrate phallic power. The sexuality of José Arcadio (the son) is described as cyclonic, as a kind of vital, elemental force.

B. The novel is equally committed to female fertility. Pilar Ternera seems to mother or mate with virtually all of the men in the book, but there is nothing abusive or exploitive in her situation. With her counterpart, Petra Cotes, Pilar shares the role of sexual assent and sexual assertion. On the far side of any constraints, they seem to relish their power and their role in the culture.

C. Desire in this novel transcends the personal. This is especially clear in the fruitfulness of Petra's relationship to Aureliano Segundo, who is married to Fernanda. Their affair is a vision of fertility and plenty.

D. The most passionate episode of the novel is its haunting final love relationship between Aureliano (the great-great grandson) and his Aunt Amaranta Úrsula.

    1. The two brave all laws of constraint, decorum, and coercion and seem to re-create their own Garden of Eden, but their lovemaking is followed by "a torrent of carnivorous ants who were ready to eat them alive."

    2. These ants bring destruction. They know nothing of human love but only follow nature's inhuman, logical dictates. The force that brings these two bodies together may well be akin to the force that devours flesh in the end.

E. But García Márquez is no dewy-eyed romantic. He is alert to the ravages and the excesses of feeling, and he has a fine sense of its labyrinths.

    1. Arcadio (the grandson) is depicted as a brutal tyrant. He is vicious and is shot by a firing squad.

    2. The great grandson José Arcadio is a sinister pedophile, meeting his just deserts at the hands of children.

    3. José Arcadio Segundo is haunted by the sights he has seen and can never be free of his indwelling fear.

IV. Returning repeatedly in the episodes of the lives of the Buendía clan during its 100-year duration is the mystical figure of Melquíades, the gypsy philosopher/tutelary divinity of the story. Melquíades presides over the mysterious, cryptic script that it seems only he can read.

    A. We see an entire line of men seeking to decipher the magic script that entails the history of the Buendía family, on the order of a Book of Revelation.

    B. García Márquez does not hide from us the fact that these men pay a price for attempting to decipher the script: They opt out of life, staying in the room for decades, in order to attend to this text. It is a severe equation. We are also struck by the fact that the script is kept in a closed-off room that has 72 chamber pots, as if the record of human doing were somehow inseparable from the waste of the human body.

    C. The book turns increasingly dark toward the end. The Catalonian bookseller, one of the wise men of the text, auctions off his books and urges the people of Macondo to disregard all that he has said earlier about art and writing:

> That wherever they might be they always remember that the past was a lie, that memory has no return, that every spring gone by could never be recovered, and that the wildest and most tenacious love was an ephemeral truth in the end.

As we come to the end of the book, we know that the curse will be fulfilled.

    D. The story ends with Aureliano and his aunt having their wild, ecstatic, yet innocent affair, yet we also realize that he has spent years decoding and deciphering the script. It's as if García Márquez brings together in Aureliano the two poles of fiction: the lusty fornicator and the reader of text.

        1. Amaranta dies, and the ants who sought to devour Aureliano and Amaranta after their lovemaking return to devour the child who is the product of their union. We feel as if God, who has seemed to be absent in this novel, finally returns to mete out punishment. But the only crime of the two seems to have been to recover Eden, to escape history.

2. At the end, Aureliano reads the text and sees that it is his own history. A storm begins to blow that will destroy Macondo. As Aureliano reads, he sees himself becoming the text: "He began to decipher the instant that he was living, deciphering it as he lived it, prophesying himself in the act of deciphering the last page of the parchment, as if he were looking into a speaking mirror."

3. Aureliano and Macondo are swept away by the storm, and we are told that there is no second chance for them. But we may find their second chance in the eternal life that literature confers; reading spawns a living world.

Essential Reading:

Gabriel García Márquez, *One Hundred Years of Solitude*.

Supplementary Reading:

Michael Bell, "The Cervantean Turn: *One Hundred Years of Solitude*," in *Gabriel García Márquez: Solitude and Solidarity*.

Eduardo Posada-Carbó, "Fiction as History: The Bananeras and Gabriel García Marquez's *One Hundred Years of Solitude*," *Journal of Latin American Studies* 30.2 (May 1998): 395–414.

Michael Wood, *One Hundred Years of Solitude*.

Questions to Consider:

1. Colonel Aureliano Buendía is the great military figure of the novel. He is also its primary example of solitude as an inevitable curse of living. Do you think there is some kind of logical connection between these two concepts: war and solitude?

2. The final sentences of this novel read like a curse or doom finally come true: Aureliano reads, at last, the script that pronounces the extinction of the Buendía clan. Yet this moment of judgment follows what is arguably the freest and most ecstatic human relationship of the novel, even if it is also transgressive. How does one square these things?

Lecture Thirty-Five—Transcript
One Hundred Years of Solitude, Part 2

I have argued repeatedly in this course that literature gives us unique access to the inner life. I argued this as far back really as Defoe's *Moll Flanders* and right on through, and it's most conspicuously the case in those difficult but fascinating and rewarding writers like Proust, Joyce, Woolf, or Faulkner. Hamlet called that, "that which passes show," all of that, which is inside of me, that no one else can know anything about. *Hamlet* is one of the great texts about all of the large realm that others are in the dark about, but what about the other side of the coin? What about the self as a tomb, as a prison? Remember again, Ivan in the *Brothers Karamazov*, cold Ivan described as a grave. What about the drama of death in life, which is another way of saying "solitude?" That drama is unforgettably rendered in this otherwise sparkling book. How do we take the measure of solitude, *soledad*, because we live as well as we die in ourselves? Further, isn't reading itself inevitably an act of solitude? In some sense, this issue of taking the measure of solitude, trying to gauge what it really means, has to do with the stakes of this entire course or the whole project of reading literature.

The gaiety, the zest, the chutzpah of this novel, *One Hundred Years of Solitude*, strikes all of its readers and constitutes one of its great claims for entering the canon and for being a kind of marker of change in the canon. One of the contributions, at least, of magic realism is to widen the Western understanding of what "reality" entails. That's a large, large contribution. I've tried to talk about that in the lecture—the contribution that is entailed by understanding dream, desire, fantasy, and imagination. All coexist with the world of contingent facts, and in fact may script that world—may, in fact, underlie that world of facts. However, the risk that a writer who goes far in the direction of dream and imagination runs is that the book that's produced might seem to be picturesque, or, to put it more uncharitably, "touristic"—a kind of facile, make-believe world where fantasy rules everything. In other words, what I'm saying is if there's too much fantasy, then it becomes make-believe and we no longer ascribe the same kind of reality quotient to it.

I've tried to make the case that this book has a very substantial dosage of hard-nosed political reality, colonial exploitation, cruelty, and abuse. These are not elided or docked or evaded in this book. They emerge powerfully and not despite, but I think because of, the discourse of magic and play, so that Conrad's tale of exploitation and ideological warfare, or Faulkner's sense of family doom, these darker realities are definitely in García Márquez's humorous and surreal rendition of life. But I think the darkest of all in this book, the richest quarry in this book, is what its title tells us—solitude—and few writers can match him, it seems to me, for giving us a picture of self-entombment, of the incurable loneliness of being alive, of the risk of being buried alive. One of the characters, Amaranta, a woman of deep, deep passions, nonetheless turns down suitor after suitor. She burns her hand black, scorches it black, and she spends her last days sewing her own shroud. She sees herself as a messenger of death, for death, into death. She enters willingly into it. She has said no to marriage, to suitors, and many are her suitors in this text, but at the end of the book we see her taking great preparations for death. This in itself is interesting—the way in which death is presented in this book, not as a kind of brutal, surprising, alien ending, but as a kind of continuation of who you are.

What does she do? She sees herself as a messenger in the sense that she acquires a carton of letters to take with her to the other side—the mail of death. Such a nice image of death as continuation, of literally commerce and exchange between life and death, of blurring that line that we think separates them. It's not an ending, and often the deaths of García Márquez's characters are a dimension of their being. I say that in part because it is so shocking to our Western sense of death as being obscene, brutal, cutting us off and stopping us, and I think that in particular is the way death comes about in some of these books, like Proust's book or Woolf's book. They're related to the Western horror of dying, our denial of death. In García Márquez, death is part of what you are. These characters in some sense choose their dying. They enter their dying. There are lots of deaths, and there are a number of living deaths in Macondo. Rebeca is the woman who carries her parents' bones with her in a sack. She is the woman who eats dirt. She is the woman who is also enormously gratified and impassioned by her very sexually powerful husband, José Arcadio, but he dies. Once he does die, it's as if her connection to the living circuit, the force field of life is in fact cut. She does become one of these immured, entombed people. She literally disappears from sight. She goes inside her house. No one sees her again. They forget about her. It's as if the insomnia plague led to the loss of memory once again.

I think that the most intriguing figure that represents solitude and entombment is one that you might not initially think of, and that's the woman, Fernanda. I think she's the only person in the book that one feels that García Márquez does not like. She's very beautiful, but she's also very haughty and pretentious. She is excessively, sort of tyrannically, pious. She is very autocratic, and she is a moralizer. When she marries Aureliano Segundo, she insists on a week's waiting period before they can make love, and then she comes to bed with a white gown that reaches all the way down to her ankles. It has a large buttonhole "at the level of her lower stomach." Her husband laughs when he sees this.

She is a woman with great social pretensions. She constantly refers to her very distinguished father, and one of the marvelous moments of the book is when the father sends them his yearly Christmas present. The whole family is excitedly awaiting it, and it comes in the form of some enormous box. It actually arrives at the house a little earlier than usual, and they've got to take out all of these copper bolts. It's a big chest, and Aureliano Segundo is busily taking them. Then they get quite a surprise when they open up the top of this chest.

> He raised the lead cover and saw Don Fernando, [that's the father, Fernanda's father] dressed in black and with a crucifix on his chest, his skin broken out in pestilential sores and cooking slowly in a frothy stew with bubbles like live pearls.

Edgar Allen Poe couldn't have improved on this. This is living death. He sends himself dead to his family to share himself dead with them at Christmas. It's quite a gift—pretty lugubrious gift. Here is the material language of decay/deterioration but also of remember to die, *momento mori*, also of guilt and fall—the death of spirit.

I said that García Márquez does not like Fernanda, and I think that this passage is there for him to really make it unforgettably clear that she represents the tradition of death. Death is the denial of life, as the denial of pleasure, as "solitude" in the sense of literally being buried alive, which is the way he arrives. I keep saying "alive" because from an organic point of view death doesn't exist. Death organically is cooking slowly in a frothy stew with bubbles like live pearls. It's quite a description, so that rot is a kind of molecular fiesta. Lots of things are happening.

Even the great matriarch of the book, Úrsula, who lives to be 145, close to Biblical issues here, and has brought up generations of children, too becomes blind in her old age and enters another form of solitude. She negotiates the world only through touch and smell. There are a number of characters that get our attention as figures of solitude, either growing into it through old age or entering it because of their denial of pleasure and of love. But the most memorable one and the one who stays with us longest, I think—long after we finish this book—is the son, Colonel Aureliano Buendía, the younger son of the patriarch. He is the war hero of the novel. I've already mentioned it before. He is the man who spent his entire life fighting for the liberal cause, and he paid the supreme price in increasing coldness of heart—a solitude that cannot be breached. Remember, I've already alluded to him as the man whose fate it is not to die at the hands of a firing squad but to die by becoming ice. That's how that first sentence of the book is—that he remembered when his father introduced him to ice. He is the man who dies in front of us as we watch him. He becomes increasingly suspicious of other people because of his activities, adventures and misadventures in the endless wars that he partakes of. When he returns home and Úrsula sees how much he has changed, how he is wrapped in this cloak like he is always cold, he makes this particular decree. "It was then that he decided that no human being, not even Úrsula, his mother, could come closer to him than ten feet." It's an amazing kind of moment. It's like he draws a circle around himself. It's like a reverse Christ, *nole me tangere*—do not touch me. He becomes untouchable. You couldn't get a more graphic image of solitude than this.

One of the most moving passages of the book is the moment when he realizes that his mother, Úrsula, fully understands, and measures, and is saddened by what he has become. He realizes that she is the only person who—and it's a key verb here—who penetrates his misery. As he realizes, he looks hard at her, and he sees everything. It's pitiless what he sees. He sees that her skin is leathery. He sees her teeth, and he sees that they're decayed. He sees her hair, and he sees that it's faded, that it's colorless, and he sees that her eyes are frightened. Yet, looking at this, it's not enough. It won't take him where he wants to go. It won't take him to something that is alive because it seems that too much of him has died.

> In an instant he discovered [this is again about his mother now] the scratches, the welts, the sores, the ulcers, and the scars that had been left on her by more than half a century of daily life, and he saw that those damages did not even arouse a feeling of pity in him. Then he made one last effort to search in his heart for the place where his affection had rotted away and he could not find it.

I think it's a heartbreaking passage. He could not find it. At first, it seems like just a straightforward indictment of him as no longer being able to feel, and it never stops being that. But it continues into something else—this effort to break through the ice, to chop through the frozen sea as Kafka might have said, that fails. He sees. He measures, and he fails. It's as if, to use Faulkner's term, "I lies dying." The sentient self is dying here in this sequence.

Aureliano is the dark conscience of the novel—solitude, *soledad*, the estate of the self. Maybe every self has a ten-foot circle around it. Maybe no one ever gets closer than ten feet to us. Maybe even when we see the damages and scars that life has given to those that we love, we only see it. We can't feel it, and when we reach out to feel it, we can't get there. He is the one who smiles throughout this book the strange smile. He is the one who is obsessed with making these little goldfish. He is the one who lives, as it were, the hundred-year history. He doesn't live to be a hundred, but one thinks that he does. It's a history of war, and war is corrosive. So, it pickles him. He knows he is living death. We know that García Márquez found it hard to kill him because that's what writers do when characters die. They kill them. How does he die? He sees a circus going by, a woman on an elephant, a camel, a dancing bear, clowns, and through it all he sees his own solitude, and he puts his forehead against the tree and he dies. This is his death. As I said, in García Márquez one owns one's death. One doesn't die in brackets—his death.

But when García Márquez wrote this, he went upstairs trembling, and his wife, Mercedes, said to him, "The colonel is dead." We are told that he wept for two hours. What can counter solitude, mummification? I think the answer is, and I've talked about this some but I'm going to talk about it a bit more, is desire, lust for life, appetite, and passion. I've already mentioned that the book celebrates phallic power. I've mentioned José Arcadio—that his sexuality is described as "cyclonic," as a kind of vital, elemental force. But the book is equally committed to female sexuality, especially female fertility. Two characters particularly stand out in this remark or this fashion, Pilar Ternera, who seems to mother or mate with virtually all of the men, but there is nothing abusive or exploitative in it. There's a sense in which this is the dance of the species. This is her role. This is a role of considerable dignity, and her counterpart, Petra Cotes, they share the role of sexual-ascent-become-sexual assertion. There's nothing boasting about it, but as I said, there's a kind of dignity, there's a kind of pride. They're on the far side of any sense of constraint. They relish their own power, their role, in the culture, in the life cycle.

When I speak of desire, I don't simply mean an itch that is inside of some human beings. I'm talking about something much larger. It goes beyond psychology. It goes beyond the personal, and we see this in particular in Petra Cotes's relationship to Aureliano Segundo. He's the one who is married to Fernanda, the kind of conservative, denying woman of the book, and so he has this long affair with Petra Cotes. Their relationship together is like a vision of fertility and plenty, like a cornucopia that when he is with her their crops are luxuriant. The animals produce triplets. The hogs are fattened. It's the procreative principle. As I said, there's nothing psychological in sight. You'd be better off thinking of photosynthesis, of the radiant heat of the sun that produces life in the plants.

The most passionate episode of the book is the one that I've already alluded to. It takes place at the end. It's the final haunting love relationship between Aureliano, the great, great grandson, and his aunt, Amaranta Úrsula. They brave all of the laws of constraint, and decorum and coercion, and they seem to create their own ecstatic Garden of Eden. As I mentioned, their ecstatic love-making is followed by extraordinarily creative activities, and in one sequence, what we read is that they daub themselves with peach jam after they have made love. They fall asleep, and they wake up to "a torrent of carnivorous ants who were ready to eat them alive," ants that come to their jam-covered bodies after making love. Those are the ants of destruction. I would compare them perhaps to the horsemen of the Apocalypse. Those ants know nothing of human love. They follow nature's savage, inhuman, but logical dictates. The force that brings two bodies together may well be akin to the force that devours flesh altogether. Yes, these two lovers have found Eden, but it is rife with its own destruction. Remember Amaranta's scorched hand. Passion, incandescent passion, can burn you alive in this book.

García Márquez is not a dewey-eyed romantic. He is alert to the ravages and excesses of feeling. He knows something about its labyrinths. One character, Arcadio the grandson, is depicted as a brutal tyrant, vicious, shot by a firing squad. Another character, the great grandson, José Arcadio, is a sinister pedophile who meets his death at the hands of children. They surprise him. They throw him fully-clothed into the pool. They grab him by the hair. They hold him under, and they steal his money. José Arcadio Segundo is haunted by the sights that he has seen. He can never be freed from his indwelling fear. Yes, this is a rich, passionate book, but it's a book that knows something about fear, anxiety, terror, and neurosis. José Arcadio Segundo all his life will remember the sad, mocking smile of a man being executed. It's a trauma he doesn't get past. This book particularly frames solitude in connection with the script, the magic text within the text. The character of Melquíades, the gypsy philosopher, is really the tutelary divinity of the book. He's the man who keeps returning over and over to the Buendías, as if to check them out, to write them down, to let them know that there's a record of their exploits. He is a figure of a kind of elusive wisdom. He never speaks much. Well, we know that he is beyond death, because he keeps coming back in these different forms. He presides over this mysterious, cryptic script written in a code that it would seem only he can read. Every reader has the feeling that this script, this mysterious script, and it's real, it's kept in a room at the Buendías' house, has to be a version of the novel itself.

So we see an entire line of Buendía men seeking to decipher—men, mind you, not women—decipher the magic script. It almost sounds rabbinical that the task of the men is to decipher the script. They're trying to decipher the history of their family. It begins to look like a book of revelation. García Márquez does not hide from us the fact that you pay a price for attending to the text, to the script—that there are characters who lose themselves in this room. They're there for decades just reading the script. They become ghostly. It's a severe equation of life, bustling, rich, fertile, passionate life, on the one hand, and this monkish, celibate tending to the script on the other. There could be a certain amount of humor in this as well, because the closed-off room where the script is kept also happens to have 72 very smelly chamber pots in it, as if García Márquez wants to sort of clue you in that there is nothing that humans can do that can be utterly separated from the body. Nonetheless, we get a sharp sense that what we are seeing here about the script, which is about writing, and reading, and art, is also about solitude, and perhaps about ice.

The book turns very dark toward the end. The Catalonian bookseller auctions off his books. He's been one of the wise men of the text, and he urges the people of Macondo to disregard all of the things he has earlier said about art and writing. He tells them to leave Macondo.

> That they forget everything he had taught them about the world and the human heart, that they shit on Horace, and that wherever they might be they always remember that the past was a lie, that memory has no return, that every spring gone by could never be recovered, and that the wildest and most tenacious love was an ephemeral truth in the end.

This is bad news. These are dark tidings. I think it takes a writer of considerable pluck to put poison like that in his text, to speak against his own vision. It speaks as well for the kind of cynicism, the kind of despair, that begins to come into this book as we reach the end, and we know that the curse is going to be fulfilled—that the prophecy will be fulfilled—that the hundred years will be over. And so, it ends.

It ends, as I've said, with Aureliano and his aunt having their wild, ecstatic, and yet I think innocent love, and at the same time we realize that this Aureliano is the man who earlier spent years decoding and deciphering the text. It's as if García Márquez were bringing together the two poles, the lusty fornicator and the reader of the text.

You remember those ants that were ready to devour the man and the woman covered with jam after their lovemaking? Those ants re-enter the text. I call them the horseman of the Apocalypse, the ants of destruction. They re-enter the text, and they devour the child who is the product of this ecstatic union between Aureliano and Amaranta Úrsula. First, she dies, and then the child dies. He saw the child. "It was a dry and bloated bag of skin that all the ants [of] the world were dragging toward their holes [in] the stone path in the garden." The curse is now coming true. It's as if the Father God who has seemed to be absent, or sleeping, or on leave in this text, finally says no. Punishment is at last meted out, but I want to say that it goes against the grain of much of this book. What has their crime been? To recover Eden, to escape history.

Aureliano now at the end reads the text. He decodes it, and he sees that it is his own history that he is reading. As he is reading it, the storm begins to come, the cyclonic strength of the wind is mentioned, and we think of the cyclonic power of sexuality. We see that Macondo is beginning to be destroyed as he reads. Listen to what he reads.

> He began to decipher," he's looking at the text, "the instant that he was living, deciphering it as he lived it, prophesying himself in the act of deciphering the last page of the parchments, as if he were looking into a speaking mirror.

He reads that now Macondo is going to be wiped off the face of the earth when he finishes the parchments, "because races condemned to one hundred years of solitude did not have a second opportunity on earth." It is a mesmerizing scene. He sees himself becoming text. He is becoming literature. This novel's ingredients are life, blood, love, and desire, and they are becoming the words on a page, the script. It is a formidable binary. Could you have both? Aureliano and Macondo are swept away by storm. We are told that there is no second opportunity, but I want to close this lecture by saying, yes, there is. Yes, there is. That is the reprieve, the eternal life that literature confers on authors in stories. You open this book, and you read it, and you reverse the curse because the text, the words, create the life, the blood, the sex, and the passion. You are there reading alone—solitude—but the magic of Magic Realism is the magic of reading. It spawns a living world: Macondo Eden.

Thank you.

Lecture Thirty-Six
Ending the Course, Beginning the World

Scope:

Our course began with a journalistic account of a woman battling heavy odds in 18th-century London, and it closed with the mythic tale of an entire family battling its fate in the rise and fall of Colombian Macondo. There have been battles throughout—economic, sexual, ideological, moral, military, spiritual, biological, emotional—and literature alone grants us access to this ongoing drama. It is through works of art and imagination that the known record (facts, dates) comes alive, in its human fullness and dimensionality.

As Richard Carstone is dying in *Bleak House*, Dickens writes that he is "beginning the world." Each of us is fated in "real life" to inhabit one body and one mind and one world, but the magic of reading enables us, over and over, to begin the world anew: with new eyes, new ears, new sights and sounds. New heart? Maybe. What is certain is this: The virtuality of art—that it is "not real," according to the skeptics—is its supreme trump card, for it opens the door to voyages we can take in no other way.

Outline

I. What we've learned in these 36 lectures on classic novels should be understood as seeding and working the soil of the brain and heart. We don't have any real way to measure the effects of this kind of education, but I believe that reading literature widens the way we look at the world, making us more dimensional.

   A. In *Fear and Trembling*, Kierkegaard says, "You must work for your bread"; he then goes on to say that, of course, this isn't always true in the real world. Some people gain their bread without working, and others labor without receiving bread. In the mind and the soul, however, Kierkegaard believes that his law holds. We must earn our truths, and one way to do so is by reading literature.

   B. What do you gain—what have you gained—by reading classic novels written over a 250-year period?

1. There is nothing crass about such a question, because we are entitled to know the possible benefits of the labors we undertake.
2. Often, we read great books too early in our lives or in situations where we are obliged to read them. Books don't speak to us then; they become dead letters.

C. One reason to read classic literature is to become culturally literate. The books we have looked at are Western classics, and knowledge of them can provide a basis for intellectual exchange. Yet knowing the plots and characters of works of fiction can also seem like a whimsical proposition. Do we take from these books something truly vital?
1. The reality of literature is not informational. In fact, we now live in a moment that seems awash in information, and it's not always clear how "good" this information is.
2. There are serious distinctions among information, knowledge, and wisdom. We're long on information and short on knowledge—and shorter still on wisdom.

II. The following are thumbnail sketches of what I take to be the enduring truths of the narratives we have read. I hope you will use these as entryways for what you might look for in these books and what they might mean.

A. Defoe teaches us about the deeper wisdom of "keeping our own books," of recognizing the spiritual dimensions of our experience. One of the great wonders of *Moll Flanders* is that it seems as if it is nothing but a description of the physical, material world, but it has moments where we see an inner realm of spirit and feeling, in which Moll herself "keeps her own books." This book points out to us the difference between the world we can see around us and what we know about ourselves.

B. Sterne reveals to us the anarchy and deliciousness of thinking in contrast to the order of normal prose and normal logic. The mind is agile, and *Tristram Shandy* tries to track its adventurous activity.

C. Laclos leaves us with a disturbing sense of intelligence-as-seduction and of all human liaisons as ungaugeable and dangerous. He asks some hard questions in this book: What is the value of intelligence? What is rewarded in our culture, intelligence or virtue?

D. Balzac dramatizes the fate of feeling in a new capitalist order with its ruthless, success-at-all-costs ethos. His *Bildungsroman* was one of the first to show us the price of success, an issue we face at all stages of our lives.

E. Brontë casts her light on the brutal and primitive reaches of human feeling, exposing the illusoriness of rules and decorum. *Wuthering Heights* is a ghoulish story that reveals the rage, anger, and hunger inside us all. It also shows us the depths of the relationship between Catherine and Heathcliff, who are so closely connected as to become one.

F. Melville sounds the metaphysical depths, shows us that the world of appearances might be a pasteboard mask, and suggests that the self can be hijacked by its passions. He also offers us a world of wonder, taking us out to sea and showing us ever-increasing depths to be plumbed.

G. Dickens makes us understand "pollution" and "ecosystem" as both literal and moral concepts: We are porous creatures, related to one another beyond our ken. *Bleak House* also points to our modern world, where events that take place far away can reverberate at home or in our souls.

H. Flaubert's *Madame Bovary* is a tough, unflinching text, embodying both romantic lyricism and an analytical, even cynical, perspective on romance. Flaubert shows us that human desire can be constructed by outside influences and, tragically, that desire cannot be gratified. Nonetheless, desire may still be what is most beautiful about us, the search for something beyond what we have.

I. Tolstoy writes the tug-of-war between the anarchy of experience and the desire for pattern, as individuals find and lose their way in historical events. He makes us understand that we always live in a historical setting that we cannot see. We do not know how our roles will be seen when the history of our moment is written.

J. Dostoevsky shines his light into the human psyche, attuned to its unpredictability, pride, violence, and tenderness in a world where all is permitted. He gives us the word *nadryv*, "strain, laceration," as the chief characteristic of human relationships. But he also tells us that if we could look properly at every single moment, in everything around us, we would find paradise.

K. Conrad's impressionist text points to the underside of European colonialism, inflected by racism, greed, and self-deification. Conrad announces an era of horror, guilt, and damage done to others and, therefore, ourselves, by the primitivism that may lurk inside the most well-regulated minds if subjected to sufficient stress.

L. Mann writes about the power of the abyss, showing that form and beauty are driven by libido. They are often a façade, behind which are hunger and desire. They point to the abyss, and the artist is inevitably en route to the abyss in his search for form and beauty. Discipline itself may be a myth, and even more disturbingly, *Death in Venice* asks the question: Have you lived a lie?

M. Kafka's weird stories enact the exit from the human, whether through metamorphosis or legal arrest; truth and justice are unreachable. Kafka is a spiritual writer in a material age, and he gives the death blow to any kind of anthropocentric and humanistic scheme.

N. Proust bequeaths to us a new entity: the creature on stilts, the view of our life-in-time, the private universe hidden in each of us, and the magic of memory. Proust tries to take the measure of temporal reaches—the length of time one has lived, the extent to which one is extended into the past.

O. Joyce stages, with unparalleled genius and exuberance, the song and dance of both mind and body, the strange melody of human thinking. He gives us the never-before-told story of the self in culture as if the traffic of our molecules and the noise of the street and the sound bytes of the media and the pulsations of the body were all brought together in a remarkable form and mesh.

P. Woolf writes, with lyricism and savage beauty, the radiance and doom of her female protagonist, Mrs. Ramsay, the mother, and about the projects of retrieval via art and memory. She tells us why art matters and shows us that we are not as bounded as we think, that the inward core of darkness is mobile.

Q. Faulkner registers, against a backdrop of rotting flesh and coursing elements, the dying of *I*, the play of consciousness, and the splendor of the land and water. It is not merely the fate of flesh that interests him, but what human beings can do to offset this entropic scheme. We also find in Faulkner's work the most violent assault on the self; what we think of as the bounded ego could, if subjected to sufficient pressure, "unravel in time."

R. García Márquez, the revolutionary, breaks all the rules; he privileges freedom, desire, and fantasy, yet acknowledges the irremediable solitude at one's core. His book is an extraordinary circus of desire, but there is a supreme penalty to be paid.

III. Despite this list, and despite these lectures, there can be no shortcuts for understanding literature. You must work to earn your bread yourself.

A. Everywhere you look (and in places where you cannot look), people are reading. Here is culture's most inexpensive, commonplace, and democratic creative act. At Richard Carstone's death in *Bleak House*, Dickens writes that he is "beginning the world." That is what we do when we read these books.

B. Reading books means converting the print into meaning. We make such conversions all the time, responding to a green traffic light, a smile, or a cholesterol count.

1. Converting the print on the page into its fuller meaning is an extraordinarily gratifying, pleasurable, even hedonistic exercise.

2. Art is the bloodstream of civilization, and reading is like a blood transfusion, in which the reality of the world of past writers—their imaginations, their hearts, and their brains—becomes available to us. We become citizens of the world—we begin the world—by reading books.

Supplementary Reading:

Arnold Weinstein, *Recovering Your Story: Proust, Joyce, Woolf, Faulkner, Morrison.*

————, *A Scream Goes Through the House: What Literature Teaches Us About Life.*

Questions to Consider:

1. We return to our initial query: What can be the value of literature? Given the diversity of materials and themes seen in this voyage through fictions, what common ground might emerge as the constants in reading? Has there been a "voyage"? If you have not read the books but only listened to the lectures, have you—or have you not—had the experience of literature?

2. I have posited semiotics—the interpretation of signs—as the core challenge of all reading, indeed, of all education and all experience. To what extent do you feel that you engage in semiotic labors during your everyday life? Do you think this key transaction is merely a mental procedure, or is it something more vital and existential?

Lecture Thirty-Six—Transcript
Ending the Course, Beginning the World

The ending ceremony of each academic year is called "Commencement." It's not called "Conclusion"; it's called "Commencement," or beginning. What you've learned in four years of college or in 36 lectures on Classic Novels should be understood as seeding, sewing, working the soil of the brain and the heart so that it might yield some kind of long-term harvest. We don't have any lights on this. We don't know anything about these matters. It's really quite strange, given how much we are able to quantify and measure, that we have no real idea as to the pay-off of what our efforts are when it comes to education—what we learn from what we do and how it is ultimately re-used, important and vitalizing in our life afterwards. I spend my life teaching books because I am convinced that they are sources not so much of wisdom but of widening our repertoire and of changing the way we look at the world—not altering us but adding to us, making us, using a word that I like to use, more dimensional.

As I say, we don't know what the reward is for reading these novels. I can certainly not write a contract with you and say, you read these books, these 18 authors, and I can guarantee you that either your income is going to be higher, or that you're going to end up in heaven, or that you'll no longer have any fights either with your family or with yourself. It could actually be the other way around. These books could be trouble.

There's a line in Kierkegaard's text, *Fear and Trembling*, where he cites a phrase that all of you have heard, "You must work for your bread he says." Then he goes on to say that we know, he knows, that in the real world, the every dayworld, the work-a-day world, people get bread without working. Perhaps you are born and have inherited bread. Perhaps you have cheated and gotten bread. Perhaps for all kinds of reasons bread has come to you without labor; and sadly, tragically, the converse is also true. We know that there are many people who toil, and labor, and work, and do not get bread. So, Kierkegaard knows that in the real world that severe law does not necessarily hold, but then he says it does hold in the world of the mind and of the soul. I think he's right. There are no freebies in the mind and the soul, and I would argue finally that the nature of understanding is such that there are no shortcuts either. You earn your truths. You work to get them. So, in that sense it seems to me that reading literature—reading it, not just hearing about it, but reading it, thinking about it, experiencing it—will yield a result. But it is not something that one can easily sort of grasp out of the air or get in some sort of nugget form. You'll see I'm going to still try to give you some nuggets, but this is going to be, therefore, my Commencement lecture, not my conclusion.

What do you gain? What have you gained by reading classic novels written over a 250-year period? That may sound crass. It may sound like I'm teaching a course in economics, but there isn't anything crass about it, because life is utilitarian. Any time we labor or work we are entitled to wonder what good it's going to do us. What is the value of it? As I said, how useful is an education? I happen to think that often we read the great books too early in our lives. We read them, if we're young, when we have other very powerful competing factors such as hormones, such as other interests in our life, and we also have other impeding factors such as perhaps immaturity, perhaps poor teaching. All of this can make the great books that we read dead letters, and I don't know how to overstate that. You have to judge for yourself. How many books have you read, and I guess the best way to phrase it is how many books have you been obliged to read, usually by teachers and maybe by your family, that are dead letters? It doesn't mean that they're lying there with blood coming out of them. It just means that they're inert on the page, that the book hasn't spoken to you, that it doesn't live. It's just a book with black characters on a white page, and it lies there like a fallow field. Then there's not much of a pay-off at all, is there? So, what could be some of the reasons to read literature? One of them, and this goes with the logic that E. D. Hirsch has made quite well known in American culture about cultural literacy, is that reading books, particularly reading the classics, makes you culturally literate. I don't want to really disagree with that. These are the Western classics, and a knowledge of them, at least a recognition of them, can lead to a basis for social/intellectual exchange. That's important. It's important to know that *Hamlet* exists. It's important to know that *Wuthering Heights* exists, or that the *Brothers Karamazov* exists. On the other hand, it seems to me, perhaps because I've spent so many years doing this, wondering about these questions, that if you simply know the plots, authors, dates and characters of works of fiction, it's not obvious to me what you've gained if that's all you know. That can seem whimsical, or it can seem worse still, like ashes or dead leaves. Or, you could say, why read these books at all? I could go to Wikipedia or to Cliff Notes and get information about these texts, and you could. There's no question about it.

So, I want to say that the reality of literature is not informational. In fact, my own belief, and it's probably a cockeyed belief, is that we live in a moment when we are awash in information. Our electronic Internet culture gives us more information than we could ever possibly process, and we also know that with Google and other instruments, it's not always clear what the status of this information is. But the point that I really want to make is that there is, in my view, a very serious difference between information and knowledge—that we're long on information and short on knowledge. I want to say now, and this will sound perhaps a little bit sermonizing, that we're still shorter on wisdom. From information, to knowledge, to wisdom is a series of arduous steps, and there are certainly no shortcuts to wisdom.

What I'm going to suggest now is a series of sort of fundamental sketches of what I take to be the enduring truths of these books, and for me these are earned truths. These are truths that have come to me by dint of reading and thinking about these books, and I hope that you will listen to this as a kind of touchstone for you. These may not be the things that matter most in these books for you. At best, I want you to think of them as entryways for you, as ways in which you might re-think these books that you've read or that you've heard me talk about and see what might be in them, what one might in fact look for in them and see what that might mean.

Let me start with Defoe. It seems to me that Defoe teaches us about the deeper wisdom of "keeping our own books," I'm using intentionally a kind of economic phrase there—to keep one's own books. I want to say that we don't always keep our own books, but that our own books can be kept only by us. It's true that you can get someone else to do your taxes for you, but the kind of books that I'm talking about, the inner books, the script of what you feel, what you believe, and what you think, the only person who can keep those books is you. One of the great wonders of *Moll Flanders*, in my view, is that this book that looked so material, it looks like it is nothing but a description of the physical, material, phenomenal world, nonetheless sort of has glints, and it has moments where we see, and they are usually shocking moments, an inner realm of spirit, an inner realm of feeling, where Moll Flanders keeps her books, where Moll Flanders takes stock. Here is a woman who's been stealing things right and left, trying to marry to get rich. These are moments when she goes inside and measures her own consciousness. That's what I think this book tells us is about the sort of difference, the incommensurateness between what the world can see about us and what we know about ourselves. Let me put this in really crass terms—about you smiling and having a conversation with someone while thinking the dirtiest or meanest thoughts in your mind. You can imagine how many extensions of that there might be. Only you see that mix of inside and outside between what is public and what is private. It seems to me that Defoe points us that way.

In Sterne's *Tristam Shandy*, we get a sense of the anarchy and deliciousness of thinking and how constructed the order is of normal prose, and perhaps even of normal logic, because the mind is full of different directionalities. Every time you remember, your mind goes backwards. Even now, as either you look or listen to me, where is your mind? Is it on me? Is it on what you had for breakfast yesterday? Is it on what kind of reward you're hoping for tomorrow? The mind is agile. It goes all over the place. Sterne has tried to write a book that follows, tracks that kind of adventurous activity. Flesh, of course, does not have all of these advantages that the mind does.

Laclos' novel, *Les Liaisons Dangereuses*, leaves us with what I think of as a disturbing sense of intelligence-as-seduction, and of all human relationships, what he calls liaisons, as ungaugeable, immeasurable and dangerous. They are forms of exposure, and he asks some hard questions in this book. He doesn't ask them directly, but he asks them of us nonetheless through the book, which is What is the value of intelligence? Now, I want to simply turn that into a contemporary question. What is rewarded in our culture, intelligence or virtue? Those are exactly the issues in this book, intelligence or virtue. I'll tell you one thing that the students who get into Brown University where I teach, they may be very decent people, but that's not how they got in. You get in to universities in this society through your intelligence, and I'd argue further you get big salaries in this society because of your intelligence, not your virtue. Now, it could also be the case that you get ulcers, a bad conscience, and breakdowns because of these matters, but it's that sort of discrepancy between these things about how intelligence is in fact a really primary force in modern life, and its particular moral ends may be rather ambiguous. That's the kind of thing it seems to me that we are getting in Laclos, and we're getting also the fact that virtue is accorded much lip service. But how much reality does it have in terms of how decisions are made and how people are recognized and rewarded?

Balzac dramatizes the fate of feeling in a new capitalist order with a kind of ruthless success-at-all-costs code. He's one of the first writers to tell us what the cost of living is, and again I use the economic term intentionally—what it costs to succeed, because succeeding is the great sort of injunction in his work. What Balzac is trying to show us is you pay something to succeed, and I think it's a problem that we face not only when we're coming out of college or coming out of high school, and that's of course the way this book is written; a *Bildungsroman* about young people determining what it is they need to do to succeed. In my view, it's a problem that we encounter at every stage of our life. We ask ourselves what we have paid to succeed in mid-life. It's often allied with "mid-life crisis." We ask ourself what we have paid to succeed at retirement and perhaps also on our deathbed. So, he is asking an absolutely basic, resonant, echoing question.

What about Emily Brontë? She casts her light on the brutal reaches, the primitive reaches, of human feeling, as if all of the things that we take to be civilization were something of a kind of polite façade, the illusoriness of rules and decorum. *Wuthering Heights* is a ghoulish story, worse than anything that Stephen King could have written, and it puts pay to any polite notions of decency and caring, as if decency and caring are wonderful to talk about and if you're lucky you may occasionally run into them. But at least in this book what we find particularly, unforgettably in the figure of Heathcliff is that deep down inside of people there is nothing but rage, anger, and hunger. It is a fierce book. It is a demonic book. It also asks a very hard question about human relationships. It tells us the word "relationship" is such a polite, namby-pamby word because Heathcliff and Catherine in this book are not simply related. Catherine says, Nelly, I am Heathcliff. Could you be so closely connected to another person that they're like a succubus? They're a part of who you are, and it makes no difference if one of you is dead, because you will continue to live on in the other.

Melville is the first to truly sound the metaphysical depths in this course, and he suggests that the world of appearances, the things that we see that we take to be real, are nothing but a paste-board mask, and that they must be struck through—this is Ahab's view of things—and can be struck through, and that might be not just a quest for truth but a kind of tragic obsession and compulsion. He also asks if the self can be completely hijacked and taken over by its own ruling obsessions. He also offers us in this book, and this is one of the great things about *Moby-Dick*, page after page, a world of wonder. He is tonic for bored land lovers, which is what I think all of us are. He takes all of us out to sea. He says that we think that we're walking on the land, on the ground, on the floor. We think there's a bottom line. Take another look, he says. Underneath there is nothing but depth. These are our depths, and he annihilates, therefore, most of the petty comfortable frames where we think things belong, where we timidly keep house. Everything he scrutinizes opens up.

Dickens helps us to understand that pollution and ecosystem, two words that he never uses in *Bleak House* but that I think we have to bring to it, are both literal and moral terms/concepts. In Dickens' world, people find themselves interrelated; Dickens' world is tentacular, miasmic. People find that they are glued to others in ways they could never have seen. They find that they have neighbors that they never knew they had. Dickens, I think, points to our modern world. It's an environmental/ecological picture of reality. It's a globalized world where events that take place far away can reverberate at home or in our souls. Dickens tells us in *Bleak House* that the slum dwellers have the keys to the city, not that they're rich, not that they have power, but that the slum will finally never be contained in the slums. They will spill out, and they will in fact infect the lives of all others. We have seen enough of the diseases in our American cities to know the truth of what Dickens is saying.

Flaubert. *Madame Bovary* is a tough, unflinching text. It's a text that has both romantic lyricism on the one hand and a kind of surgical, analytic, and sometimes quite cynical perspective on the other. So, Flaubert shows us that human desire, which we want to think of as something that is spontaneous, innate, and beautiful inside of us, what we know today in a world of advertising, and things like that, and marketing—we know that desire can be constructed. It can be constructed by the books that we read, by the newspapers that we read. Today we would know that it can be constructed by the sports that we watch, or the films that we see, or the videos, or the music. This is a very provocative model, that desire does not belong to us— that we are in a sense porous in that way as well. Dickens never got at it from that angle, but it's the same view. We can be invaded, and in fact we can be sort of conditioned by things that come to us in forms that appear to be as innocuous as the books that we read. Yes, desire can be constructed. Yes, as well, tragically, it seems that desire in *Madame Bovary* cannot be gratified. I think Flaubert suggests that inherently desire is ungratifiable. But—and I tried to make this argument in my lectures—ultimately desire may be what is still most beautiful about us. It still may express the deepest hunger in our lives, the search for something beyond what we have.

Tolstoy writes the tug-of-war between the anarchy of experience, the murkiness of experience on the one hand, and the desire for pattern—something that I think is a dialectic that rules all lives. In particular, he locates this in a historical framework, as his individuals find and lose their way in historical events.

History is funny. I was never a great history student. You look at the history texts, and for me it was a series of memorizing dates, memorizing events, and these were dead letters. I've talked about dead letters. For me this was dead letters. I could pass tests because I have a good memory, but I could not see why this was important.

What I think Tolstoy makes us understand is that we always, by definition, of necessity, live in a historical setting that we cannot see. When our history is written, when the history of our moment is written, what figure will we make? What role will we be seen to have played? Will you be Hamlet? Will you be Guildenstern? Will you be a groundling? Will you even appear on the scene? We don't have any lights about this. We cannot see how our own individual coming, going, and doing possibly fits, or doesn't fit, in the larger frame. We are, of course, taken up with our own wants, our own agenda, but history happens onto us. Certainly, the people in the Twin Towers all had plans, agendas, and notions about what they were going to do with their private lives when calamity/disaster struck. I think Tolstoy points us in that direction.

Dostoevsky shines his light into the human psyche, and it goes deep, deep, deep, deep down. He looks at a world in which everything might be permitted because God might be dead, and what he finds there is not so much evil as unpredictability, pride, violence, tenderness, and a fact that some things taste good that we shouldn't think they would. That is to say that he has the child, Lisa, who imagines crucifying a little boy and eating pineapple compote at the same time. This out of the lips and mouth of a child. Here is a view of human nature, and he doesn't say this child is evil. He is trying to say (as Ivan says, "Who doesn't wish for his father's death?"), he's trying to tell us some very unwelcome home truths about what the human psyche might be like.

He finds fireworks, like Melville. He dives deep. He gives us that word, or at least it's a word that I've tried to emphasize in my lectures, *nadryv*, strain, laceration, as the characteristic sort of complexion of human relationships. But he also finds paradise. He says that life is paradise. He says that if we could look properly at every single moment in everything around us we would find paradise.

With Conrad we move into something different. Conrad begins to point to the underside of Europe, European colonialism, racism, greed, and self-deification. With Conrad we begin to see that the West is in trouble, as we now continue to hear of it being in trouble. He is the bell toller for the good conscience of the West. He announces already an era of horror, guilt, and of damage done both to others and therefore to ourselves, about the kind of primitivism that may lurk inside the most well-regulated minds if subjected to sufficient stress.

Thomas Mann writes about the power of the abyss showing that form and beauty, which we take to be lovely aesthetic terms not having really any other kind of moral valence, certainly not having any libidinal valence. No, says Mann. They're driven by libido. They can often be a façade behind which there is hunger and desire. They point to the abyss, and the artist is inevitably en route to the abyss in his search for form and beauty. Discipline itself may be a myth, and even more disturbingly I think *Death in Venice* asks the question, Have you lived a lie? Do you find out late in life that you've lived a lie? When do you know your own truth? Is there any calendar for that? Certainly, his hero, Aschenbach, discovers in Venice a dreadful truth, a remarkable truth, about his life and about his art.

Then we get to Kafka, the weirdest figure of the course. I said over and over Kafka's stories enact an exit from the human whether it's through metamorphosis, turning into a bug, or whether it is through being arrested in your bed. These are all ways in which you exit the human community that you thought was unexcitable. Truth and justice seem to be unreachable. Kafka in my view is a spiritual writer in a material age, and he gives the deathblow to any kind of anthropocentric and humanistic scheme that we want to believe in. We can be altered in Kafka's world. As I said in one of my other lectures, in Kafka we are ushered into the world of Chicken Little, where the sky can fall in.

What about Marcel Proust? He gives us, I think, a new entity. He calls it at the end of his book "the creature on stilts." It's a circus image—that we live on stilts. Stilts are in fact time, and the longer we live the higher up the stilts go. At some point, they take us higher even than church steeples, so high that eventually we must fall off of those stilts. Try to imagine your estate temporally. Heaven knows we have accountants and others who help us to imagine our estate financially. Try to imagine your estate temporally, and you see something of the enormity of Proust's new vision—to try to take the measure of our temporal riches, which is true for even the youngest among those who may be hearing this lecture or seeing it—how long we have lived, how much we are extended into the past, how illusory it may seem to us today—that is to say just snapshots. We can't make it real. We can't get to it. Proust is about accessing that— accessing it in a way that our electronic culture can never access things. Make it real. Proust says late in his book, "There was a precious ore in me, but would it be brought to light?" That's the private, personal script that must be finally expressed because he says, "With my death would disappear both the miner and the ore."

Joyce gives us in *Ulysses*, with unparalleled genius, the song and dance of both our mind and our body, the buzzing, never-yet-told story of the self in culture, as if the traffic of our molecules and the noise of the street, and the sound bytes of the media, and the pulsations of the body, all were brought together in some sort of remarkable form and mesh. That's why Joyce looks so strange on the page, and then we realize he's giving us that plenary picture of ourself in culture, of ourself as a mix of body, mind, thought, and sensation.

Virginia Woolf writes, with a kind of lyricism and beauty, the radiance and doom of her magnificent female protagonist, Mrs. Ramsay, the mother, and about the projects of retrieval via art and memory. She, more than any other writer perhaps, tells us why art matters, that the retina itself, what the eye can see, misses all of the splendor of what happens under the skin, and the tempest in our feelings that goes on 24/7 as we respond to the world that no camera could possibly photograph. This is what we find visible to us in her marvelous language. She also tells us about that inward core of darkness, which is the self, the promiscuity of a self that moves into the world inwardly just through thought and feeling—that we are not bounded as we think.

Then Faulkner, who writes, against the backdrop of rotting flesh and coursing elements and the dying of "I," the play of consciousness and the splendor of the land, and of the water, and of the elements. It is not merely the fate of flesh that interests him. It's also, it seems to me, what it is that human beings can do to offset this entropic scheme, this treadmill toward decay and death that no one can offset or reverse. In Faulkner's work, as well, we see, I think, the most violent assault on what we call "I." That's why his title is so significant, *As I Lay Dying*. What we think of as the bounded ego that we are could, if subjected to sufficient pressure, implode, explode, fissure, dissolve, "unravel in time," to use his words.

Then García Márquez, the revolutionary, the last writer of the course, the man who breaks the rules, who privileges freedom, desire and fantasy in order to give us a different picture of things in which a certain kind of freedom finally could be possible in which desire finally might rule. You could overcome gravity. You could overcome law. You could overcome logic. Can you? His book has an extraordinary circus of desire, magnificent depictions of human sexuality, and yet there is a supreme penalty that is paid, which is solitude, as if you still can't leave you.

But this list and these lectures only take us so far. This is a journey that you have to make yourself. These are just the notes that I'm giving you. Literature is incurably labor-intensive, words on a page that we negotiate by opening the book. We negotiate these words, and we transform them into the meanings that these books give us or that we give these books. In other words, we work to get our bread, but you know what's wonderful is that we get bread through these books. Everywhere you look, and in many places where you never look, people read. Reading is the greatest, most inexpensive, commonplace and democratic creative act in modern life. At Richard Carstone's death in *Bleak House*, Dickens writes that he is beginning the world.

What I want to say is that literature is a way of beginning the world. As I said, this is my Commencement lecture. It's a way of beginning the world. In a completely secular sense, literature is an afterlife. These books, once read, inside of you, ingested, will live. This is my cannibal motif again. They will live because they will add to the furnishings of your mind and your way of seeing.

Reading books means converting the print into meaning. It takes the signs that are on the page and converts them to meaning. We do this all the time. If I see a green light, I convert it into meaning. If I see a smile, I convert it into meaning. If I get a particular cholesterol count, I convert it into meaning, and of course we see words on a page and we convert them into meanings. Some of the great religious exercises in our culture are bar mitzvah and confirmation, where young people stand up and read the great books of the community, the great books of the culture. Often enough, they do not understand exactly what they are reading. That is what literature is. These are the great books of the culture that we read, and we convert those signs, the print on the page, into its fuller meaning. It is an extraordinarily gratifying, pleasurable, hedonistic exercise. Art is the bloodstream of civilization. We enter the text with our capacity to think, feel, and imagine. There is no other voyage like it. Reading is like a blood transfusion in which the reality of the world of the past of writers who are long dead now, of their imaginations, their hearts, and their brains, all of that becomes available to us. It flows into us. You become a citizen of the world by reading books. You get your estate by reading books. You begin the world by reading books. Art is arterial.

Thank you.

Timeline

1660 ....Daniel Defoe probably born
in London.

1707 ....Union of England, Scotland, and
Wales as the United Kingdom of
Great Britain.

1713 ....Laurence Sterne born in
Clonmel, Ireland.

1721 ....Defoe's *Moll Flanders* published by
W. Chetwood and T. Edling
in London.

1731 ....Defoe dies in London.

1741 ....Pierre Ambroise François Choderlos
de Laclos is born in Amiens, France.

1759–1767 ....Sterne's *Tristram Shandy* published
serially in nine volumes in London.

1768 ....Sterne dies in London.

1775–1783 ....American Revolution.

1776 ....U.S. Declaration of Independence.

1782 ....Pierre Choderlos de Laclos's *Les
Liaisons Dangereuses* published in
Paris by Durand.

1789 ....The French Revolution begins.

1799 ....Honoré de Balzac born in
Tours, France.

1801 ....Establishment of United Kingdom
of Great Britain and Ireland,
superseding earlier
United Kingdom.

1803 ....Choderlos de Laclos dies in
Taranto, Italy.

1848 ....Revolutions in France overthrow the
July Monarchy and instate the
Second Republic; Emily Brontë dies
in Yorkshire, England.

1850 ....Balzac dies in Paris.

1851 ....Melville's *Moby-Dick; or, the
Whale* published in London and
New York.

1852–1853 ....Dickens's *Bleak House* published in
20 monthly serials by Bradbury and
Evans in London.

1853–1856 ....Crimean War.

1857 ....*Madame Bovary* published by
Michel Levy Frères; Joseph Conrad
born Jozef Teodor Konrad Nalecz
Korzeniowski in Berdiczew,
Podolia, Russia (now Ukraine).

1861–1865 ....American Civil War.

1865–1869 ....*War and Peace* published in
six volumes.

1867 ....Establishment of the Austro-
Hungarian (Hapsburg) Empire.

1870 ....Dickens dies in London.

1870–1871 ....Franco-Prussian War.

1871 ....Marcel Proust born in
Auteuil, France.

1875 ....Thomas Mann born in
Lübeck, Germany.

1879–1880 ....*The Brothers Karamazov* published
in St. Petersburg.

1880 ....Gustave Flaubert dies in
Croisset, France.

1922 ....Formation of the Union of Soviet Socialist Republics (USSR); independence of the Republic of Ireland; *Ulysses* published in book form in Paris; Marcel Proust dies in Paris.

1924 ....Joseph Conrad dies in Bishopsbourne, Kent, England; Kafka dies in Kierling, Klosterneuberg, Austria.

1925 ....*The Trial* published.

1927 ....*To the Lighthouse* published by Harcourt in New York.

1928 ....Gabriel García Márquez born in Aracataca, Colombia.

1929 ....The New York Stock Exchange crashes; Thomas Mann wins the Nobel Prize in Literature.

1930 ....*As I Lay Dying* published by J. Cape and H. Smith.

1933 ....Hitler comes to power in Germany.

1939–1945 ....World War II.

1941 ....Joyce dies in Zurich, Switzerland; Virginia Woolf dies in Lewes, Sussex, England.

1945 ....Germany divided by the Allies; decolonization of most European empires begins; atomic bombs fall on Hiroshima and Nagasaki in Japan.

1950 ....Faulkner wins the Nobel Prize in Literature.

1955 ....Mann dies in Zurich, Switzerland.

1959–1975 ....Vietnam War.

1962 ....Faulkner dies in Byhalia, Mississippi.

1967 ....*One Hundred Years of Solitude* published in Buenos Aires, Argentina.

1982 ....García Márquez wins the Nobel Prize in Literature.

1989 ....Fall of the Berlin Wall.

1991 ....Dissolution of the USSR.

Glossary

Defoe, *Moll Flanders*

episodic: rambling, unstructured plot.

homo economicus: man defined by economic forces.

picaresque: satirical narrative genre devoted to the adventures of the *picaro* (rascal, rogue).

plain style: unembellished, straightforward language with few allusions.

Sterne, *Tristram Shandy*

digression: narrative strategy of breaking the linear flow.

double-entendre: use of words with more than one meaning, often obscene.

free association: mental process of moving from one idea immediately to another.

hobbyhorse: Sterne's term for the compulsive, associative character of thinking.

Laclos, *Les Liaisons Dangereuses*

ancien régime: the pre-Revolutionary French class-based society.

contrapuntal: a narrative strategy of clashing perspectives.

epistolary novel: the narrative tradition of the novel-in-letters.

Heisenberg theorem: a modern scientific model of the observer's impact on the observed.

Nietzschean: cult of the amoral "superman" figure.

Scientism: materialist view of humans as regulated by biological forces.

Sturm und Drang: tempestuous pre-Romantic German literary culture.

Balzac, *Père Goriot*

"Ariadne's thread": derived from the Theseus myth, the path through a labyrinth.

Bildungsroman: narrative genre of novels about the education/formation of the young.

La Comédie Humaine: the cumulative title Balzac gave to his many novels.

ennui: French for "boredom," "emptiness."

exposition: Balzac's method of laying out his story.

parvenir: French for "succeed."

pension: French term for a boarding house.

Realism: literary school devoted to descriptive accounts of social settings.

Satanic: literary term derived from Milton, denoting a powerful, evil, yet seductive figure.

Brontë, *Wuthering Heights*

Byronic male: literary term depicting a mysterious, powerful, romantic male figure.

moor: the primitive area of Yorkshire where Brontë situated her novel.

"raw versus cooked": anthropological term from Lévi-Strauss, denoting primitive versus civilized.

seer/scribe: narrative strategy of a distanced observer relating a mysterious story.

Thrushcross Grange: civilized abode of the refined Lintons in *Wuthering Heights*.

Wuthering Heights: primitive abode of the Earnshaws and Heathcliff in *Wuthering Heights*.

Melville, *Moby-Dick*

cetology: the science of whales.

cyclopic: reference to the one-eyed giants of Greek mythology.

Emersonian legacy: impact on American thinking of R. W. Emerson's transcendentalism.

epic: grand narrative of nation-building or larger-than-life heroes.

semiotics: the interpretation of *signs* (as a model of human and social behavior).

soliloquy: Shakespearean device of speaking one's thoughts to the audience.

stereophonic: narrative strategy of multiple speakers.

sultanism: imagery, derived from the Middle East, of powerful male rulers.

Dickens, *Bleak House*

"angel in the house": Victorian notion of the angelic, pure, sexless women.

Chancery court: London law court that decides civil cases; considered mysterious and powerful.

ecological: term denoting a scheme in which interdependency rules.

epistemological: the science or project of "knowing."

Foucault, Michel: French theorist of the shaping value of institutions upon subjectivity.

pollution: environmental term connoting the porousness of the individual human being.

Victorian period: mid-19th-century British culture of high ideals and sexual repression.

Flaubert, *Madame Bovary*

bovarysme: term coined from this novel; a propensity to project one's desires onto the world.

Don Quixote: hero of Cervantes's 17th-century novel, synonymous with seeing-via-books.

Enlightenment legacy: ethos of rationality and logic stemming from 18th-century thinkers.

free indirect discourse: narrating personal feelings indirectly via third-person prose.

Romance: idealist view of life as ecstasy and passion, often based on literary depictions.

Tolstoy, *War and Peace*

"fox versus hedgehog": a singular vision of particulars versus a "global" overview of the whole.

Freemasons: quasi-religious cult, operative in Europe since the Middle Ages.

positivist: a view of events determined rigorously by discernible cause/effect.

metacritical: term denoting authorial self-awareness signaled in the text.

metahistory: modern view of history as "constructed" (rather than recovered).

War of 1812: meant here especially as Napoleon's European and Russian campaigns.

Dostoevsky, *The Brothers Karamazov*

Bernard, Claude: scientist and figure for the scientific atheist worldview.

buffoon: key figure in Dostoevskyan psychology: fool/trickster of ridicule.

Grand Inquisitor: figure of religious authority derived from the 17th-century Spanish Inquisition.

"insult and injury": Dostoevskyan psychology of pride as a ruling force, can be sadistic.

nadryv: Russian term denoting "laceration"; used in a psychological sense by Dostoevsky.

patriarchal rule: system of socio-moral authority based on a figure of the father/God.

Conrad, *Heart of Darkness*

colonialism: term denoting (here) the European exploitation of Africa.

deconstruction: modern theory of reality as "constructed" and undecidable.

imperialism: term denoting the political regime and ambitions of the British Empire.

impressionism: literary/artistic term for denoting the subjective immediacy of phenomena.

postcolonial: refers to modern inquiry into the practices of imperialist societies.

Mann, *Death in Venice*

The Birth of Tragedy: Nietzsche's account of Greek tragedy as an interplay of order/chaos.

Dionysus: Greek god of inebriation and frenzy.

Eros: Greek god of desire.

marmoreal style: a polished, "worked" style that "contains" what is inside it.

Phaedrus: text of Plato that discusses both beauty and gender.

Kafka, "The Metamorphosis" and *The Trial*

bureaucratic: referring, in Kafka, to the anonymity of a complex power structure.

metamorphosis: transformation.

Ovid's *Metamorphoses*: classic Latin text about humans transformed into other shapes.

sacrificial logic: a social logic of the rationale behind human sacrifice.

"topography of obstacles": in Kafka, a predictable landscape of resistance.

Proust, *Remembrance of Things Past*

Balbec: the Norman seaside resort where Marcel and his grandmother go.

Combray: the village of the protagonist's childhood memories.

Faubourg Saint-Germain: the elegant aristocratic area/culture of Paris.

inverti: French morphological term for "inverted"; used to label/signify homosexuals.

madeleine: particular French pastry.

oubli: French for "oblivion," for all-that-is-not-remembered.

reversals: the defining rhythm of Proust's work.

Joyce, *Ulysses*

"artful dodger": Dickensian term for ducking the forces of authority, rethought by Joyce as strategy for avoiding painful truths.

"Circe": Homer's goddess who transformed men into swine; Joyce's metamorphosis.

Daedalus and Icarus: Greek figures of the father and son who flew using wings made with wax; when Icarus, the son, flew too close to the Sun, his wings melted and he fell to his death.

"Ithaca": Odysseus's native island, homeland; Joyce's homecoming chapter.

Non serviam!: "I will not serve!" Lucifer's famous cry of revolt and emancipation.

"Penelope": Odysseus's faithful wife; Joycean final chapter on Bloom's wife.

stream of consciousness: writing that taps into the (ungrammatical) flow of thoughts.

voyeurism: the libidinal pleasure involved in seeing or spying on others.

Woolf, *To the Lighthouse*

Donne, John: English metaphysical poet who wrote "No man is an island."

mimetic art: the realist notation of "copying" reality.

The Social Contract: Rousseau's 18th-century tract about civic liberty.

Stephen, Leslie and Julia: Virginia Woolf's famous parents.

Faulkner, *As I Lay Dying*

Antigone: Sophoclean play about burying the dead, and moral responsibility.

baptism: religious rite of naming, reconceived by Faulkner as the crisis of *un-naming*.

Jefferson: central town in Faulkner's Mississippi scheme.

Lacan, Jacques: French poststructuralist theorist of language sundered from substance.

sign-system: view of language (from Ferdinand de Saussure) as sign/referent, reworked by Faulkner.

Yoknapatawpha: Indian word used by Faulkner as the name of his fictitious Mississippi county.

García Márquez, *One Hundred Years of Solitude*

boom: term used to describe the explosion of Latin American fiction in the 1960s.

Macondo: the name given by García Márquez to his imaginary Colombian community.

Magic Realism: term used to designate a modern movement in Latin American fiction.

Script: the mysterious written record that contains the entire Buendía history.

Biographical Notes

Honoré de Balzac (1799–1850): Balzac's masterpiece, *La Comédie Humaine*, written between 1830 and 1850, includes almost 150 interconnected novels and short stories and constitutes a vast portrait of early-19th-century French society. Balzac's meticulous descriptions and intricately interwoven plots notably classify social types in the same way that 19th-century naturalists classified zoological species. Throughout his career, Balzac worked both days and nights, drinking enormous amounts of strong black coffee to maintain his productivity. Despite his genius as a novelist, Balzac led a turbulent personal life, unsuccessfully seeking acceptance from the nobility, taking mistress after mistress, and accumulating staggering debts to finance his flamboyant wardrobe, antique collection, and large printers' bills. Yet the story of his troubled life only renders his enduring and international influence on the novel more remarkable.

Emily Brontë (1818–1848): Of the three Brontë sisters who wrote novels, the least is known about Emily. She lived most of her life at the family house in Haworth, and of all the Brontë sisters, Emily spent the most time there. She undertook various brief stints at boarding school, both as a student and teacher, and spent several months in Brussels in 1842 with her sister Charlotte, learning French and German while teaching young pupils. As children, Emily and her sister Anne wrote an ongoing saga about an imaginary land called Gondal; Emily also wrote some excellent poetry. *Wuthering Heights* was not well received upon first publication, which may have discouraged Emily from writing and publishing a second novel. After caring for her brother, Branwell, during his fatal illness, Emily herself fell ill yet refused medical treatment and continued her daily household tasks until the day of her death.

Joseph Conrad (1857–1924): Conrad was born in Russian-occupied Poland to an aristocratic family that was forced into exile to avoid retaliation for its involvement in nationalist uprisings. His parents died when he was young and he was placed in an uncle's care. Conrad joined the French Merchant Marine in 1874–1875 and traveled to Martinique and the West Indies. With the British Merchant Marine from 1878–1894, he sailed to Africa, Australia, India, and Indonesia. He became a naturalized British citizen and rose to the rank of captain in 1886. His experiences as captain of a

Congo River steamboat for a Belgian company in 1890 loosely contributed to the plot details of *Heart of Darkness*. He eventually settled in England, married, and devoted himself full-time to writing. Between 1894 and 1924, he produced more than a dozen novels and almost 30 short stories, as well as novellas, essays, memoirs, and plays.

Daniel Defoe (1660?–1731): Although Defoe is best known today for his perennially popular novels, including *Robinson Crusoe* (1719), *Moll Flanders* (1721), *A Journal of the Plague Year* (1722), and *Roxanna* (1724), he was famous in his lifetime as an outspoken journalist, whose religious and political writings led him at times to be convicted for libel and treason and subjected to fines, imprisonments, and one instance of pillorying. In addition to his work as a journalist and novelist, Defoe, who was born into the merchant class, worked at various times as a stockings vendor, merchant, investor, importer, propagandist, pollster, and spy for England and Scotland. His fortunes rose and fell; he experienced lawsuits, terms in prison, and bankruptcies; participated in a failed rebellion against King James II in 1685; and later served the court of William III.

Charles Dickens (1812–1870): Dickens was sent to work in a blacking (shoe polish) factory in London when he was 12, after his father was imprisoned for debt. This experience fueled his ambition as a writer and led him to criticize debtor's prisons and the British legal system. After secondary school, Dickens educated himself by reading history and literature in the British Museum Library while working as a law clerk, court reporter, and journalist; this introduction to law, politics, journalism, and theater provided the background for many of his novels. In addition to novel writing, Dickens served briefly as editor of the *London Daily News* and founded and edited the reviews *Household Words* (1883–1885) and *All the Year Round* (1859–1870). At once critical and emblematic of Victorian society, his novels, especially *Oliver Twist* (1839), *A Christmas Carol* (1843), *David Copperfield* (1849–1850), *Bleak House* (1852–1853), *Hard Times* (1854), *A Tale of Two Cities* (1859), and *Great Expectations* (1861), continue to enjoy large readerships today.

Fyodor Dostoevsky (1821–1881): Dostoevsky grew up in a middle-class family in Moscow and graduated from engineering school but began a career in writing with a translation of Balzac's *Eugenie Grandet* in 1844. He became a member of the Petraschevsky Circle, a radical group of socialist thinkers who were arrested in 1849. They faced a death squad, but just as they were to be killed, orders from the czar arrived, commuting their death sentences to labor in Siberia. Dostoevsky's time as a political prisoner in the labor camp in Tobolsk, Russia (1850–1854), and his subsequent service in a Siberian army outpost for five years haunted the rest of his life and writing. Upon his return to St. Petersburg, he suffered professional and personal losses: His journals were shut down by the authorities, his wife and brother died, and he lost much of his fortune to a gambling addiction. Despite these troubles, he wrote steadily, producing such well-known works as *Notes from Underground* (1864), *Crime and Punishment* (1866), *The Idiot* (1869), and *The Brothers Karamazov* (1880).

William Faulkner (1897–1962): The foremost writer of the American South, Faulkner established his reputation among critics with *The Sound and the Fury* (1929) and *As I Lay Dying* (1930). Yet he did not capture the American public's attention until the publication of the novel *Sanctuary* (1931), a sensational thriller that he wrote with the sole intention of making money. He wrote remarkable, complex novels, including *Light in August, Absalom, Absalom!, The Wild Palms, The Hamlet*, and *Go Down, Moses* in the 1930s and 1940s but made little money from them and lived instead on his work as a screenwriter in Hollywood. He continued, however, to be critically applauded in the United States and, especially, in France. The 1946 publication of *The Portable Faulkner* created a renewed interest in his work. In 1949, his acceptance speech for the Nobel Prize in Literature won him international admiration for his humanism.

Gustave Flaubert (1821–1880): Although *Madame Bovary* portrays French provincial life with painstaking realism and Flaubert admitted that he shared much of Madame Bovary's temperament, famously declaring, "Madame Bovary, *c'est moi*" ("Madame Bovary is me"), he rejected the identification of his novel with the term *Realism*. The novel caused a sensation in 1857 and Flaubert was put on trial for offending public morality; he was acquitted, but the scandal put him in the public eye. His subsequent works, including *Salammbo* (1863), *Sentimental Education* (1870), *The Temptation of Saint Anthony* (1874), and *Bouvard et Pécuchet* (1881), received critical acclaim. Flaubert shared friendships with other important literary figures, including George Sand, Ivan Turgenev, Henry James, and Guy de Maupassant, and his voluminous correspondence with Louise Colet and others embodies a valuable range of his observations on aesthetics.

Gabriel García Márquez (b. 1928): Born in Aracataca, Colombia, García Márquez began his writing career as a journalist, and acknowledges that his fiction and journalistic writing reciprocally influence each other. When *One Hundred Years of Solitude* (1967) first appeared, the demand for the novel was so high that it constantly required new printings. As one of the novels of the "boom" that brought Latin American literature to international attention, it won García Márquez the 1982 Nobel Prize in Literature. His magisterial intergenerational portrait of Macondo often garners comparisons to Faulkner's depiction of Yoknapatawpha County. Every subsequent novel by García Márquez has been immediately published in substantial editions and translated into several languages. He currently lives in Mexico City.

James Joyce (1882–1941): Joyce received a Jesuit education at Clongowes Wood College outside Dublin (which is featured in *A Portrait of the Artist as a Young Man*) and attended University College, Dublin. As evidenced by his ever-popular short-story collection, *Dubliners* (1914), and first novel, *A Portrait of the Artist as a Young Man* (1916), Joyce harbored ambivalence toward the Irish nation: Although interested in the Irish nationalist movement, he condemned the Irish for developing what, in his view, was a narrow provincialism. To "fly by those nets," Joyce lived most of his adult life abroad, first in Trieste, Italy, where he composed much of *A Portrait*, then in Zurich, where he wrote most of *Ulysses*, and eventually in Paris. With *Ulysses* (1922), Joyce pioneered the stream-of-consciousness technique. Although it was hailed as a masterpiece, its humorous and unabashed portraits of sexuality led to censorship in many countries. Joyce's last work of fiction, *Finnegan's Wake* (1939), is considered one of the most difficult texts in English literature.

Franz Kafka (1883–1924): Born into a middle-class Jewish family in Prague, Kafka endured a lifelong conflicted relationship with his father, an uneducated, domineering owner of a dry-goods store. At university, Kafka studied law and became friends with the writer-to-be Max Brod, with whom he explored Prague's intellectual and artistic scene. After his studies, Kafka worked in an insurance agency and managed his father's factory part-time. The monotony of his bureaucratic profession, his father's mismanagement of the factory, and the interference of these responsibilities with his writing exacerbated his anxiety and his health problems. Kafka spent months at a time in sanatoriums, regaining his health and returning to Prague only to fall ill once again. He also experienced several personal disappointments: Although he proposed to several women, none of his proposals culminated in marriage. Kafka stipulated in his will that his manuscripts should be destroyed, but Brod ignored the will and brought Kafka's unpublished stories and unfinished novels to light.

Pierre Ambroise François Choderlos de Laclos (1741–1803): Laclos attended the Royal Artillery School in La Fère and served as an officer in the army for much of his life, specializing in fortification projects. A posting in Grenoble allowed him to interact with aristocratic society and provided background for his only novel, *Les Liaisons dangereuses* (1782). Notoriously successful as a critique of the *ancien régime* and in its interweaving of multiple perspectives, *Les Liaisons dangereuses* is considered the pinnacle of the 18th-century epistolary novel tradition. Laclos also wrote poetry, literary reviews, and essays on literature, politics, military science, and women's education, the last of which were published posthumously in the collection *De l'Éducation de femmes* (1903). During the French Revolution, Laclos served as the secretary of the Duc d'Orléans and was a Jacobin club member. Imprisoned twice during the Terror, he escaped the guillotine and went on to serve in Napoleon's army until his death.

Thomas Mann (1875–1955): Influenced by artists and philosophers, including Wagner, Schopenhauer, and Nietzsche, while remaining skeptical of all of them, Mann is known for his distant, ironic narrative style and philosophical investigations into Western aesthetics and history. His first novel, *Buddenbrooks* (1901), a realist portrait of his merchant ancestors, garnered critical acclaim. The novella *Death in Venice* (1912) was variously received, and Mann's reputation languished until the publication of *The Magic Mountain* (1924), which was placed on a par with Proust's *Remembrance of Things Past* and won him the 1929 Nobel Prize in Literature. Although Mann was able to publish during the first few years of Nazi power, his German citizenship was revoked in 1936 when he published invectives against Nazism, after which he inadvertently became a symbolic leader of German progressives and exiles. He lived in the United States for several years and spent his last years in Switzerland.

Herman Melville (1819–1891): Eclectically educated and an avid reader, Melville taught secondary school briefly before undertaking his first whaling voyage in 1841. Sailing with the merchant service, whaling ships, and the U.S. Navy, he became one of the most traveled 19th-century American men of letters. The early novels *Typee* and *Omoo* draw from his experiences in Tahiti and other South Sea islands; other voyages took him to Hawaii and South and Central America. He wrote fiction prolifically for 11 years; in addition to *Moby-Dick* (1851), his works include the novels *Mardi* (1849), *Redburn* (1849), *White-Jacket* (1851), and *Pierre* (1852) and such shorter works as "Bartleby, the Scrivener," *Benito Cereno*, and the essay "Hawthorne and His Mosses" (1850), a manifesto of American literature. After this intense period, Melville traveled again, became a customs inspector in New York, and wrote poetry, not returning full-time to fiction until the writing of *Billy Budd* in the late 1880s.

Marcel Proust (1871–1922): Proust's happiest days were his childhood vacations at the family's country home in Illiers, which he depicts as Combray in *Swann's Way*. Yet most of the time, this son of a successful doctor and an overprotective mother suffered from serious ailments, especially asthma. Despite his illnesses, Proust managed to frequent Parisian society regularly, attending salons, concerts, dinners, and parties that would be novelized in *Remembrance of Things Past*. After studies at the Sorbonne in both law and literature, he began his literary career by publishing essays and stories in literary reviews, collected with additional stories in *Les Plaisirs et les jours* (1896). He attempted an autobiographical novel, *Jean Santeuil*, which was later reworked in his *chef d'œuvre*. *Remembrance of Things Past* took more than 15 years to write, and although he did not live to see it published in its entirety, in 1919, Proust won the prestigious Prix Goncourt for *Within a Budding Grove.*

Laurence Sterne (1713–1768): Born in Ireland, Sterne spent his early childhood traveling between Ireland and England until his family settled in North Yorkshire when he was 10. After attending Cambridge, he spent most of his adult life as clergyman in a rural village north of York. In 1759, he anonymously published *A Political Romance*, which masterfully satirized the pettiness of church officials in York. Sterne's most important works, *Tristram Shandy* (1760–1767) and *A Sentimental Journey* (1768), were written at the end of his life. The former draws extensively on his experiences in rural York, as well as such literary influences as Rabelais, Cervantes, Swift, Montaigne, Burton's *Anatomy of Melancholy*, and Locke's *Essay Concerning Human Understanding*. His voyages to France and Italy (intended to help him recover from tubercular episodes) inspired *A Sentimental Journey.*

Leo Tolstoy (1828–1910): Tolstoy lived almost all his life on his family's estate, Yasnaya Polyana. Widely read and educated at the universities in Kazan and St. Petersburg, he spent his youth in leisurely pursuits with other aristocrats in Tula, Moscow, and St. Petersburg. The experience of fighting with the Russian army in the Crimean War led to his first novel, *The Cossacks* (1863). After his marriage in 1862, Tolstoy entered a period of intense creativity that produced *War and Peace* (1863–1869) and *Anna Karenina* (1875–1877). In the late 1860s, the deaths of several family members and his own near-death experience precipitated a spiritual crisis that prompted him to practice a rigorous, self-styled form of Christianity. He abandoned Russian Orthodoxy; rejected violence and institutional authorities, including the state, the church, the military, and private property; and embraced pacifism, simplicity, inner conscience, and the personal relationship with God. Writing prolifically on his spiritual views, he attracted several followers; his post-conversion fiction, such as the novellas *Ivan Ilyich* (1886) and *The Kreutzer Sonata* (1890), reflects his concern with living a morally correct life.

Virginia Woolf (1882–1941): Woolf's father, Leslie Stephen, a noted scholar and biographer, encouraged her to read widely from a young age. Her childhood was tragically punctuated by instances of insanity in her family and sexual abuse by her older half-brother. Woolf herself did not escape mental illness: Her mother's death sparked a mental breakdown, and after her father's death, she attempted suicide. After her parents' deaths, she and her siblings moved to a house in the London neighborhood Bloomsbury. There, they formed the Bloomsbury Group, a regular gathering of intellectuals, at which she met her husband, Leonard Woolf, a critic and economist. Together, they founded Hogarth Press and published some of the most important avant-garde writers of the day. Writing alternately assuaged and provoked Woolf's depressive episodes, and she ultimately committed suicide. In addition to her novels, for more than 30 years she wrote reviews and essays for the *London Times Literary Supplement*. Woolf is also remembered for her vigorously feminist essays, including *A Room of One's Own* (1929) and *Three Guineas* (1938).

Bibliography

Note: The entries in this bibliography are grouped according to the authors covered in the lectures.

Defoe, *Moll Flanders*

Defoe, Daniel, and Albert J. Rivero. *Moll Flanders: An Authoritative Text, Contexts, Criticism.* New York: W.W. Norton, 2004. A comprehensive edition that includes contextual documents, a range of criticism, a chronology, and a selected bibliography.

Richetti, John. *The Life of Daniel Defoe: A Critical Biography.* Oxford: Blackwell, 2005. A thoughtful, well-written biography that presents the influence of Defoe's historical context and personal concerns in his fiction.

Weinstein, Arnold. *The Fiction of Relationship.* Princeton: Princeton University Press, 1988. This broad study of the relationship theme in literature explores Defoe's novel in terms of its depiction of the inner life, arguing for a sense of existential honesty and responsibility at the core of the book, despite its apparent focus on disguise and deceit. This argument informs much of the lecture in this course.

Sterne, *Tristram Shandy*

Sterne, Laurence. *The Life and Opinions of Tristram Shandy, Gentleman.* Melvyn New and Joan New, eds. London: Penguin, 2003, 1997. Includes an introductory essay by Christopher Ricks and an introduction and notes by Melvyn New.

Iser, Wolfgang. *Laurence Sterne: Tristram Shandy.* David Henry Wilson, trans. Cambridge Landmarks of World Literature. Cambridge: Cambridge University Press, 1988. A readable analysis focusing on the paradox of subjectivity as the guiding principle of the book.

Keymer, Thomas. *Sterne, the Moderns, and the Novel.* Oxford: Oxford University Press, 2002. A thorough examination of the contemporary developments of narrative discourse and print culture, the serialization of the novel, and Sterne's role in the literary culture of England in the 1760s.

New, Melvyn. *Tristram Shandy: A Book for Free Spirits.* New York: Twayne Publishers, 1994. A fascinating, in-depth analysis of the novel, featuring close readings and highlighting the novel's intertextuality and issues in the history of ideas.

Ross, Ian Campbell. *Laurence Sterne: A Life*. Oxford: Oxford University Press, 2001. An engaging biography, situating Sterne's life in the political concerns of the day and covering his involvement in local political and clerical events, the controversial reception of his work, and his impact on contemporary literary movements.

Weinstein, Arnold. *Fictions of the Self: 1550–1800*. Princeton: Princeton University Press, 1981. This early discussion of Sterne positions him as the groundbreaking figure whose experiments with narration are in the service of a kind of individual freedom to be achieved in no conventional way. Offers many of the insights to be found in the lecture given in this course.

Laclos, *Les Liaisons dangereuses*

Laclos, Pierre Choderlos de. *Les Liaisons dangereuses*. P. W. K. Stone, trans. and intro. New York: Penguin, 1961.

Rosbottom, Ronald C. *Choderlos de Laclos*. Boston: Twayne, 1978. This general account of Laclos's masterpiece in the Twayne series, a readable and informative discussion written by a distinguished scholar of 18th-century French literature, is among the few English-language texts on this classic.

Roussel, Roy. "*Les Liaisons dangereuses* and the Myth of the Understanding Man." In *The Conversation of the Sexes: Seduction and Equality in Selected 17th- and 18th-Century Texts*. New York: Oxford University Press, 1986, pp. 94–123. An interesting reading of seduction as the trope by which the characters attempt to free themselves from (social and sexual) determinism and to make themselves understood by one another.

Weinstein, Arnold. *The Fiction of Relationship*. Princeton: Princeton University Press, 1988. This account of the relationship theme in literature includes a discussion of Laclos's novel in terms of power and erotic control. Contains the seeds of the two lectures in this course.

Balzac, *Père Goriot*

de Balzac, Honoré, Burton Raffel, and Peter Brooks. *Père Goriot: A New Translation: Responses, Contemporaries and Other Novelists, Twentieth-Century Criticism*. New York: W.W. Norton & Co., 1998.

Includes an editor's introduction, a map of Paris in the 1820s, responses to the novel from contemporaries and other novelists, a substantial selection of the best 20th-century criticism, a chronology, and a selected bibliography.

Kanes, Martin. *Père Goriot: Anatomy of a Troubled World*. New York: Twayne Publishers; Toronto, New York: Maxwell Macmillan Canada, Maxwell Macmillan International, 1993. An overview of standard approaches to reading the work; generally humanist in its view of the novel.

Brontë, Emily, *Wuthering Heights*

Brontë, Emily, and Richard J. Dunn. *Wuthering Heights: The 1847 Text, Backgrounds and Contexts, Criticism*. 4th ed. New York: Norton, 2003. This authoritative edition contains excerpts from Emily Brontë's diary, correspondence, and reviews concerning both the 1847 and the 1850 editions; the poems included in the 1850 edition; a selection of rigorous criticism of the novel; and a chronology of Emily Brontë's life.

—————. *The Poems of Emily Brontë*. Derek Roper with Edward Chitham, eds. Oxford: Clarendon Press, 1995. The standard edition; thoroughly annotated.

Berg, Maggie. *Wuthering Heights: The Writing in the Margin*. New York, London: Twayne Publishers, Prentice Hall, 1996. A thoughtful, detail-oriented, and thoroughly readable study exploring the spatial, corporeal, textual, and critical margins of the novel as its most productive arenas of signification.

Chitham, Edward. *The Birth of Wuthering Heights: Emily Brontë at Work*. Houndmills, Basingstoke, Hampshire; New York: Macmillan Press; St. Martin's Press, 1998. An ambitious investigation into the conditions of writing and sources that made it possible for Emily Brontë to write the novel. This book traces Emily's adaptation of the Gondal sagas written in her adolescence with Anne Brontë and her translations of poems from Latin and minutely examines the manuscript for clues to the process of writing the novel.

Winnifrith, Thomas John, ed. *Critical Essays on Emily Brontë*. New York: G.K. Hall & Co., 1997. Classic essays covering Emily's biography and poetry, and criticism of *Wuthering Heights* from its publication in 1847 until 1995.

Melville, *Moby-Dick*

Melville, Herman. *Moby-Dick*. Hershel Parker and Harrison Hayford, eds. New York: Norton, 2002. Includes an editor's introduction, significant maps and visual materials, responses to the novel from contemporaries and other novelists, a substantial selection of the best 20th-century criticism, a chronology, and a selected bibliography.

Higgins, Brian, and Hershel Parker. *Critical Essays on Herman Melville's Moby-Dick*. New York: G.K. Hall; Toronto, New York: Maxwell Macmillan Canada, Maxwell Macmillan International, 1992. A voluminous compilation of contemporary reviews, articles, and essays dating from the novel's publication to the present, with special sections on literary influences and affinities, the whale, Ahab and Ishmael, and the writing of the novel.

Markels, Julian. *Melville and the Politics of Identity: From King Lear to Moby-Dick*. Urbana: University of Illinois Press, 1993. A compelling reading of the novel as staging an ideological battle central to American cultural politics; draws on the philosophies of Locke and Hobbes.

Peretz, Eyal. *Literature, Disaster and the Enigma of Power: A Reading of 'Moby-Dick.'* Stanford, CA: Stanford University Press, 2003. A powerful, compelling reading of the novel as a paradoxical attempt to testify, through language, to unspeakable events of literature and history.

Sten, Christopher. *Sounding the Whale: Moby-Dick as Epic Novel*. Kent, OH: Kent State University Press, 1996. Contends that *Moby-Dick* brings together the two epic traditions: the ancient, nation-building epic of battle and the more modern, universally oriented epic of the spiritual journey.

Thomson, Shawn. *The Romantic Architecture of Herman Melville's Moby-Dick*. Madison, NJ; London: Fairleigh Dickinson University Press; Associated University Presses, 2001. Explores the Romantic aesthetic of the novel, reading it as the confrontation of two Romantic tendencies: Ahab's "passionate idealism" and Ishmael's "grounded intellect and Romantic spirit."

Dickens, *Bleak House*

Dickens, Charles. *Bleak House*. Nicola Bradbury, ed. London: Penguin, 1971. This paperback edition includes an introduction by the editor, original illustrations by Hablot K. Browne, a chronology, bibliography, notes, and appendices on Chancery, spontaneous combustion, and Dickens's number plans for the novel.

Allan, Janice M. *Charles Dickens's Bleak House: A Sourcebook.* London: Routledge, 2004. Includes sections on context, interpretations, a selection of key passages, and a bibliography of further reading. Written/compiled for the undergraduate writing a research paper on the novel but clear, informative, and useful for anyone interested in the novel and its historical and literary contexts.

Bigelow, Gordon. "Market Indicators: Banking and Housekeeping in *Bleak House.*" In *Fiction, Famine and the Rise of Economics in Victorian Britain and Ireland.* Cambridge: Cambridge University Press, 2003. An intelligent analysis of Dickens's representation of the Chancery court as a legal system that exists simply to perpetuate itself, at the expense of the characters' well-being.

Weinstein, Arnold. *A Scream Goes Through the House: What Literature Teaches Us About Life.* New York: Random House, 2003. This book about the representation of feeling and pain in literature contains an essay on *Bleak House* that grafts Dickens's book into a discourse about plague, infection, and human connection reaching back to Sophocles and continuing to Tony Kushner. Expresses many of the ideas central to the two lectures in this course.

Flaubert, *Madame Bovary*

Flaubert, Gustave, Margaret Cohen, and Paul De Man. *Madame Bovary: Contexts, Critical Reception.* 2nd ed. Margaret Cohen, ed. New York: W.W. Norton, 2004. A truly impressive edition, featuring a revised translation, a generous sampling of earlier versions of key passages, Flaubert's letters on *Madame Bovary*, the trial against Flaubert, and a judicious selection of groundbreaking critical essays. An introduction, chronology, and selected bibliography are also included.

Vargas Llosa, Mario. *The Perpetual Orgy: Flaubert and Madame Bovary.* Helene Lane, trans. New York: Farrar Strauss Giroux, 1986. A pleasurable account of another novelist admiring and learning from his reading of this novel; analytically precise and presented with humor and imagination.

Tolstoy, *War and Peace*

Tolstoy, Leo. *War and Peace*. Anthony Briggs, trans. New York: Penguin, 2006.

———. *War and Peace*. Norton Critical Edition, 2nd ed. Louis Shanks Maude and Aylmer Maude, trans. George Gibian, ed. New York: W.W. Norton & Co., 1996. Supplementary materials include relevant historical maps, a summary of the publication history of the novel, several of Tolstoy's diary entries and letters pertaining to the novel, drafts of the introduction, and a comprehensive selection of criticism. A chronology and selected bibliography are also included.

Berlin, Isaiah. "The Hedgehog and the Fox: An Essay on Tolstoy's View of History." Chicago: *The Elephant*, Ivan R. Dee, 1953, 1978. This provocative and oft-cited essay argues that if there are two kinds of thinkers, those who believe in a unifying central vision of the world (hedgehogs) and those who see the world as having many different ends without any definitive unity (foxes), then Tolstoy is caught in between: He sees the world like a fox but wants to believe in the organizing principle of a hedgehog.

Morson, Gary Saul. *Hidden in Plain View: Narrative and Creative Potentials in War and Peace*. Stanford, CA: Stanford University Press, 1987. An excellent study that examines Tolstoy's critiques of and innovations in language, history, and psychology through this novel.

Dostoevsky, *The Brothers Karamazov*

Dostoevsky, Fyodor. *The Brothers Karamazov*. Constance Garnett, trans. Ralph E. Matlaw, ed. New York: Norton, 1976. Includes a broad range of critical essays and a selected bibliography.

———. *The Brothers Karamazov*. Richard Pevear and Larissa Volokhonsky, trans. New York: Farrar, Straus and Giroux, 2002.

Blackmur, R. P. *Eleven Essays in the European Novel*. New York: Harcourt, 1964. This early collection of essays by a distinguished poet/critic has some of the most illuminating pages on *The Brothers Karamazov* ever written. Blackmur is especially alert to the deeper rhythms and philosophical significance of the text, while also paying special attention to its figures and metaphors.

Holquist, Michael. *Dostoevsky and the Novel*. Princeton: Princeton University Press, 1977. Contends that Dostoevsky emerges at a crossroads at which Russian literature's predominant concern with defining Russian nationalism and Russian national history gives way to a preoccupation with more modern and universal issues.

Jackson, Robert Louis. *The Art of Dostoyevsky: Deliriums and Nocturnes.* Princeton: Princeton University Press, 1981. An insightful study that covers all the short fiction and novels, with special attention to character development, Russian literary and historical context, and Dostoevsky's preoccupation with ethical and metaphysical dilemmas.

Conrad, *Heart of Darkness*

Conrad, Joseph. *Heart of Darkness.* New York: Penguin, 1999.

————, and Robert Kimbrough. *Heart of Darkness: An Authoritative Text, Backgrounds and Sources, Criticism.* 3rd ed. New York: Norton, 1988. This comprehensive volume includes a historical map, primary and secondary historical sources on the Congo, excerpts from Conrad's Congo diary and relevant correspondence, contemporary authors' accounts of Conrad's writing process, passages from Conrad's writings on life and art, a generous selection of critical essays, and a guide to bibliography.

De Lange, Attie, Gail Fincham, and Wieslaw Krajka. *Conrad in Africa: New Essays on "Heart of Darkness."* Boulder, CO: Social Science Monographs; Lublin, New York: Maria Curie-Sklodowska University, distributed by Columbia University Press, 2002. A newer collection of critical texts, international in scope, that emphasizes postcolonial and intertextual readings of Conrad.

Mann, *Death in Venice*

Mann, Thomas. *Death in Venice.* New York: Vintage, 1954.

————. *Death in Venice.* Clayton Koelb, trans. and ed. New York: W.W. Norton, 1994. Supplementary materials include relevant historical maps, Mann's working notes and relevant excerpts from letters and essays, a sampling of criticism available in English, a chronology of Mann's life, and a selected bibliography.

Kafka, "The Metamorphosis" and *The Trial*

Kafka, Franz. *The Metamorphosis.* Norton Critical Edition. Stanley Corngold, trans. and ed. New York: W.W. Norton & Co., 1996. Supplementary materials include Kafka's manuscript revisions, relevant excerpts from Kafka's letters and diaries, a good selection of critical essays, a chronology, and selected bibliography.

―――. *The Trial*. Willa Muir and Edwin Muir, trans. New York: Schocken, 1984.

Corngold, Stanley. "The Structure of Kafka's *Metamorphosis*." In *The Commentators' Despair: The Interpretation of Kafka's Metamorphosis*. Port Washington, NY: Kennikat Press, 1973, pp. 1–38. A seminal essay that reviews the major criticism of the text and argues that its innovation lies in the transformation of the metaphor into the fact of fiction, the counter-metamorphosis of the metaphor.

Deleuze, Gilles, and Felix Guattari. *Kafka: Towards a Minor Literature*. Dana Polan, trans. Minneapolis: University of Minnesota Press, 1986. Fascinating account of Kafka's work that refuses all discussion of transcendence and metaphor and insists on examining the actual topography of the writing itself in order to achieve an immanent reading of Kafka.

Spilka, Mark. *Dickens and Kafka: A Mutual Interpretation*. Bloomington: Indiana University Press, 1963. Early but provocative effort to link Kafka's bureaucratic, nightmarish labyrinths to the penal world of the late Dickens, especially as seen in *Bleak House*.

Weinstein, Philip. *Unknowing: The Work of Modernist Fiction*. Ithaca: Cornell University Press, 2005. This brilliant account of modernism situates the breakthrough work of three key authors—Kafka, Proust, and Faulkner—against the backdrop of Enlightenment premises in order to argue that the new prose of these three 20th-century figures annihilates our assumptions of mastery, or our view of literature-as-knowledge.

Proust, *Remembrance of Things Past*

Proust, Marcel. *Remembrance of Things Past*. C. K. Scott-Moncrieff and Terence Kilmartin, trans. New York: Random House, 1981.

Beckett, Samuel. *Proust*. New York: Grove Press, 1957. A beautifully written and insightful essay from a not-yet-famous Beckett (he was only 25 years old at the time of writing), demonstrating how involuntary memory in Proust shocks individuals out of the complacent structures of time (ultimately, mortality) and habit in which everyday experiences are otherwise mired.

Bersani, Leo. *Marcel Proust: The Fictions of Life and Art*. London: Oxford University Press, 1965. An elegantly written analysis that shows how the narrator's failed attempts to novelize life have allowed him to develop an aesthetic of novelistic reminiscence. Careful and precise attention is given to the motif of homosexuality in the novel.

De Botton, Alain. *How Proust Can Change Your Life*. New York: Vintage, 1998. An original approach to Proust's novel and a delightful read; de Botton explores how Proust's wisdom can be applied to daily life and argues that the novel audaciously demonstrates that suffering can make one's life a richer experience.

Shattuck, Roger. *Proust's Way: A Field Guide to In Search of Lost Time*. New York: Norton, 2000. Incorporating insights from Shattuck's earlier *Marcel Proust* (1974) and *Proust's Binoculars* (1963), this book navigates various editions and translations, foregrounds Proust's innovative approach to visuality and optics in the novel, and offers a unified vision of this sprawling novel.

Weinstein, Arnold. *Recovering Your Story: Proust, Joyce, Woolf, Faulkner, Morrison*. New York: Random House, 2006. Articulating more fully and more concretely the issues developed in these lectures on Proust, this study focuses on the discovery of a universe of interiority in Proust, outfitted with a logic and a language at odds with traditional narrative discourse.

Weinstein, Philip. *Unknowing: The Work of Modernist Fiction*. Ithaca: Cornell University Press, 2005. This brilliant account of modernism situates the breakthrough work of three key authors—Kafka, Proust, and Faulkner—against the backdrop of Enlightenment premises in order to argue that the new prose of these three 20th-century figures annihilates our assumptions of mastery, or our view of literature-as-knowledge.

Joyce, *Ulysses*

Joyce, James. *Ulysses*. New York: Random House (Vintage), 1986.

Blamires, Harry. *The New Bloomsday Book: A Guide Through Ulysses*. Revised edition keyed to the corrected text. New York and London: Routledge, 1988. A useful reading companion. Provides an exhaustive chapter-by-chapter account of the novel, covering plot summary; thematic highlights; explanations of colloquialisms;

correspondences with Homer's *Odyssey*; and cultural, religious, historical, and literary allusions.

Budgen, Frank. *James Joyce and the Making of Ulysses*. Bloomington: Indiana University Press, 1960. In this volume, Budgen recalls his daily conversations with Joyce in Zurich in 1918–1919, delivering, all at once, a memoir of their friendship, a bystander's account of the novel's development, and a perspicacious reading of *Ulysses* in its own right. Includes essays on *Finnegan's Wake* and Budgen's obituary on Joyce.

Hart, Clive, and David Hayman, eds. *James Joyce's Ulysses: Critical Essays*. Berkeley: University of California Press, 1974. A collection of classic essays with contributions from many important Joycean scholars.

Weinstein, Arnold. *Recovering Your Story: Proust, Joyce, Woolf, Faulkner, Morrison*. New York: Random House, 2006. Tackling the critique of Joyce as esoteric and unreadable, this study emphasizes the humor and everyday wisdom of *Ulysses*, while attending as well to the trailblazing innovations in narrative history that this novel inaugurates.

Woolf, *To the Lighthouse*

Woolf, Viriginia. *To the Lighthouse*. New York: Harcourt, Brace, Jovanovich (Harvest), orig. copyright 1927.

Bowlby, Rachel. *Virginia Woolf: Feminist Destinations*. New York: Blackwell, 1988. A magisterial career-length study that defines Woolf's commitments to feminism and modernism.

Lee, Hermione. *Virginia Woolf*. New York: Vintage, 1999. This biography offers a complex and comprehensive portrait of Woolf as a literary genius and profoundly human being. Drawing extensively on correspondence and journals, it is notable for describing how Woolf's experiences of the advent of modernity in her lifetime affected her work and how Woolf was able to overcome personal suffering to generate her greatest artistic achievements.

Snaith, Anna. *Virginia Woolf: Public and Private Negotiations*. Basingstoke, England: Macmillan; New York: St. Martin's, 2000. Explores the convergences and divergences of public and private in both Woolf's life and her writing, and discusses Woolf's feminism, her narrative techniques, her view of the evolving history of gender roles, and her attitudes toward publication and participation in public debate. Introduces previously unexamined manuscript material, and letters written to Woolf by her readers.

Weinstein, Arnold. *Recovering Your Story: Proust, Joyce, Woolf, Faulkner, Morrison*. New York: Random House, 2006. This discussion of Woolf's novel is paired with an account of *Mrs. Dalloway*, with an emphasis on the creation of a language of interiority that stakes out new ground in modern fiction.

Faulkner, *As I Lay Dying*

Faulkner, William. *As I Lay Dying*. New York: Random House (Vintage International), 1991.

Bleikasten, André. *Faulkner's As I Lay Dying*. Bloomington: Indiana University Press, 1973. This book-length study of Faulkner's novel remains the fullest and most readable critical account of the text, encompassing a wide spectrum of philosophical and writerly issues and particularly attuned to Faulkner's stylistic virtuosity.

Wagner-Martin, Linda, ed. *William Faulkner: Four Decades of Criticism*. East Lansing: Michigan State University Press, 1973. This early collection of essays includes the classic studies of Faulkner's work, when his reputation as an American novelist was at its peak. Later Faulkner criticism is more attuned to issues of ideology, but this volume is a useful starting point for sizing up the Mississippian's achievement.

Weinstein, Arnold. "Faulkner's *As I Lay Dying*: The Voice from the Coffin." In *Nobody's Home: Speech, Self and Place in American Fiction from Hawthorne to DeLillo*. New York: Oxford University Press, 1993. Offers a more extended and close-grained reading of Faulkner's novel, developing the central issues and motifs that are sounded in the two lectures of this course. Reads Faulkner in terms of a long American discourse about self-making and self-extinction.

Weinstein, Philip. *Faulkner's Subject: A Cosmos No One Owns*. New York: Cambridge University Press, 1992. Although it does not deal directly with *As I Lay Dying*, Weinstein's study of Faulkner remains one of the most lucid and persuasive efforts to situate Faulknerian writing within the context of poststructuralist theory. The treatment of race, gender, and consciousness is superb.

García Márquez, *One Hundred Years of Solitude*

García Márquez, Gabriel. *One Hundred Years of Solitude*. New York: Harper Perennial, 2006.

Bell, Michael. "The Cervantean Turn: *One Hundred Years of Solitude*." In *Gabriel García Márquez: Solitude and Solidarity*. New York: St. Martin's Press, 1993. Offers a beautiful reading of the Macondo characters as sleepwalkers, unaware that their strange behavior attests to their repressed fears of confronting reality. Addresses the influence of surrealism; the inadequacy of the term *Magical Realism*; the value of the local, developing nation's perspective within the globalizing present; the similarities between Cervantes and García Márquez; and, as indicated by the title of the book, the interplay of solitude and solidarity in the text.

Posada-Carbó, Eduardo. "Fiction as History: The Bananeras and Gabriel García Marquez's *One Hundred Years of Solitude*." *Journal of Latin American Studies* 30.2 (May 1998): 395–414. Examines the critical reception of García Márquez's account of the banana workers' strike as history against more accurate historical accounts and explores the effects of the acceptance of García Márquez's fictional account as history.

Wood, Michael. *One Hundred Years of Solitude*. Cambridge: Cambridge University Press, 1990. A thoroughly readable companion to the novel, covering historical context, literary affinities, and the major themes and stylistic innovations in the text.

Notes

Notes